This edition published in 1997 by
The Southwestern Company UK Ltd
Goldsmiths House,
Broad Plain, Bristol BS2 OJP

Reprinted 1998

A CIP catalgue record for this book is available from the British Library

ISBN 0-87197-456-8

Produced by Miles Kelly Publishing Ltd.
Designer: Smiljka Surla
Editors: Rosie Alexander, Kate Miles,
Angela Royston
Assistant Editors: Susanne Bull, Lynne French
Picture Research: Yannick Yago

Printed in France

Kingfisher

Encyclopedia of QUESTIONS and ANSWERS

1

Earth and Space Science

SOUTHWESTERN

CONTENTS

1 EARTH AND SPACE

SCIENCE

2 ANIMALS AND PLANTS

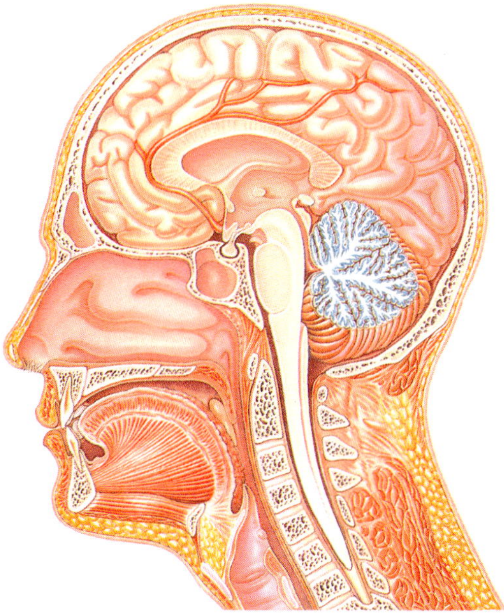

HUMAN BODY

3 PEOPLES AND COUNTRIES

HISTORY

Acknowledgments

The publishers wish to thank the artists who have contributed toward this book. These include the following:

Susanna Addario; Hemesh Alles; Marion Appleton; Hayward Art Group; Craig Austin; David Barnett; Peter Bull; Vanessa Card; Tony Chance; Kuo Kang Chen; Harry Clow; Stephen Conlin; Peter Dennis; Richard Draper; Eugene Fleury; Chris Forsey; Mark Franklin; Terry Gabbey; Sheila Galbraith; Mark George; Jeremy Gower; Ruby Green; Ray Grinaway; Nick Harris; Nicholas Hewetson; Adam Hook; Christian Hook; Christina Hook; Richard Hook; Tony Kenyon; Mike Lacey; Claire Littlejohn; Mick Loates; Bernard Long; Alan Male; Shane Marsh; Jamie Medlin; Nicki Palin; Alex Pang; Roger Payne; Mel Pickering; Maurice Pledger; Bryan Poole; Sebastian Quigley; Claudia Saraceni; Guy Smith; Tony Smith; Michael Steward; Simon Tegg; Ian Thompson; Ross Watton; Steve Weston; Linda Worrall; David Wright;

Photographs

The publishers wish to thank the following for supplying photographs for this book:

Page 14 (BC) Corbis; 20 (TR) Corbis; 21 (BC) Rich Kirchner/ NHPA; 25 (BR) Corbis; 26 (TR) Corbis; 29 (B) ZEFA; 33 (BC) ZEFA; 34 (BR) David Frazier/ Science Photo Library; 45 (TR) ZEFA; 49 (TR) NHPA; 50 (TR) Corbis; 62 (C) Mehau Kulyk/ Science Photo Library; 65 (CL) Firework Ltd; 68 (T) ZEFA; 71 (TL) Jerome Yeats/ Science Photo Library; 73 (TR) Geoff Tompkinson/ Science Photo Library; 75 (BC) Corbis; 78 (TL) Yves Baulieu/ Publiphoto Diffusion/ Science Photo Library; 81 (TL) Corbis; 96 (CR) Ford; 111 (T) Henry Ausloos/ NHPA; 116 (TL) Bill Coster/ NHPA; 122 (BC) Kevin Cullimore/ Tony Stone Images; 123 (TL) David B. Fleetham/ Oxford Scientific Films; 126 (BR) G.I. Bernard/ Oxford Scientific Films; 131 (B) Hans Reinhard/ Bruce Coleman Ltd.; 136 (C) Georgette/ Douwma/ Planet Earth Pictures; 139 (BL) Stan Osolinski/ Oxford Scientific Films; 142 (BR) Eric Soder/ NHPA; 145 (CR) Alain Compost/ Bruce Coleman Ltd.; 146 (TC) Linda Burgess/ The Garden Picture Library; 146 (C) John Glover/ The Garden Picture Library; 147 (R) Tim Ridley/ Larousse Archives; 149 (TL) E.A. Janes/ NHPA; 149 (CR) Jerry Pavia/ The Garden Picture Library; 150 (TR) Michael Tweddie/ NHPA; 150 (B) David Middleton/ NHPA; 151 (TR) Jerry Pavia/ The Garden Picture Library; 163 (BR) Science Photo Library; 167 (TR) Simon Fraser/ Science Photo Library; 167 (BR) Jeremy Mason/ Science Photo Library; 179 (TL) Will & Deni McIntyre/ Science Photo Library; 182 (BL) Ian West/ Bubbles; 183 (TL) Jeremy Bright/Robert Harding Picture Library; 183 (BL) Robert Harding; 188 (BL) David Hanson/ Tony Stone Worldwide; 189 (TR) Simon Potter/Telegraph Colour Library; 189 (BL) Andy Cox/ Tony Stone Images; 191 (TR) AKG Photo; 193 (BL) Donna Day/ Tony Stone Images; 194 (BR) Tony Stone Images; 195 (BR) David Joel/ Tony Stone Worldwide; 198 (BR) F. Rombout/ Bubbles; 199 (TL) St. Bartholomews Hospital/Science Photo Library; 199 (R) Dave Bartruff/Corbis; 202 (TL) Peter Lambert/ Tony Stone Worldwide; 202 (BR) The Hutchison Library; 203 (TR) c 1996 Corel Corp.; 204 (TL) c 1996 Corel Corp.; 204 (TR) Christine Osborne Pictures; 206 (BR) Jean-Leo Dugust/ Panos Pictures; 207 (BL) Carla Signorini Jones/ Images of Africa Photobank; 207 (BR) Jeremy A. Horner/The Hutchison Library; 209 (TL) Hugh Sitton/ Tony Stone Images; 209 (BR) Spectrum Colour Library; 210 (TL) Oldrich Karasck/ Tony Stone Images; 212 (CL) Paul Harris/ Tony Stone Images; 212 (BR) c 1996 Corel Corp.; 213 (TL) Alain le Garsmeur/ Panos Pictures; 214 (BC) Paul Chesley/ Tony Stone Worldwide; 215 (TR) c 1996 Corel Corp.; 216/7 (CR) Spectrum Colour Library; 218 (TL) ZEFA; 218 (BL) Spectrum Colour Library; 219 (CR) Spectrum Colour Library; 222 (BL) Rohan/ Tony Stone Images; 223 (TL) ZEFA; 225 (TR) ZEFA; 225 (BR) D. Saunders/ Trip; 228 (CR) c 1996 Corel Corp.; 231 (TR) ZEFA; 231 (BL) Jaemsen/ ZEFA; 232 (BR) Spectrum Colour Library; 235 (C) ZEFA; 237 (CR) Spectrum Colour Library; 238 (BR) The Hutchison Library; 238 (BL) ZEFA; 239 (BR) Paul Chesley/Tony Stone Worldwide; 239 (BL) Jeff Britnell/Tony Stone; 241 (TR) Luc Delahaye/ Sipa Press/ Rex Features; 242 (TC) Sipa Press/ Rex Features; 242 (BR) John Lamb/ Tony Stone Images; 242 (BL) Persuy/ Sipa Press/ Rex Features; 243 (TL) Spectrum Colour Library; 245 (BL) Images Colour Library; 245 (CR) Marian Morrison/ South American Pictures; 246 (CL) Eric Lawne/ The Hutchison Library; 247 (TL) Robert Harding Picture Library; 247 (BR) Jon Burbank/The Hutchison Library; 254 (CR) Andrew Hill/ The Hutchison Library; 260 (C) Palais de Versailles, Musee Historique AKG Photo; 260 (BR) Peter Newark's Historical Pictures; 261 (TL) Peter Newark's American Pictures; 261 (C) Popperfoto; 261 (BC) Popperfoto; 266 (TR) The Hulton Getty Picture Collection Ltd.; 268 (CR) Corbis; 271 (BR) Simon Krectmem/Reuter Popperfoto; 275 (BL) AKG Photo; 278 (CT) E.T. Archive; 278 (B) AKG Photo; 279 (CT) AKG Photo; 279 (BL) E.T. Archive; 279 (BR) Popperfoto; 281 (TL) The Hulton Getty Picture Collection Ltd.; 281 (BL) Mary Evans Picture Library; 281 (BR) AKG Photo; 282 (BR) Mary Evans Picture Library; 282 (CL) Disney Video; 283 (TC) The Bettman Archive/ Corbis; 284 (BR) Ancient Art & Architecture Collection Ltd.; 285 (BR) Leipzig Museum/ AKG Photo; 286 (CT) Peter Newark's American Pictures; 286 (BR) Corbis; 286 (CL) Peter Newark's American Pictures; 288 (CL) Steve Etherington/ EMPICS; 288 (BR) Mike Blake/ Reuters Popperfoto; 289 (TL) The Times/ Rex Features; 289 (BR) Popperfoto; 293 (TL) Nelson Museum, Monmouth; E.T Archive 293 (R) AKG Photo London; 294 (BL) BFI Stills, Posters & Designs; 295 (TL) Peter Newark's American Pictures; 295 (BC) Peter Newark's American Pictures.

EARTH FACTS

How big is the Earth?

The Earth's circumference (the distance around the world) at the Equator is 40,091 kilometres. Its diameter (the distance across the centre of the Earth) at the Equator is 12,756 kilometres. The Earth is slightly smaller when measured between the poles (12,713 kilometres), so it is not an exact sphere. If you could put the world on scales, it would weigh nearly 6,000 million million million tonnes.

▼ This cutaway of the Earth shows the upper rocky layer or lithosphere. The crust beneath the oceans is much thinner than the crust beneath the continents.

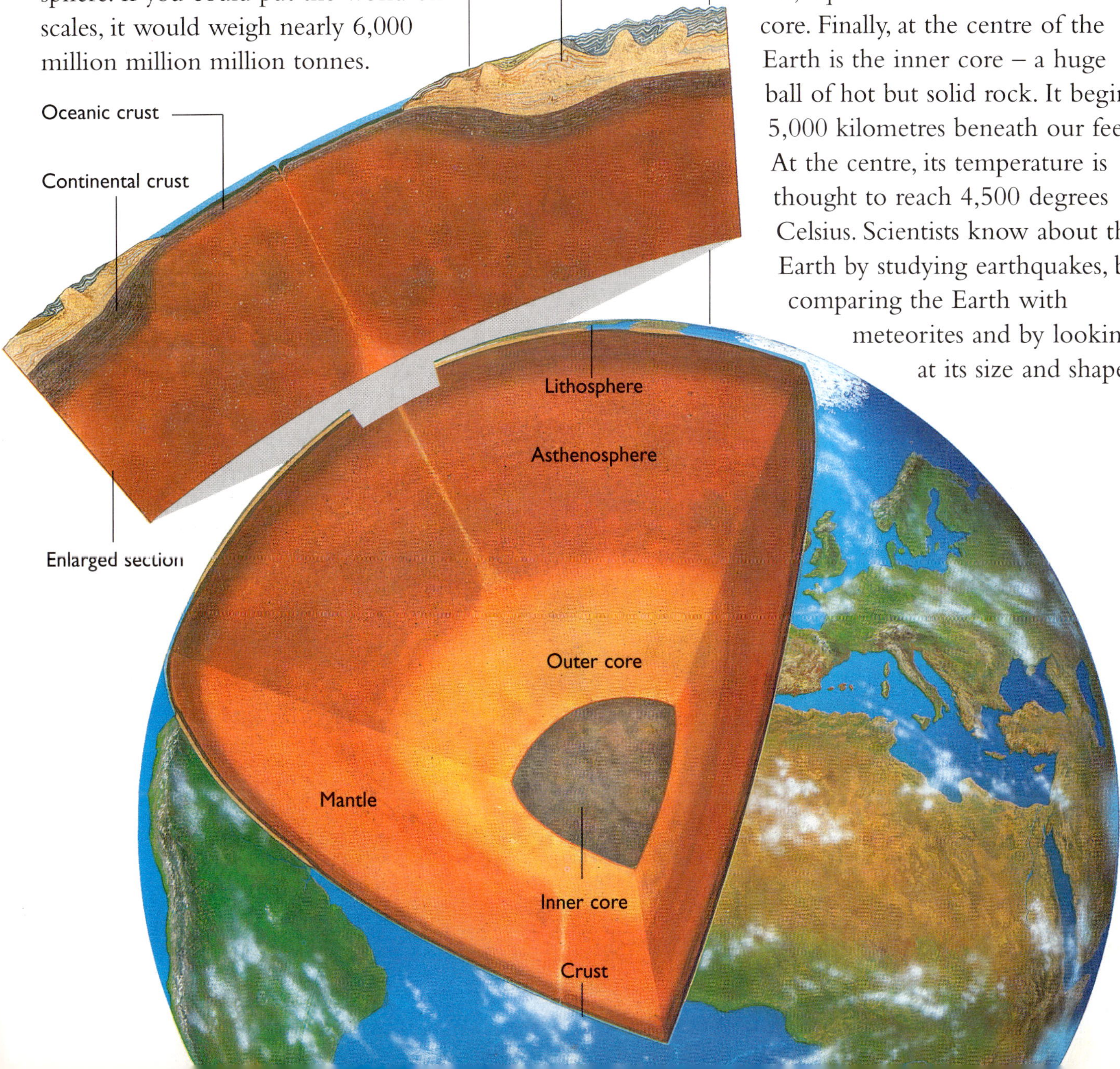

What is the Earth made of?

The Earth is a huge ball of rock. The top layer is the crust of the Earth. It is as little as 6 kilometres thick beneath the oceans. Then comes a thick layer of rock called the mantle, which goes almost halfway down to the Earth's centre. As it gets deeper, it gets hotter and beneath the mantle is a layer of hot, liquid rock called the outer core. Finally, at the centre of the Earth is the inner core – a huge ball of hot but solid rock. It begins 5,000 kilometres beneath our feet. At the centre, its temperature is thought to reach 4,500 degrees Celsius. Scientists know about the Earth by studying earthquakes, by comparing the Earth with meteorites and by looking at its size and shape.

▲ **The Earth was formed at the same time as the Sun. Material around the Sun cooled and collided to build up bodies that in time became planets.**

How old is the Earth?

The universe began to form over 15 billion years ago. The Earth is much younger. It is about 4.6 billion years old. Scientists have worked this out by studying rocks in meteorites which have landed on Earth from outer space. Meteorites are lumps of rock which were formed at the same time as the Earth. Scientists have also calculated the Earth's age from the rate at which elements of the radioactive metal uranium decay (break down) into lead.

Why is the Earth round?

The world is round for the same reason that a raindrop and a bubble are round. If possible, a liquid naturally shapes itself into a ball. When the Earth formed, it was hot and liquid. Because it was floating in space, it became round. When the liquid rock cooled and hardened into solid rock, the Earth stayed round.

Actually, the Earth is not perfectly round, but is slightly flattened at the poles. This flattening is caused by the speed of its spin.

The Earth is the only planet known to have enough oxygen for living things. In sunlight, plants give off oxygen, keeping the planet alive.

Is the Earth solid?

The crust is solid, but the rocks of the mantle are so hot that they are partly molten, rather like hot toffee. The outer core is hotter still (between 2,200 degrees Celsius and 5,000 degrees Celsius) and is completely molten and liquid. At the very centre is a ball of hot rock, squashed so tightly that it is solid. The core is far too hot and solid to drill through.

What are rocks made of?

The Earth's crust is made up of rock. Rocks are solid clusters of minerals (chemical substances composed of crystals). The minerals quartz, feldspar and mica are found in granite rocks, for example.

Is the Earth a unique planet?

No other planet orbiting the Sun is like the Earth. Only the Earth has the necessary conditions for life (as we know it) to exist.

What is the biosphere?

The biosphere is the Earth's 'skin' of soil, water and air. Within it live all the planet's plants and animals. No other planet in the Solar System has such a biosphere.

Why does the Earth orbit the Sun?

Like other planets, the Earth is held in a path, or orbit, around the Sun. The Sun's gravity is the force which holds the Earth in place. The Earth travels 958 million kilometres around the Sun in 365 days 6 hours and 9 minutes. This is called a year.

How much land is there?

Less than one-third of the Earth is covered by land. The land is older than the oceans. The rocks of the largest landmasses – the continents – are up to 3.8 billion years old. The oldest rocks in the ocean are less than 200 million years old. The Earth's surface is about 71 percent water. This water includes the oceans, ice and water vapour in the atmosphere.

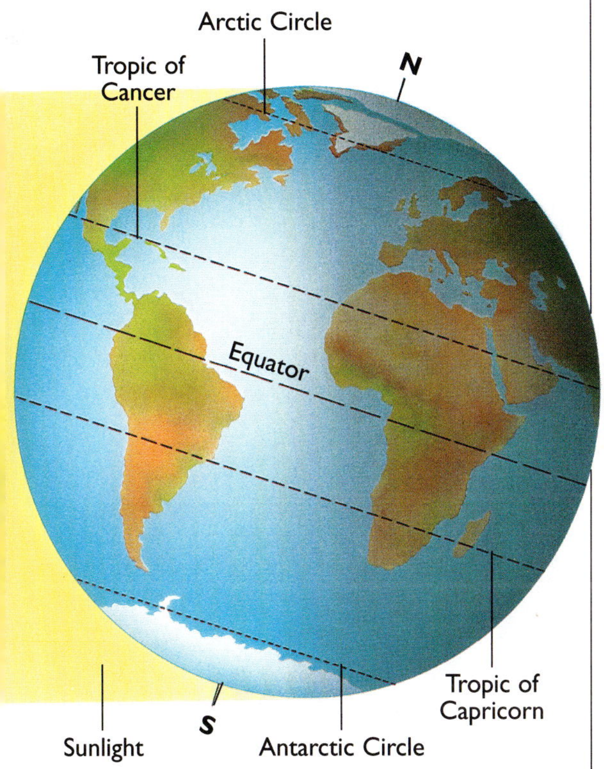

◀ **This picture of the Earth shows the tropics, the polar circles, and the Equator. The Earth turns on its axis (an imaginary line between the North and South poles). More sunlight reaches the Equator than the poles.**

Where is the Equator?

The Equator is an imaginary line around the middle of the Earth. It is the line of 0 degrees latitude. The fattest part of the Earth is just below the Equator where the planet bulges.

Where is the North Pole?

The North Pole is near the middle of the Arctic Ocean. It is the point where all the lines of longitude meet on the map. The South Pole is in the Antarctic continent.

EARTH FACTS

- Diameter: 12,713 km at the poles, 12,756 km at the Equator.
- Circumference: 40,091 km.
- Surface area: 510 million sq km.
- Area covered by water: 71 percent.
- Age: 4.6 billion years.
- Oldest rocks: 3.8 billion years.
- Thickness of crust: 20 km (average).
- Temperature at centre: 4,500°C.
- Distance from Sun: 152 million km (average).
- Distance from Moon: 385,000 km (average).

Where are the tropics?

The tropics are regions of the Earth that lie north and south of the Equator. Each of the tropics is about 2,600 kilometres wide. The Tropic of Cancer is 23°27′ north of the Equator. The Tropic of Capricorn is 23°27′ south of the Equator. These two lines of latitude (imaginary lines on the Earth's surface) mark the boundaries of a region where the Sun shines directly overhead.

What are the hemispheres?

A hemisphere is half of a globe. On maps and globes, the Equator (0 degrees latitude) divides the planet into two halves – the Northern and Southern hemispheres. An imaginary line around the Earth from the North Pole to the South Pole (the line of 0 degrees longitude) divides the Eastern and Western hemispheres.

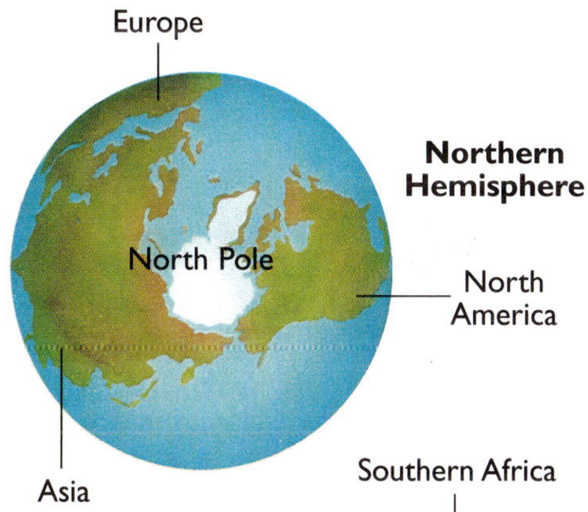

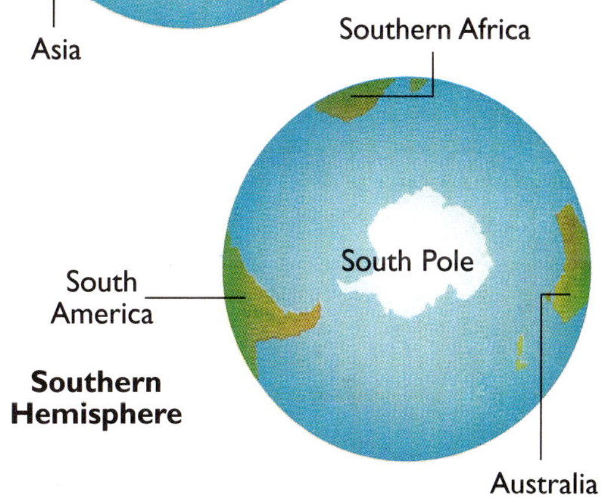

▶ **The Northern Hemisphere includes Asia, North America and Europe. The Southern includes Australia, southern Africa and most of South America.**

What is the Earth's axis?

Take an orange and push a stick through its middle. The stick marks the axis of the orange. There is of course no stick through the Earth – its axis is an imaginary line between the poles. The Earth's axis is tilted about 23.5° from the vertical.

Why do we have day and night?

The Earth turns on its axis as it orbits the Sun, therefore part of the Earth is sunlit (day) while part is in shadow (night). Since the Earth spins all the time, day and night follow each other continually. Sunrise marks the start of day, and sunset the coming of night.

In mid-summer in the Arctic (facing the Sun), it is always daylight and northern Europe and North America have long summer days. In the Antarctic, it is always night. In mid-winter it is the other way round. The Antarctic has permanent daylight, while the Arctic is in darkness, and northern Europe and North America have short winter days.

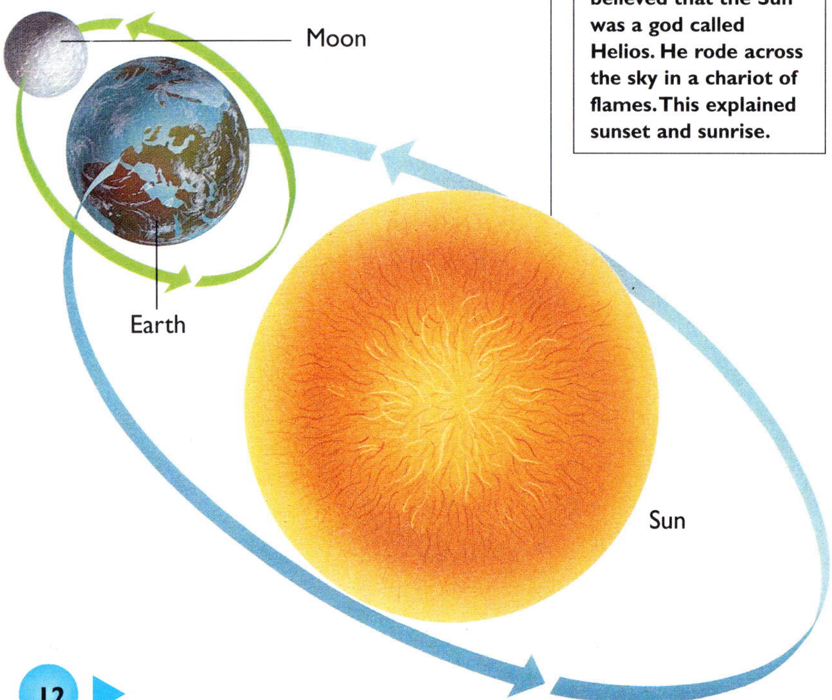

▲ We have seasons because of the way the Earth orbits the Sun. The Earth is tilted and so first one pole, then the other, leans towards the Sun.

The Ancient Greeks believed that the Sun was a god called Helios. He rode across the sky in a chariot of flames. This explained sunset and sunrise.

Why do we have seasons?

The seasons (spring, summer, autumn, winter) occur because the Earth is tilted on its axis. As the Earth moves around the Sun, the hemisphere that is tilted towards the Sun gets more of the Sun's rays and so is warmer and has summer. The people in that hemisphere see the Sun passing higher across the sky, and the days are longer. Meanwhile the part tilted away from the Sun has winter because it is less warm. There the days are shorter. At the Equator, the length of a day varies very little.

◀ The Moon moves in orbit around the Earth (green arrow). The Earth travels in orbit around the Sun (blue arrow). All three are spinning like tops at the same time.

▲ **Since the Earth's axis is tilted, the hemispheres are at different angles to the Sun. In the hemisphere tilted towards the Sun, daylength is longer. This is why days are longer in summer.**

How is the Earth like a magnet?

The Earth acts like a giant dynamo. Movements inside it create electrical currents that make a magnetic field with north and south poles, rather like a bar magnet. The Earth's magnetic field stretches far into space for about 60,000 kilometres. The Sun and the other planets also have magnetic fields.

Does a compass needle point to the North Pole?

No. The magnetized needle of a compass always turns to point in the direction of the Earth's north magnetic pole. The north magnetic pole is not the same as the geographic North Pole.

Changes in the Earth's magnetic field make the magnetic poles change positions, following circular paths with diameters of about 160 kilometres, but they never stray far from the geographical poles. The north magnetic pole is in northern Canada. The south magnetic pole is in Antarctica. About 450 million years ago the south magnetic pole was in what is now the Sahara Desert.

Every 200,000 to 300,000 years the magnetic poles reverse. North becomes south and south becomes north.

▼ **The Earth's magnetic field stretches far into space. Like all magnets, the Earth has north and south magnetic poles.**

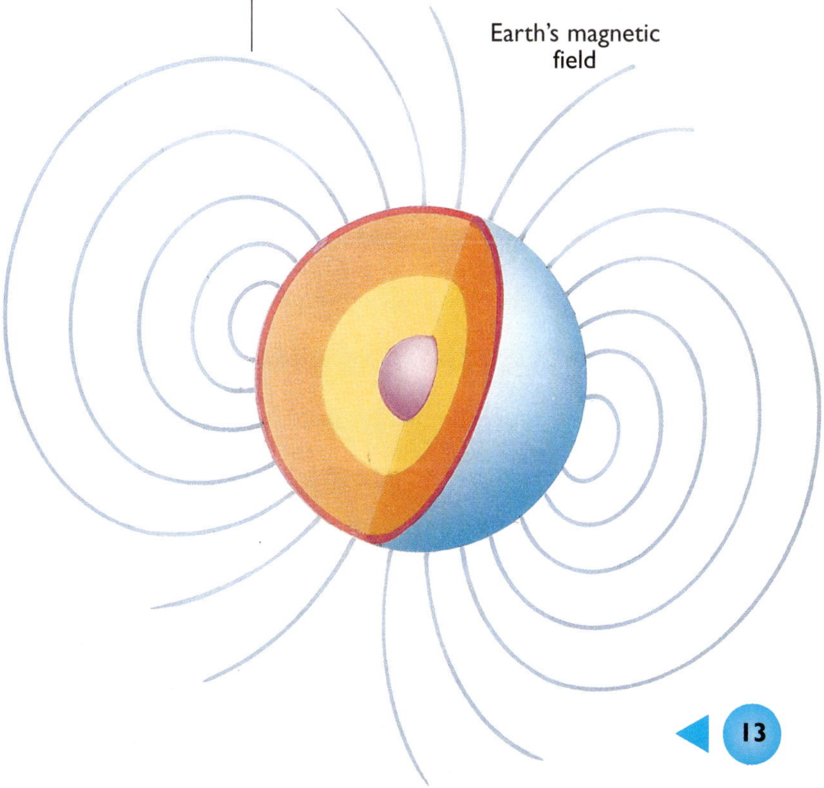

GEOGRAPHY

What do geographers do?

Geographers study the Earth, its features and living things. They look at the Earth's landscapes: where people, animals and plants live. They study such features as rivers and deserts. They study where cities are built, what industries produce, how humans and nature alter the landscape. Using survey equipment, they make precise measurements of the Earth's features. From these measurements, accurate maps of various kinds are made. Geographers help plan the cities and countryside in which we live.

When was the Earth first measured?

About 200 BC the Greek scientist Erastosthenes measured the distance around the Earth. He found the angle of the Sun's rays at different places that were a known distance apart. Using geometry, he worked out the Earth's circumference as 252,000 stadia (about 46,000 kilometres). His measurements were a little inaccurate: in fact the modern figure for the Earth's greatest circumference is 40,091 kilometres.

When were the first maps made?

People probably drew rough maps of their own lands over 5,000 years ago. A clay tablet made about 2500 BC in Babylonia (now part of Iraq) appears to show what looks like a river valley with mountains either side.

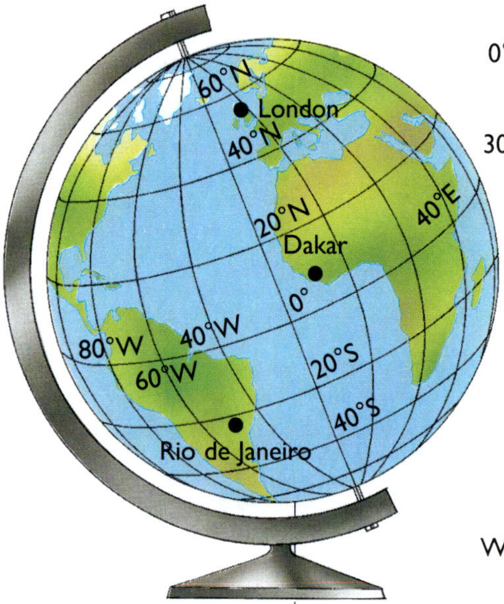

▶ Lines of latitude and longitude form a network that can be used to pinpoint places. The lines are measured in degrees. Greenwich, in London, is at 0° longitude, the Equator is at 0° latitude.

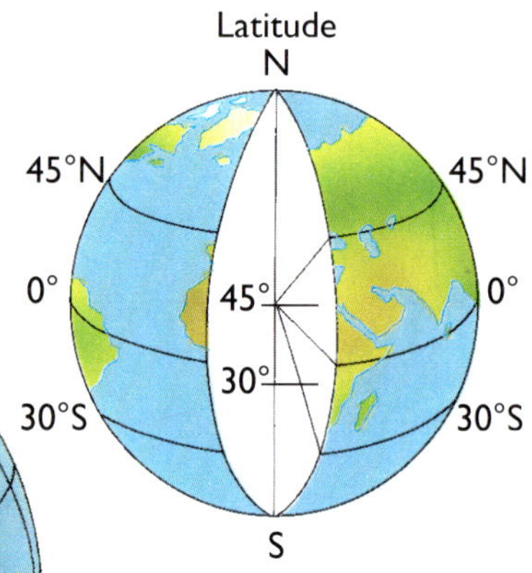

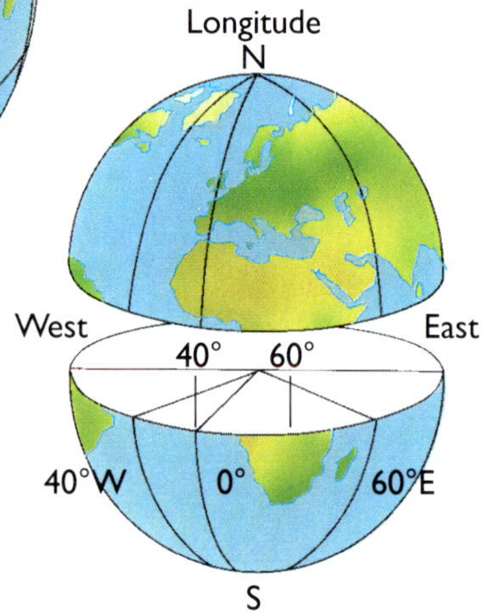

What are lines of latitude and longitude?

A map has a network of lines across it. The lines running east–west are lines of latitude, or parallels. The north–south lines are lines of longitude, or meridians. The lines make it easier to find a place on the map. The Ancient Greek geographer Ptolemy was the first mapmaker to draw such lines.

◀ The first reasonably accurate maps of the world were drawn in the 1500s. Most were based on the tales of seamen and travellers in distant lands.

When did America first appear on maps?

Before 1500, maps made in Europe did not show America. It was unknown to Europeans until Christopher Columbus sailed across the Atlantic Ocean in 1492. Soon mapmakers began to show the coast of the eastern Americas. The name America was first used on a German map in 1507.

When did sailors first use maps?

The first charts (sea maps) were made in Europe in the 1300s. They were called portolan charts and showed the Mediterranean coast in some detail. Sailors could recognize bays and headlands. A web of lines joined the various ports shown on the map, to help sailors find the right direction.

How is height shown on a map?

Height is difficult to show on a flat map. Colour shading shows areas that are the same height above sea level. Contour lines on a map also show height. The closer together contour lines are, the steeper the slope.

What is a map projection?

No flat map can be entirely accurate because the Earth's surface is curved. A map projection is a means of transferring the curved surface onto a flat map. One map projection can be imagined by wrapping a cylindrical roll of paper around a globe. It was made popular (though not invented) by the Flemish mapmaker Gerardus Mercator (1512–1594).

▶ Taking aerial photographs is one way to make maps. The photos are taken with an overlap, as shown in this picture. Viewing pairs of photos together gives a 3-D image, so contours can be plotted.

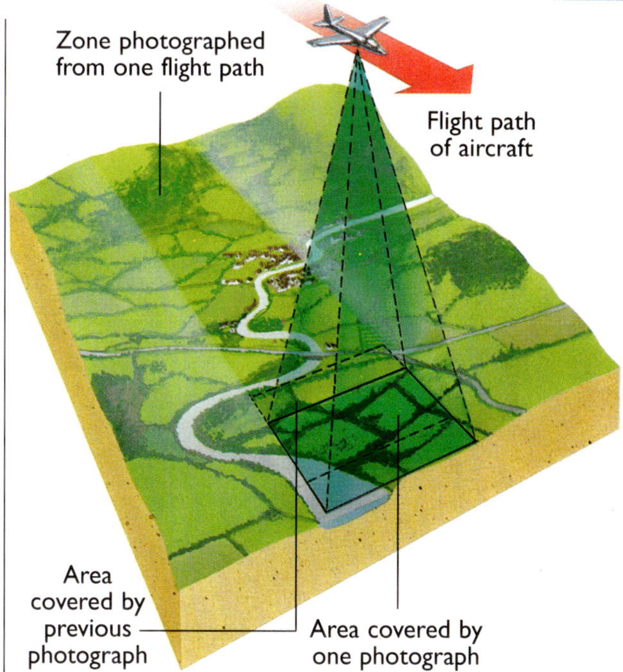

How are modern maps made?

Most maps are made from photographs taken from aircraft or from satellites orbiting the Earth. They show the land and sea in great detail.

▼ Two common map projections are Mercator's and the zenithal or azimuthal. In the zenithal projection, the paper is flat and touches the globe at one point.

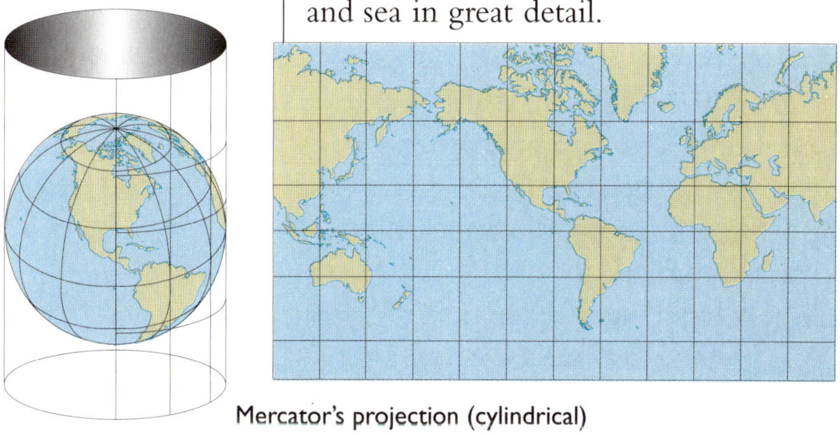

Mercator's projection (cylindrical)

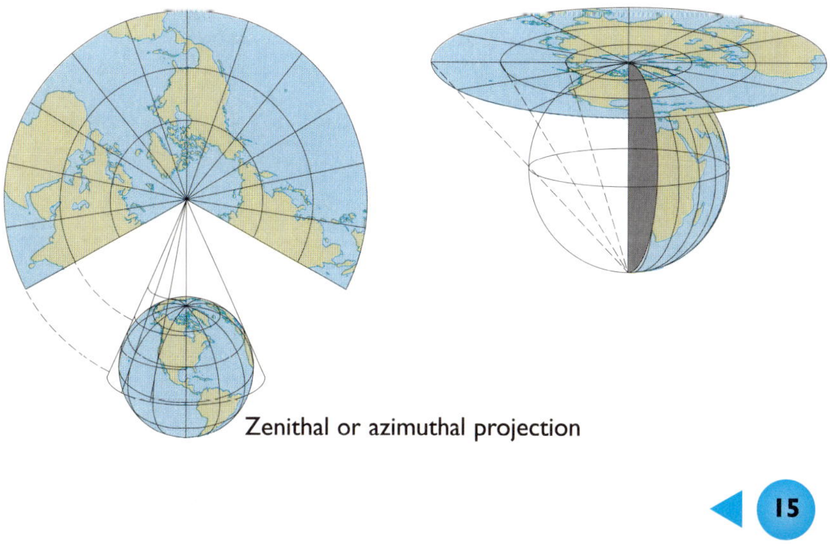

Zenithal or azimuthal projection

EVER-CHANGING EARTH

How is the Earth always changing?

Since the Earth was formed over 4.6 billion years ago, it has changed in many ways. Some changes happen so slowly that they are not noticeable in a person's lifetime. Earthquakes and volcanoes, however, can alter landscapes in hours. Glaciers, rivers and the oceans also alter the face of the Earth but they may take thousands of years.

How can continents move?

The Earth's crust is formed of a number of separate curved plates. The plates float like giant rafts on a thick treacly mass of molten rock. Heat from within the Earth sends currents moving through the 'treacle', and these cause the plates to move. As the plates move, so do the continents resting on them.

All seven continents on the Earth today – Africa, Asia, Antarctica, Australia, Europe, North and South America – were once part of one gigantic super-continent called Pangaea, which later broke up.

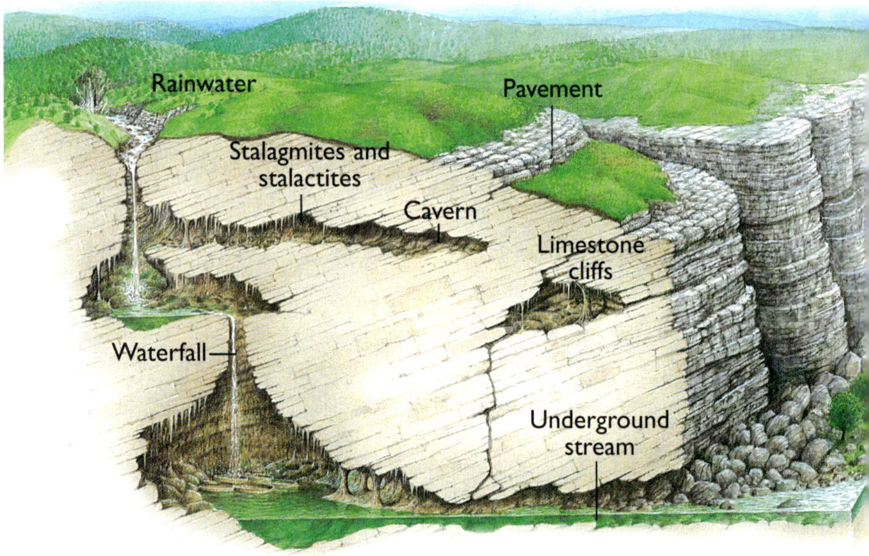

▲ Caves, caverns and potholes are formed by water wearing away soft limestone rocks. Drips of lime-bearing water form stalactites and stalagmites.

How are caves made?

Most caves are hollowed out of rock by underground water. The water trickles down from the Earth's surface, dissolving some of the rock to form small passages and openings. Carbon dioxide in the air can make the water slightly acidic, and this acid eats away at the rock. Streams may also flow into and through the cave, making it bigger.

▼ Pangaea began to break up about 200 million years ago, to form the continents we know today.

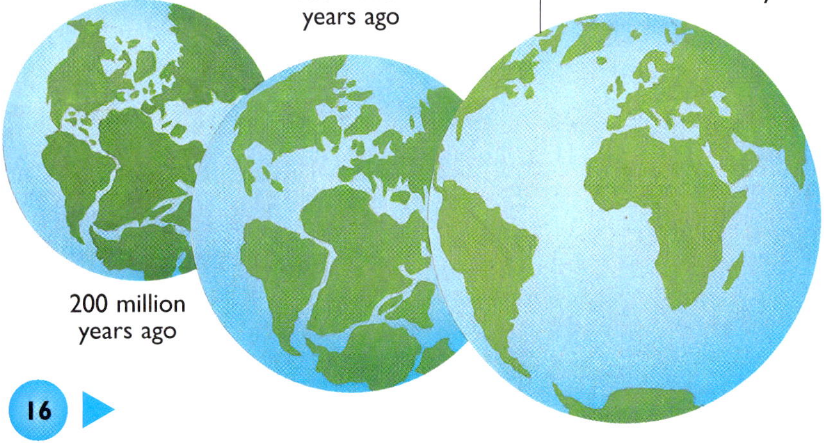

What makes a landslide?

Landslides are falls of rock and mud sent cascading down a mountain or hillside. The cause is often an earthquake or volcanic eruption. The movement of the surface causes loose or wet surface material to break away and slide downhill. A big landslide can bury a whole valley. Heavy rains can send mud slipping down a hillside. The risk of this kind of landslide is greater when trees on mountain slopes are felled – a major problem in some developing countries.

How can we tell stalactites from stalagmites?

Stalactites and stalagmites form inside limestone caves. The water that drips steadily from the roof contains a mineral called calcite. The water dries, but the calcite remains and slowly builds into a column. Stalactites grow downwards, from the cave roof. Stalagmites grow upwards, from the cave floor. Sometimes the two columns meet to form a pillar.

Why are high mountain tops covered in snow?

High mountain tops are surrounded by very cold air. For every 1,000 metres in height, the temperature falls by 5 degrees Celsius. The highest mountains are snow-covered all year round. The highest mountains in the world are found in long ranges such as the Himalayas (Asia), the Andes (South America), the Rockies (North America) and the Alps (Europe).

▶ Stalactites and stalagmites look like long icicles of rock. Stalactites grow down from the cave roof, stalagmites grow up from the floor.

ICE AND CAVE FACTS

- In the mountains of eastern Italy is a cave known as the Room of Candles. It is full of white stalagmites that look like candles.
- Don't sit and watch a stalactite grow. It can take 1,000 years to get 1 cm longer!
- During the last Ice Age, 28 percent of the Earth was ice-covered. Today, about 10 percent is covered by ice.
- The world's longest glacier is the Lambert Glacier in the Antarctic which is over 400 km in length.
- The world's deepest cave is at Rousseau Jean Bernard in France. It is 1,535 m deep.
- The longest cave system is beneath Mammoth Cave in Kentucky, USA. It is at least 530 km long.
- Sarawak Chamber in Indonesia is the world's biggest cavern. It is 700 m long, 300 m wide and 70 m high.

What is a glacier?

A glacier is a moving 'river' of ice. Glaciers are found in polar regions and in high mountains, wherever more snow falls in winter than is lost through melting and evaporation in summer. The icy mass creeps slowly downhill. Glaciers shape landscapes, flattening hills and carving out valleys. When a glacier reaches the sea in very cold regions, huge blocks of ice break off to form floating icebergs. The largest icebergs in the world are found in the ocean around Antarctica.

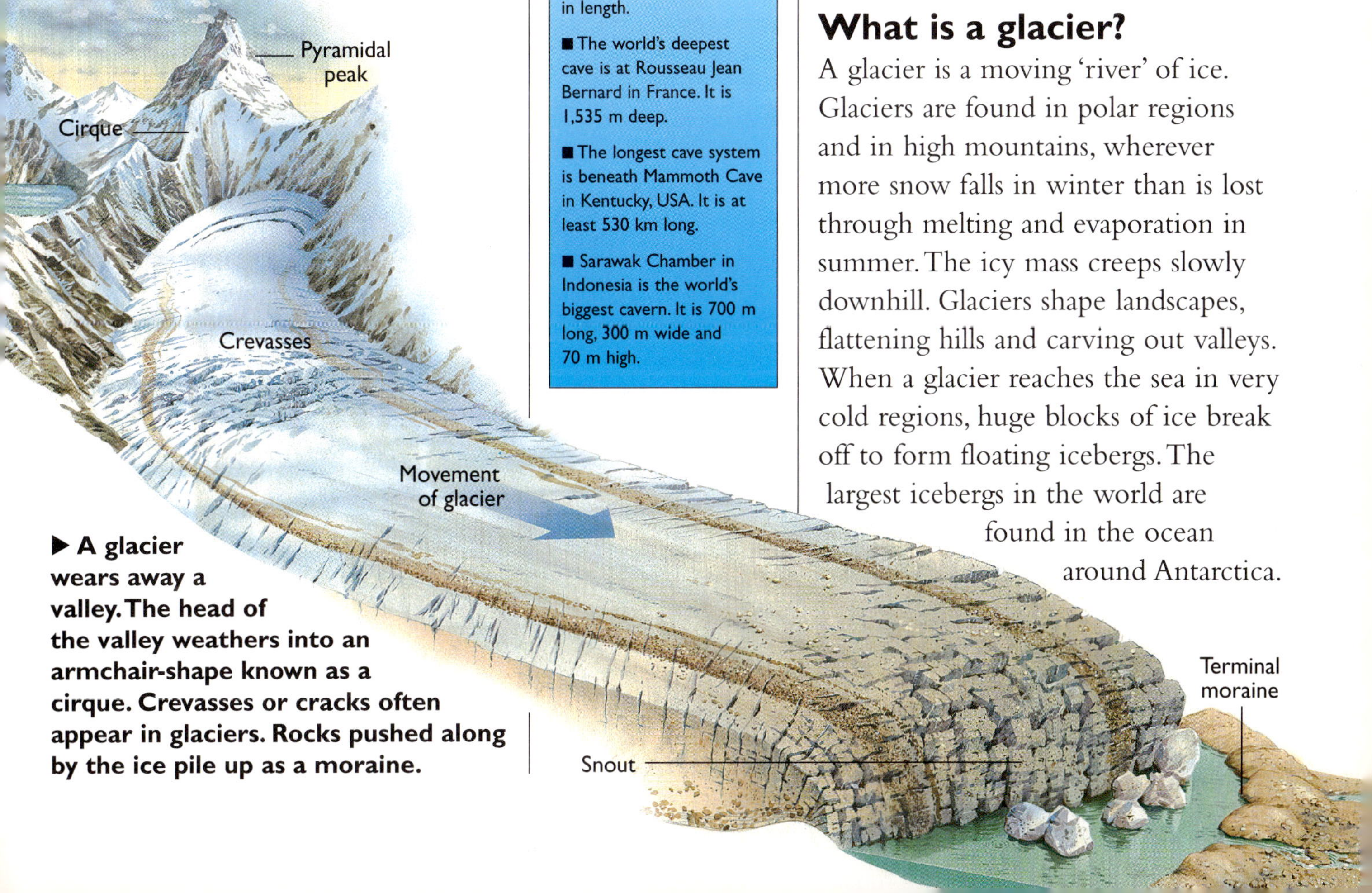

▶ A glacier wears away a valley. The head of the valley weathers into an armchair-shape known as a cirque. Crevasses or cracks often appear in glaciers. Rocks pushed along by the ice pile up as a moraine.

What is an avalanche?

An avalanche is a sudden fall of snow and ice down a mountainside. Avalanches are very dangerous because they can bury and kill people. They happen when so much snow falls that the layers of snow on the mountainside become too heavy and suddenly give way and slide or fall down. Avalanches also happen in spring when the warm weather begins to melt the snow so that it slides more easily. Earthquakes, and even sudden loud sounds, can also cause avalanches.

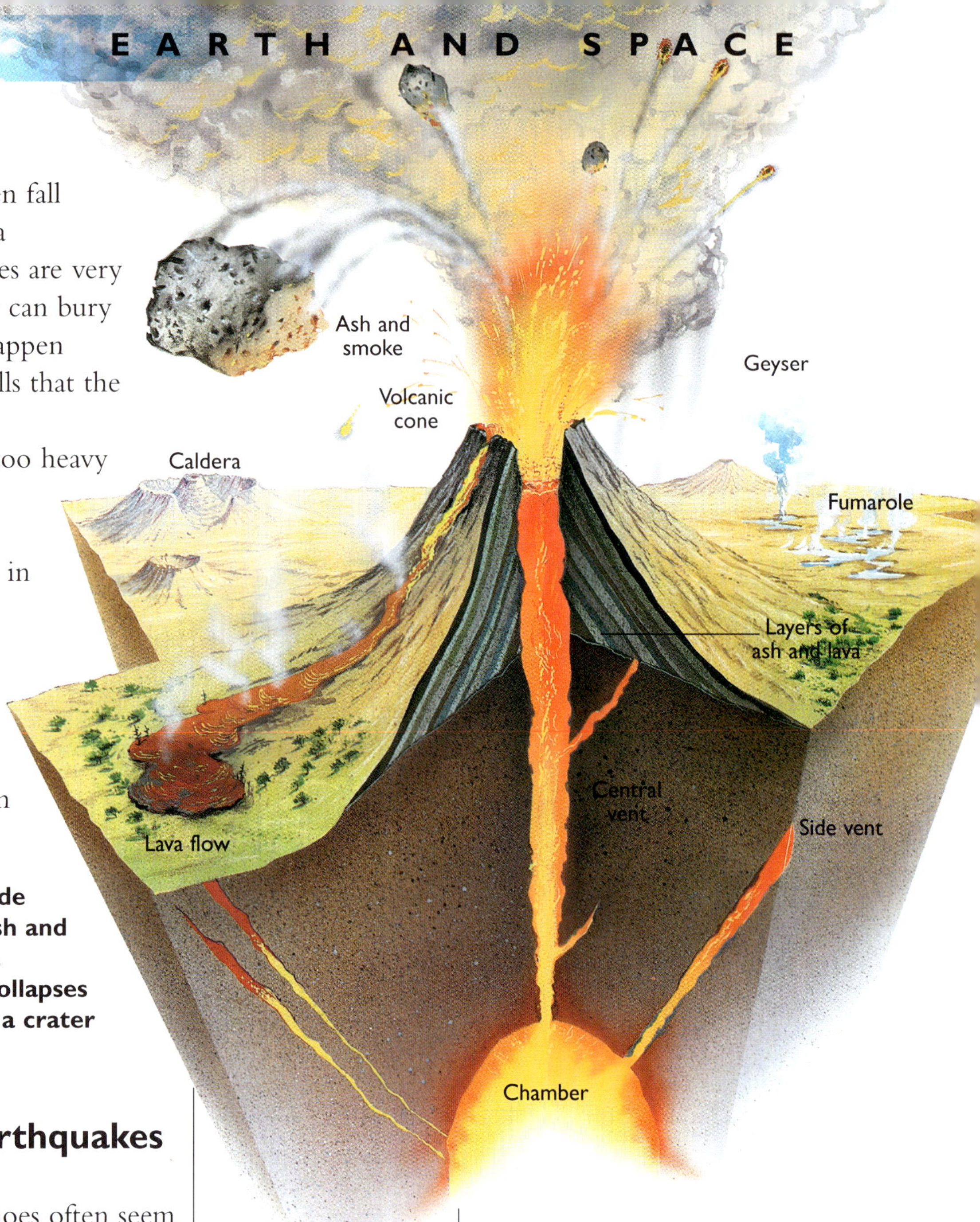

▶ A volcano may explode violently, blowing out ash and steam and red-hot lava. Sometimes a volcano collapses around its vent, leaving a crater called a caldera.

What causes earthquakes and volcanoes?

Earthquakes and volcanoes often seem to occur together. They happen most often in parts of the Earth where two of the plates making up the crust meet. Rocks are either pushed up to form mountains or ridges, or sink down into the Earth's mantle to create trenches. This movement makes the Earth's surface unstable, and earthquakes and volcanoes are likely to occur. Scientists can tell where earthquakes and volcanoes are likely to happen, but they cannot predict exactly when.

The people of Ancient China believed that the Earth was balanced on the shoulders of a giant ox. Earthquakes happened when the ox shifted the Earth from one shoulder to the other.

Why do geysers spout hot water?

A geyser is a gushing fountain of hot water and steam. Geysers are found in areas of volcanic activity, such as Iceland. Hot volcanic rocks heat underground water, which bubbles up as a hot spring. If water deeper down is heated further, it turns to steam and pushes up the cooler water above it to form a geyser. 'Old Faithful' geyser in the United States has spouted every 76 minutes for the last 80 years.

Why do some volcanoes explode?

When a volcano erupts, magma (molten rock) from deep inside the Earth is pushed up towards the surface. Red-hot lava (the name given to magma when it pours out above ground) flows out of the volcano. Smoke and ash belch upwards, darkening the sky.

An explosive volcano contains very thick lava. The lava is pushed upwards very slowly and may form a plug, sealing the volcano. Pressure builds up inside until gas and ash burst through, blowing the top off the volcano in a huge explosion.

What happens in an earthquake?

In an earthquake, the ground begins to shake. This shaking may last for only a few seconds or for minutes. Buildings may shake, crack and collapse. Surface cracks open up across fields and rocks and whole chunks of land may sink suddenly.

Earthquakes happen in places where there are great cracks, or faults, in the rocks below ground. These places are at the edges of the huge plates, or sections, in the Earth's crust. The plates slowly move past or towards each other. Where two plates meet, the rocks on either side of the gap slide past each other, which can make the ground shake.

VIOLENT EARTH FACTS

- The largest volcano is Mauna Loa in the Hawaiian Islands. It measures 119 km across its base.
- When Krakatoa volcano exploded in 1883, the sound was heard in Australia, 5,000 km away.
- There are more than 500 active volcanoes.
- In 1201 there was a terrible earthquake in the eastern Mediterranean. It is possible that over a million people were killed.
- In 1906 the San Francisco earthquake started fires that destroyed much of the city.
- In 1995 an earthquake struck Kobe, Japan. Over 5,000 people died and a third of the city buildings were destroyed.
- Every year there are 1,000 earthquakes strong enough to cause some damage.

Where do the worst earthquakes happen?

Some of the worst earthquakes have happened in China. In 1556, an earthquake at Shensi killed over 800,000 people. Then in 1976, history repeated itself. An earthquake at Tangshan killed about 750,000 people. This is the worst earthquake disaster of modern times.

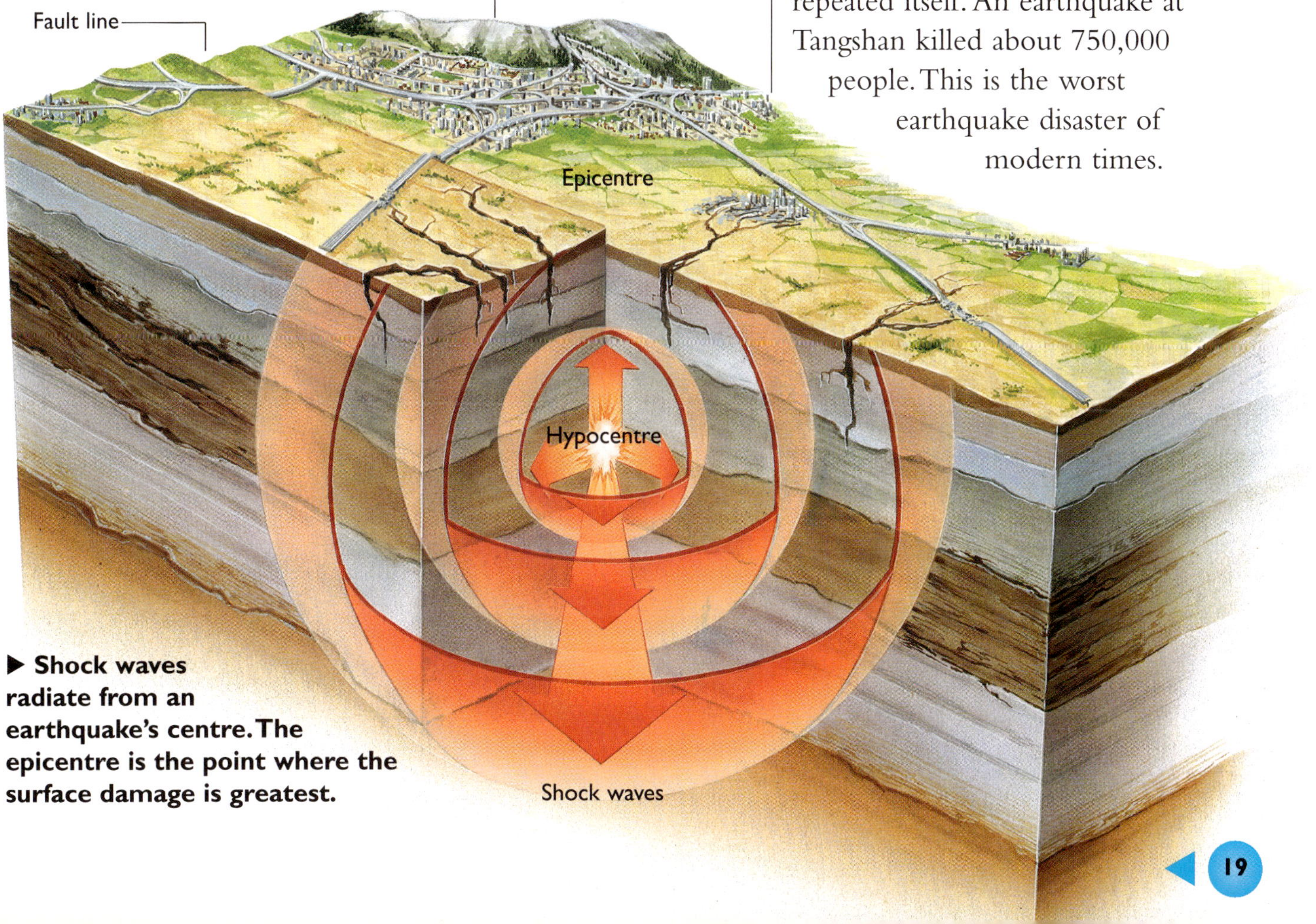

▶ **Shock waves radiate from an earthquake's centre. The epicentre is the point where the surface damage is greatest.**

LANDSCAPES

What is a desert?

A desert is a region that has less than 25 centimetres of rain a year. Deserts cover between one-eighth and one-seventh of the Earth's land surface. Hot deserts lie between 20 and 30 degrees either side of the Equator. There are cold deserts too, covered with snow and ice. Cold deserts cover one-sixth of the world's surface.

What is an oasis?

An oasis is a patch of green in the desert. Plants grow there because there is water from a well or an underground spring. The water is trapped deep down in the rocks beneath the desert. Palm trees and vegetables can be grown in an oasis. Some oases support quite large towns.

Which is the biggest desert?

The Sahara in northern Africa is easily the biggest desert in the world. Look at a map of Africa and you will see how much of northern Africa is covered by the Sahara. It fills a vast area of 9.1 million square kilometres, which is bigger than the whole of Australia.

Where are seas of sand?

In some hot deserts, an erg or 'sand sea' may form. The biggest is the Grand Erg Oriental in Algeria and Tunisia, covering 196,000 square kilometres with dunes 300 metres high.

▲ **In sandy deserts, winds blow the sand into wave-like shapes known as dunes. The dunes move and form different shapes.**

DESERT FACTS

- Death Valley, in the Mojave Desert of California, USA, is the hottest spot in North America. A high of 57°C has been recorded there.
- The Sahara was not always dry. Prehistoric paintings show it as a fertile land with grass and rivers.
- The Sun is a cheap source of power in the desert. In Saudi Arabia, there are solar-powered payphones for desert travellers.
- Desert ostriches eat sand. It probably helps them digest their food.
- Desert nights are cold. In winter, temperatures often fall below freezing.
- Australia has large areas of desert. The two largest are the Gibson and Great Victoria deserts.
- Only about 20 percent of the world's hot deserts are sandy.

What is sand?

Sand is made up of tiny mineral grains, the biggest of which are only two millimetres across. Sand is rock broken apart and crumbled by weathering. The most common mineral in sand is quartz. However, not all deserts are sandy. Only about one-fifth of hot deserts are covered with sand. Other deserts are rocky, stony or scrubby.

Are all deserts hot?

Most deserts are found in hot countries, but not all. One of the world's largest deserts, the stony Gobi Desert in central Asia has short, hot summers but cold winters. The Antarctic is a frozen desert.

How are islands made?

Some islands are chunks of land that became separated from continents. The British Isles, for example, were once joined to Europe. Others are volcanoes that have risen up above the sea. The islands of Japan are volcanic islands.

How are coral reefs formed?

The tiny coral animals of warm seas create some of the oceans' most spectacular sights – coral reefs. The limestone remains of the animals build up into walls and ridges of coral. Plants and animals move in to colonize the coral reef. Coral reefs are found only in tropical oceans; coral animals cannot live in cold water.

The Great Barrier Reef off the coast of northeastern Australia is the world's longest reef. It is over 2,000 kilometres long.

What is an atoll?

An atoll is a doughnut-shaped coral island. First, a fringing reef of coral forms on the outer rim of a volcanic island that is slowly sinking into the ocean floor. In time, mud and sand pile up on top of the reef and plants begin to grow. The central volcanic island has by now sunk completely under the water. Only the circular reef remains. There are many coral atolls in the Pacific Ocean.

What is it like at the South Pole?

The polar regions of the Arctic and the Antarctic are vast frozen deserts. At the South Pole there is no life of any kind. Snow and ice lie thousands of metres thick. For half the year there is permanent darkness.

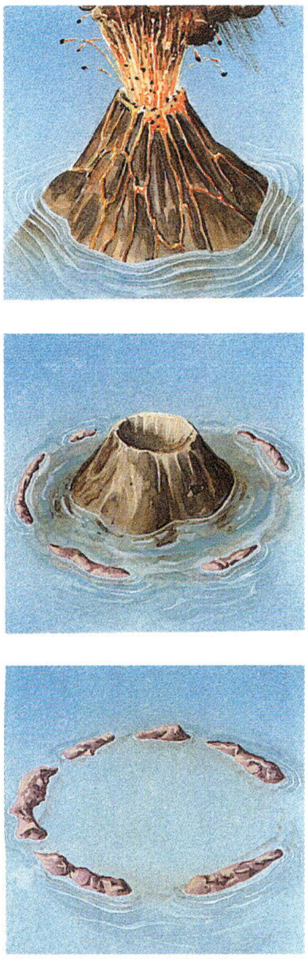

▲ Coral reefs form when a volcanic island rises from the sea. A fringing reef of coral grows, forming a ring or atoll which remains after the island has sunk.

How thick is the Antarctic ice?

The thickest ice in the Antarctic is 4,800 metres deep. That is more than ten times the height of the world's tallest skyscraper. The Antarctic covers about 14 million square kilometres – bigger than either Europe or Australia. However, the land of Antarctica is actually smaller than Australia. Its huge size is due to the enormous mass of ice covering it. Antarctica contains almost nine-tenths of all the ice on Earth.

How big was the biggest iceberg?

The biggest icebergs are the great, flat bergs that break away from the Antarctic ice sheet. Along the edge of the Ross Ice Shelf in the Antarctic the rise and fall of the tide cracks the ice. Icebergs break loose. The largest iceberg ever seen was over 31,000 square kilometres, bigger than the country of Belgium.

◀ The South Pole is one of the coldest and bleakest places on Earth. There is now a permanent scientific base there, where modern polar explorers can find a warm welcome.

How much of the Earth is forested?

In prehistoric times, people had not begun to clear forests to make room for their cities, farms and factories. About 60 percent of the Earth's land area was forested then. Today only about 30 percent is covered by forest.

Which forests have the most trees?

The richest forests on Earth are the tropical rainforests. In North America or Europe a small area of typical forest might contain about ten kinds of tree. The same area in a Brazilian or Indonesian rainforest might have over 100 different kinds of tree.

Where is the canopy in a rainforest?

The tops of the tall trees in a rainforest make up the canopy. The canopy receives the most sunlight and it grows thickly. It can form a dense roof, shadowing plants lower down. The tallest trees grow up through the lower layers, towards the sunlight. In the canopy live many animals such as monkeys, birds and insects.

What is tundra?

The tundra is a zone near the Arctic where the climate is mostly too cold and dry for trees. Most of the tundra is snow-covered much of the year. Mosses, lichens and tough grasses grow on the tundra, seen briefly during summer when the snow melts.

▶ Tundra plants are small. Their roots can grow only to about 30 cm deep before meeting frozen ground. Many plants flower during the brief summer.

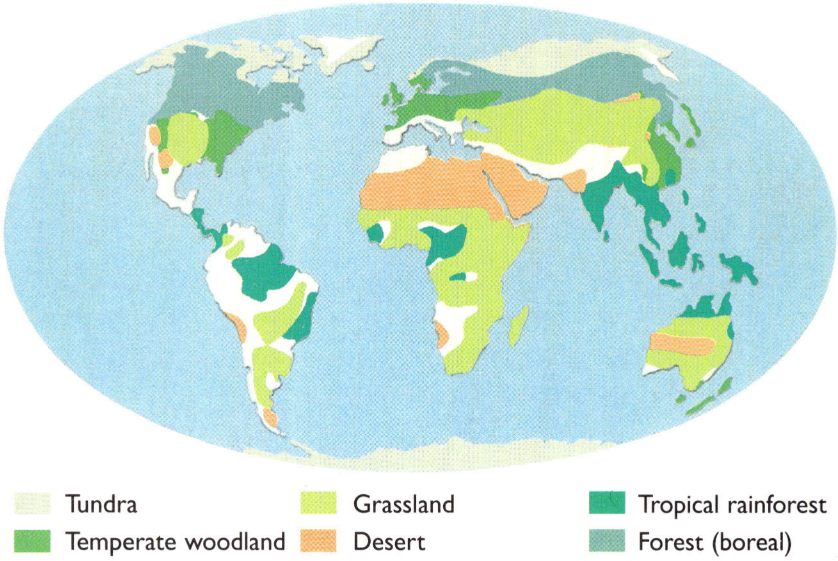

▲ The world's main vegetation zones.

It rains almost every day in a rainforest. It gets hotter and stickier, until in the afternoon there's a thunderstorm. Then it's dry again.

Where was the world's largest prairie?

The great prairie of the American Midwest once stretched from southern Texas northwards into Canada. It was the biggest on Earth and in places the grass was as tall as a person. Today little remains of the original prairie. Since the 1800s, people have ploughed it and planted it with crops such as wheat. This means there are fewer prairie animals too.

Where is the Grand Canyon?

The Grand Canyon is in Arizona in the United States. It is as much as 29 kilometres wide and 1,700 metres deep in places. It is the longest gorge in the world, being 349 kilometres in length. The Grand Canyon was formed by the Colorado River cutting deep into the rock.

▲ **The Grand Canyon is one of the natural wonders of the world.**

Which mountain range has the highest peaks?

The world's 20 highest mountains are all in the Himalaya-Karakoram range in Asia. All these mountains are over 8,000 metres high.

The highest mountain above sea level is Mount Everest in the Himalayas. Working out the exact height of such great mountains in remote regions is difficult. In 1860 surveyors calculated that Everest was 8,840 metres high. In 1973 this was corrected to 8,848 metres. In 1987 satellite measurements gave the height of Mount Everest as 8,863 metres.

Why are there fiords in Scandinavia?

During the Ice Ages, glaciers and ice sheets covered Scandinavia. Glaciers and ice sheets grind and cut into the landscape across which they move. Glaciers seek out the easiest paths down a mountain, such as river valleys. The ice deepens the valleys, and after it melts, water flows in from the sea. These deep, narrow inlets are called fiords. There are also fiords in Chile and Alaska.

▼ **These are the highest mountains on the seven continents, ranged in order of size.**

Atmosphere and Weather

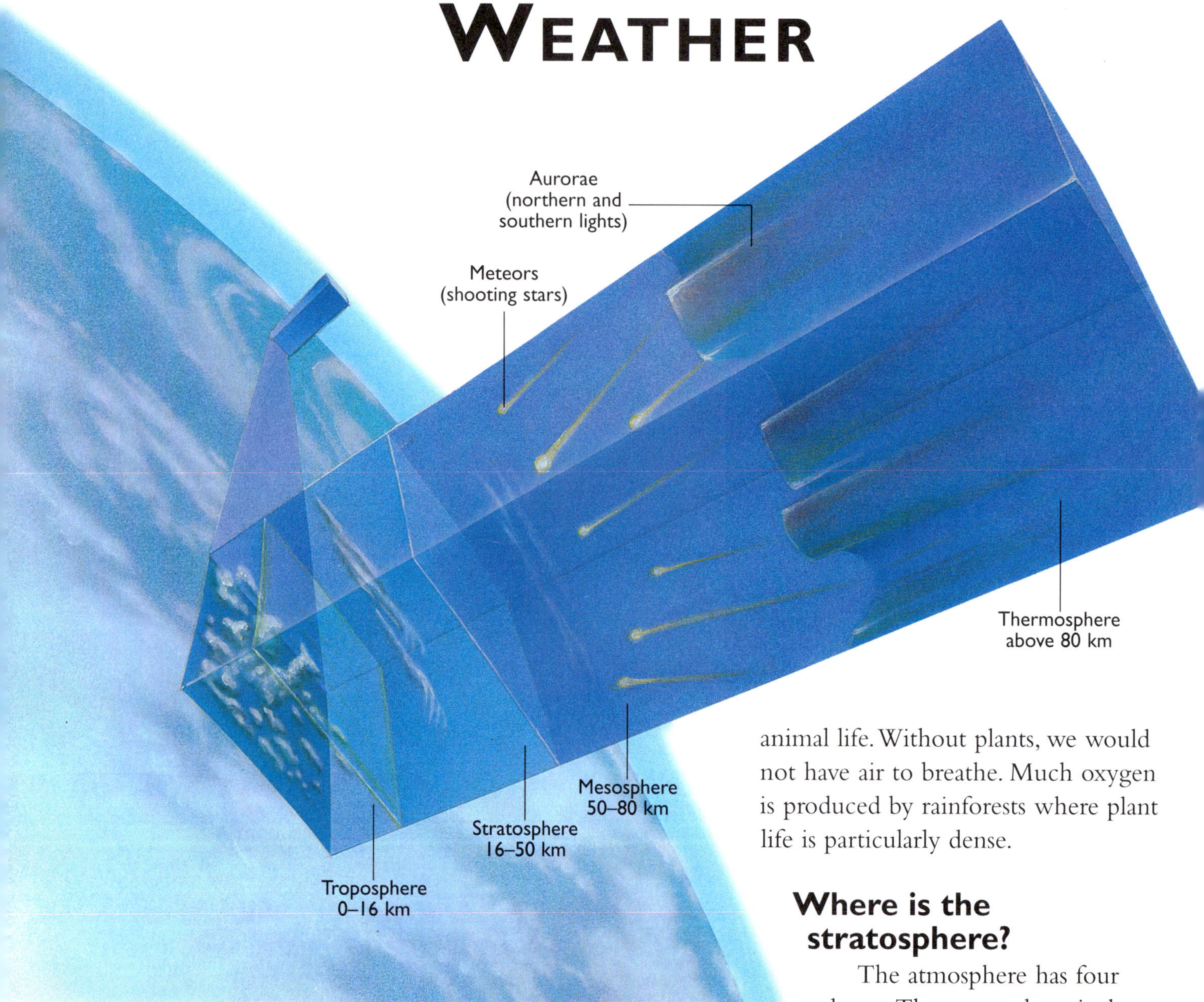

What is the atmosphere?

The atmosphere is the layer of gas surrounding the Earth. The layer is surprisingly thin, yet without it there would be no life on Earth. When the Earth was young, the atmosphere consisted mainly of poisonous gases. Plants (which give off oxygen during photosynthesis) have made the atmosphere capable of supporting animal life. Without plants, we would not have air to breathe. Much oxygen is produced by rainforests where plant life is particularly dense.

▲ Air surrounds the Earth like a transparent shell. The layers of the atmosphere shield us from most of the Sun's dangerous rays.

Where is the stratosphere?

The atmosphere has four layers. The troposphere is the lowest layer. It is up to 16 kilometres thick. Above it is the stratosphere, which reaches to about 50 kilometres high. Higher still is the mesophere, to about 80 kilometres. The upper layer is called the thermosphere. The thermosphere has two parts, the ionosphere and the exosphere. Temperature differences mark the boundaries between the layers.

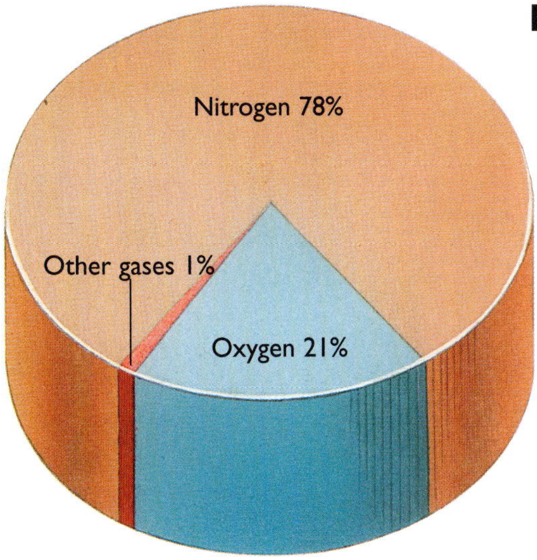

◀ **Our air is mostly nitrogen gas, which makes up nearly four-fifths of the air. About one-fifth of the air is oxygen, the gas we need to breathe. Other gases and water vapour make up the rest.**

What is air?

Air is a mixture of gases. The most plentiful gases in air are nitrogen (78 percent) and oxygen (21 percent). The remaining 1 percent is made up of water vapour and very small amounts of ozone, carbon dioxide, argon and helium.

Why is the sky blue?

Light reaches the Earth from the Sun. Sunlight looks white, but is actually a mixture of all the colours in the rainbow. When light rays from the Sun pass through the atmosphere, some are scattered by the tiny bits of dust and water in the air. Blue rays are scattered most and reach our eyes from all angles. We see more blue than any other colour and this makes the sky look blue.

Why are sunsets red?

At sunset the Sun is low in the sky and farther away from us as we look towards it. The light rays from the Sun have to pass through more layers of air to reach our eyes. This extra air scatters out all the colours in the sunlight except red. Only the red rays come straight to our eyes and so we see a red sunset.

ATMOSPHERE FACTS

- The lowest layer of atmosphere is where weather happens.
- Planes fly above the clouds. Here the skies are clear and the air is thin.
- Air is heavier than you think. The average roomful of air weighs more than 45 kg – as much as 20 bags of potatoes!
- The ozone layer is in the stratosphere.
- In the mesosphere, 50 to 80 km above our heads, it is freezing cold, down to –80°C.
- The outer layer of the thermosphere is called the exosphere. It extends as far as 8,000 km. Here it is very hot, above 2,200°C.

Where is the ozone layer?

Ozone is a form of oxygen. In the atmosphere, ozone forms when oxygen reacts under the influence of sunlight. Most ozone forms near the Equator and is shifted by the winds around the Earth. The ozone layer is an invisible screen. The ozone filters out harmful ultraviolet rays from the Sun. Scientists have discovered holes in the ozone layer, over the Antarctic and Arctic. These holes are believed to be caused by harmful gases given off by aerosol sprays, refrigerators and factories.

Who went up in a balloon to study air?

No one had explored the atmosphere before balloons were invented. The French chemist Joseph Louis Gay-Lussac (1778–1850) made balloon flights over Paris to study the air. He found that air is the same mixture at different heights, although its pressure, temperature and moistness change the higher you go.

▶ **'Red sky at night, shepherd's delight.' This old rhyme suggests that a brilliant red sunset (with few clouds) means a fine day tomorrow.**

What are the northern and southern lights?

The northern lights, or aurora borealis, are marvellous displays of coloured lights in the sky, like an enormous laser show. You can see them in or near the Arctic. The southern lights, or aurora australis, are seen in or near the Antarctic. The lights are caused by electrical particles from the Sun hitting the atmosphere and giving off bursts of light.

Why does sunlight tan the skin?

Sunlight contains ultraviolet rays. We cannot see them, but they are vital to health. They enable skin cells to make vitamin D. However, ultraviolet rays damage the outer layer of skin. The body reacts by making more of a brown pigment called melanin. This darkens the skin. The ozone layer acts as a sun-block, shielding us from most of the ultraviolet rays.

What do we mean by climate?

Climate is the usual weather of a place over a long time. Weather can change from day to day, but climate stays the same. The Earth has five major climatic zones. They are polar (cold); cold forest (cold winters); temperate (mild winters); desert (dry); and tropical rainy (warm and moist).

What makes rain?

Water from the oceans, lakes, rivers and plants is evaporated by the Sun's heat to form water vapour. This vapour, or gas, is held in the air. Air rises when warm, or when forced to rise over mountains, or when heavier cold air pushes underneath it. As the warm, moisture-laden air rises, it cools. The water vapour condenses back into water droplets, which mass together to form clouds. As the air rises, more vapour turns to water. The clouds grow bigger. When the water droplets are too big for the air to carry, they fall as rain and the cycle begins again.

▶ The northern lights produce a brilliant light show in the sky, as energized particles hit the atmosphere.

The melanin pigment that gives us a tan is missing in some people. They are albinos and can be of any race. Their skin and hair are very pale and because the iris of the eye is colourless, blood vessels show through. Albinos cannot develop a protective suntan, so they have to avoid the sun if they can.

WEATHER FACTS

- Dust and smoke from volcanoes or forest fires can make the Sun and Moon appear green or blue.
- Every snowflake is a unique six-sided crystal of frozen water molecules.
- Even in summer, clouds contain ice. Most of the ice melts as it falls, except during occasional summer hailstorms.
- One of the world's wettest places is Cherrapunji, India, which has nearly 11,000 mm of rain a year.
- The Atacama Desert in Chile is the driest, with less than 0.1 mm a year. London has about 600 mm a year.

What are the highest clouds in the sky?

High clouds include cirrus, cirrostratus and cirrocumulus. These clouds are formed mainly of ice crystals. Cirrus clouds are wispy clouds and can form at heights up to 10,000 metres. The rare nacreous or mother-of-pearl clouds can be over 20,000 metres high.

Why do some lands have monsoons?

A monsoon is a wind which blows from sea to land in summer, and from land to sea in winter. In hot lands near the Equator the air heats up in summer and rises. Cool air, carrying moisture from the ocean, is drawn inland to take the place of the rising warm air. The cool winds bring rain which is often torrential. In India the monsoon lasts from three to four months, bringing rain in summer. In winter, there is much less rainfall.

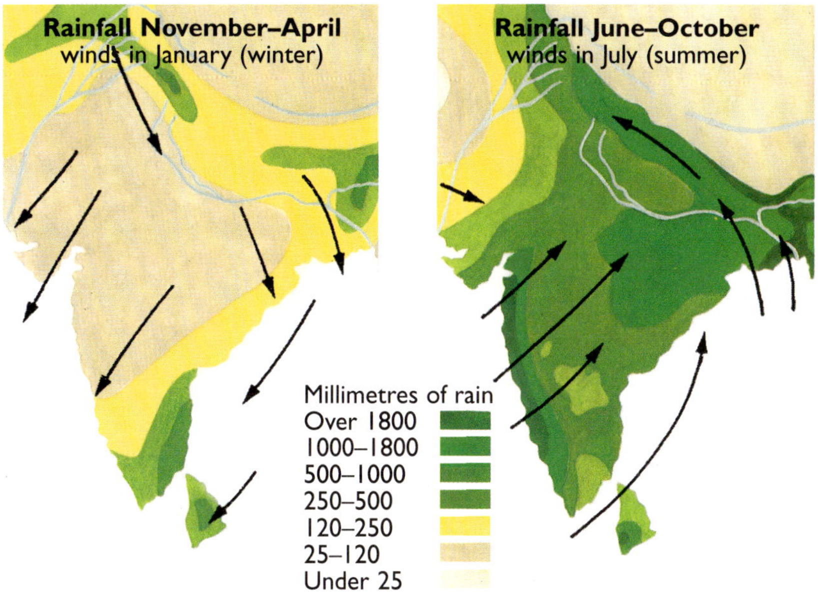

▲ The Indian sub-continent receives rain-carrying winds from the Indian Ocean during the monsoon season. In winter, the winds blow in the other direction.

◀ Whether water falls as drizzle, rain, sleet (a mixture of snow and rain) or snow, depends on the temperature of the air and the ground.

It may not rain cats and dogs, but it can rain frogs and fish! The animals are sometimes sucked up from ponds by extra-strong winds and fall with the rain.

What makes a rainbow?

Sunlight is a mixture of colours. When the Sun's rays pass through falling raindrops, the raindrops act like tiny mirrors or glass prisms. They bend and scatter the light into all its colours. We see a rainbow when the Sun is behind us and the rain in front of us. You can make your own rainbow with a water sprinkler or hose on a bright, sunny day.

▶ A rainbow is caused by sunlight shining on a screen of water droplets. Light rays are bent (refracted), reflected and then refracted again as they strike each droplet.

Where is the hottest place on Earth?

The hottest places are near the Equator, which receives the Sun's strongest rays. In 1922 a temperature of 58 degrees Celsius in the shade was recorded in the Libyan Desert in North Africa. Another very hot place is Death Valley in California, USA, where a temperature of 57 degrees Celsius was measured in 1913.

Which is colder: the North or South Pole?

The South Pole gets colder than the North Pole ever does. The coldest spot on Earth is at the Vostok base in Antarctica, near the South Pole. In July 1983 the temperature there fell to minus 89.2 degrees Celsius.

What is frost?

The layer of white frost that covers the ground on cold mornings is made by moisture in the air. On cold nights the water vapour in the air freezes when it meets the cold ground. A thin layer of ice crystals forms frost.

What causes lightning?

Lightning is a huge electric spark. During a thunderstorm, very large electric charges build up inside clouds and on the ground. The charges build up until a flash of lightning shoots through the air between them. Lightning can flash from the cloud to the ground, or between two clouds.

Lightning is a sequence of flashes. First a leader stroke zigzags to the ground. The main flash then surges upwards. Other flashes may follow in quick succession.

WEATHER FACTS

- The biggest thunderclouds tower 16 km high, nearly twice the height of Mt Everest.
- Weather forecasting is not easy. A small change in the air over the Arctic can cause a hurricane in the tropics!
- Wind force is measured on the Beaufort Scale, invented in 1806 by an English admiral. On this scale, calm is 0 and a hurricane is force 12.
- Warm, dry air flowing down the side of a mountain range can raise temperatures suddenly. Such winds are called fohns or chinooks.

Never shelter under a tree in a thunderstorm. It could be struck by lightning. You are safest inside.

What is thunder?

People once believed thunder was the sound of the gods' anger. In fact, thunder is the sound air makes as it expands when it is warmed by the heat of a flash of lightning. We see the lightning flash almost as it happens. The sound of the thunderclap travels much more slowly and we hear it a few seconds later.

The nearer you are to a thunderstorm, the closer together are the lightning and thunder. Count the seconds between them, divide by three and you have an estimate of how many kilometres away the thunderstorm is.

Why do winds blow?

As the Sun heats the air it causes winds. Warm air expands, making it lighter than cold air. Because it is lighter it rises and cool air flows in to take its place. The Sun's heat is greatest at the Equator. The warm air here therefore rises, cools as it does so and moves outwards. Cooler air moves in underneath it, to create the winds of the world. Winds move at different speeds. A slow wind is a breeze. A fast wind is a gale, strong enough to damage houses.

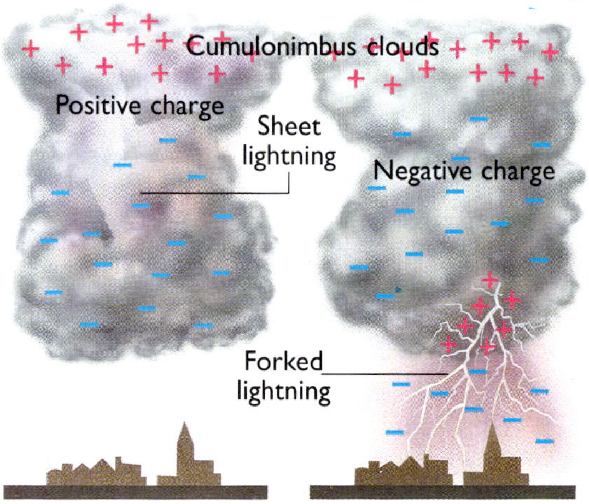

◀ Positive electrical charges collect at the top of clouds, negative charges at the bottom. Sheet lightning flashes inside or between clouds. Forked lightning flashes to the ground.

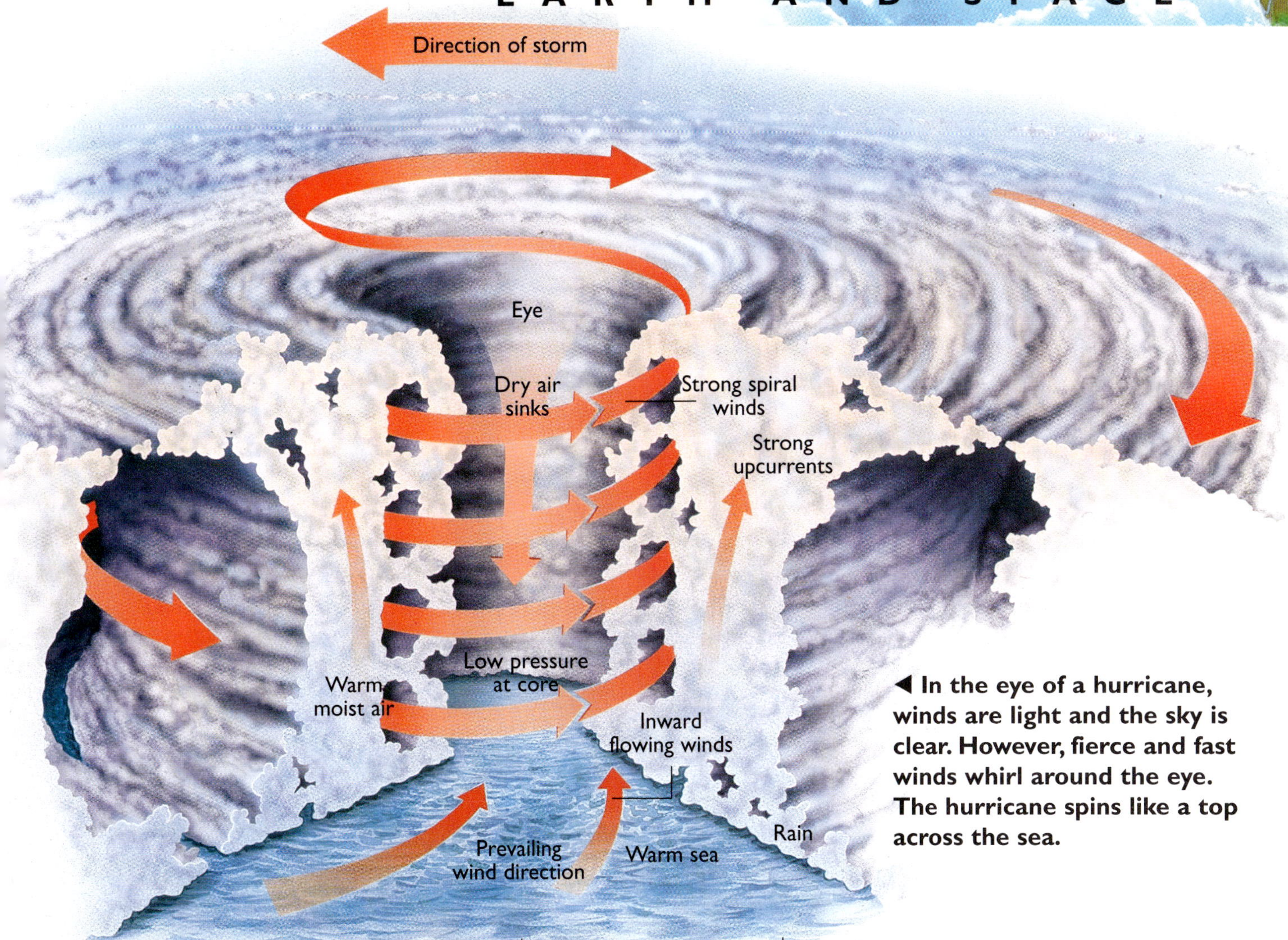

◀ In the eye of a hurricane, winds are light and the sky is clear. However, fierce and fast winds whirl around the eye. The hurricane spins like a top across the sea.

Why do hurricanes begin over the ocean?

A hurricane is a violent tropical storm. In a hurricane winds spiral round very rapidly. Hurricanes form over the ocean near the Equator, where the air is very warm and moist. The warm air rises rapidly and cooler air rushes in beneath it. The air begins to move like a giant whirling top. Hurricanes form in the Atlantic Ocean. Similar storms in the Pacific Ocean are called typhoons, in the Indian Ocean cyclones. Hurricanes are usually about 650 kilometres across. The winds in these storms travel at up to 200 kilometres/hour. The most likely time for hurricanes is late summer and autumn.

▼ Tornadoes can cause terrible damage as they twist across the countryside.

What is a tornado?

A tornado is a storm wind similar to a hurricane. It forms over the land when huge masses of clouds meet. The clouds whirl around each other. Then they join to create an enormous funnel. The tip of the funnel spins down to the ground, where it sucks up everything in its path. Tornadoes in the central United States rip across the country at 50 kilometres/hour and can be heard as far away as 40 kilometres.

OCEANS, RIVERS AND LAKES

What is a current?

A current is a stream of water moving through the ocean. There are surface currents and deep water currents. Great surface currents carry warm water from the Equator. The water cools and mixes with colder water as it moves away from the heat of the Equator. When the current turns towards the Equator again, its waters are cold. Offshore currents are caused by tide movement. Winds cause the much larger currents circling in the oceans in regular patterns. The Gulf Stream is a warm water current which begins in the Gulf of Mexico, then runs north-east towards Europe.

▼ Ocean currents are moved in regular patterns by the winds. Near the Equator, the main currents are blown westwards. Near the poles they are blown eastwards.

How big can waves be?

Each wave in the ocean is made up of water particles moving in a circle. The wind pushes the wave upwards, forming a crest. Then gravity pulls it down again, into a trough. It is the up and down movement of water in waves that has been used to drive generators. Storm waves, driven by high winds, often rise 12 metres or more in an open sea. The highest sea wave seen from a ship and officially recorded was 34 metres high, during a hurricane in 1933. The biggest wave measured by instruments was 26.2 metres high in 1872 in the North Atlantic. Such waves are rare.

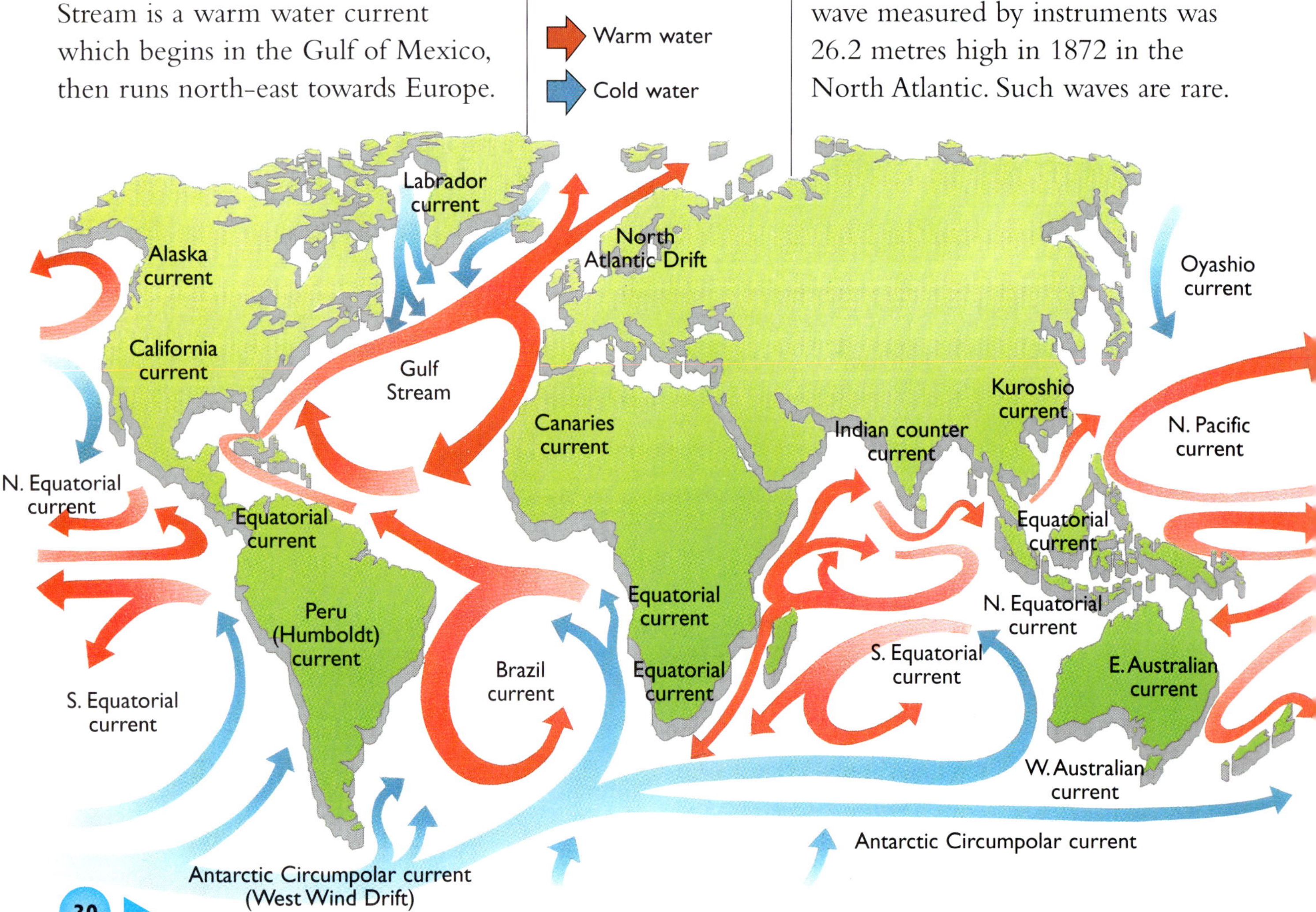

Why is seawater salty?

The saltiness of the sea comes from minerals. Minerals are washed into the sea from the land by rivers, which dissolve minerals from the rocks over which they flow. The most plentiful mineral in seawater is sodium chloride, or common salt.

Why do the tides rise and fall?

Ocean tides rise (flood) and fall (ebb) about twice every 24 hours. Tides are caused by the gravitational pull of the Sun and Moon on the Earth. They pull the oceans towards them. The land is pulled too but water moves more easily, making a giant wave. As the Earth spins, the wave travels around the Earth, causing the tides.

Away from the shore, the ocean plunges to a depth of about 4 km in most places. It's like going down a high mountain!

▼ The sea bed is cut through with valleys (trenches) and also has mountains (guyots) and volcanoes. The continental shelf slopes down gradually.

Where is the deepest point in the oceans?

The deepest point in the oceans is the bottom of a deep trench called the Mariana Trench in the Pacific. Measurements of the trench have varied from 11,034 metres to 10,916 metres below the surface.

Where is the continental shelf?

In most places, land does not stop suddenly at the coast. It slopes gently away beneath the sea to a depth of about 180 metres. This undersea land is called the continental shelf. At the outer edge of the shelf the steeper continental slope begins, leading down to the deep ocean floor known as the abyss.

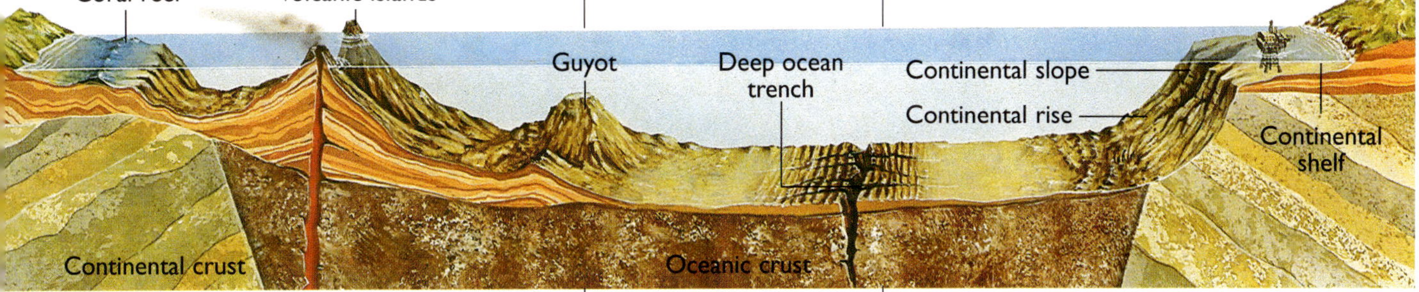

Which is the biggest ocean?

The three great oceans are the Pacific, the Atlantic and the Indian. The Pacific Ocean is by far the biggest ocean on Earth. It covers over 166 million square kilometres.

▼ The five world oceans compared: the Pacific is by far the largest.

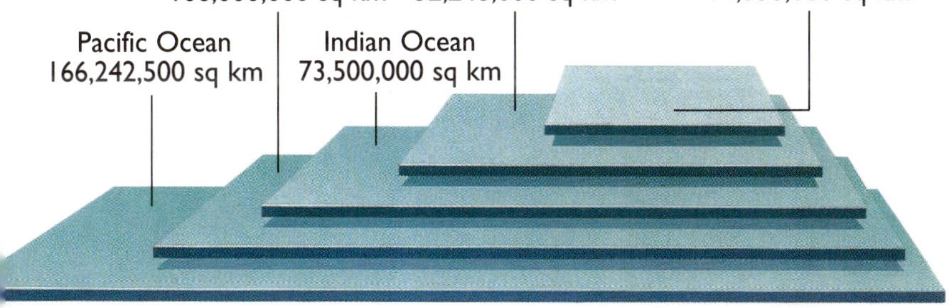

What is the ocean bottom like?

The deep basins of the ocean floor are formed from heavy rock called basalt. Layers of mud overlie the deep oceanic trenches and level parts of the ocean floor. Some of the muds are filled with the remains of dead plants and animals. Such muds are called oozes. They are hundreds of metres deep in places. There are great mountain ranges too beneath the oceans. Many undersea mountains are volcanoes, the tops of which form islands on the surface.

How can seawater be made drinkable?

Seawater is about seven times more salty than water that is safe to drink. Anybody who drank only seawater would die. Their body would dry out as it tried to rid itself of all the salt. Many ways to remove the salt from seawater (desalinate it) have been tried. The simplest way is to distil it. This can be done by boiling seawater in a container and leading off the steam into a cold bottle. The steam leaves the salt behind in the container so that fresh water condenses in the bottle. Large desalination plants do produce drinking water from the ocean, but they are expensive to operate and produce relatively small amounts of fresh water.

WATER FACTS

- In 1960 the bathyscaphe *Trieste* dived into the deepest part of the Pacific Ocean: the Mariana Trench, about 11,000 m down.
- The longest river is the Nile in Africa, which is 6,670 km long.
- Next longest is the Amazon in South America, which is 6,448 km long.
- The world's largest delta is formed by the Ganges and Brahmaputra rivers. It is 480 km long and 160 km wide.
- The Amazon pushes out so much water that fresh water from this great river is found up to 180 km out at sea.

What is a delta?

A delta forms where a river meets the sea. The river flows more slowly, and deposits mud, sand and even boulders. This material piles up, forming new land. The delta is shaped like a triangle. It derives its name from the letter Δ (delta) in the Greek alphabet.

How are canyons made?

A canyon is a deep valley cut by a river. A narrow canyon with steep rocky walls is a ravine or gorge. The biggest canyon in the world is the Grand Canyon in Arizona, USA.

Which is the longest river?

The Nile in Africa and the Amazon in South America are close rivals for the title of the world's longest river. Most measurements make the Nile the longest (see box).

◀ A river's course can take it through various stages, from its source to its mouth.

Where does a river begin?

River water comes from rain, from lakes and springs, and from melting ice and snow. A river begins as a trickling stream. Its starting point is called the source and is often on a mountain. All rivers start on high ground and flow downhill, under the pull of the Earth's gravity.

How are swamps formed?

When a slow-moving river moves through lowlands, it may form a swamp – an area of wetland. A swamp has more woody plants (trees and shrubs) than a marsh. Close to the sea, salt water and fresh water often mingle and mix in a swamp. A swamp is always waterlogged. A marsh is only water-covered part of the time (by the incoming ocean tide).

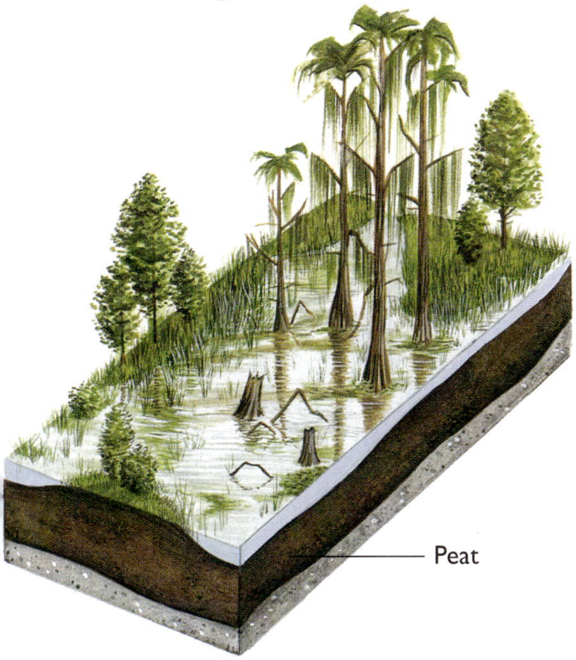

◀ **Leaves falling into a shallow lake form a peat ooze at the bottom. This ooze gets thicker, forming a bog or swamp.**

Where is the highest waterfall?

Waterfalls are found in the upper part of a river's course. They are made in places where the river crosses a layer of hard rock. The hard rock is worn away more slowly than the softer rock downstream, forming a 'step' which gets gradually deeper. Water plunges over the step, creating a waterfall. At the Angel Falls, or Cherunmeri, in Venezuela, South America, the water falls 807 metres in a single drop. This is the world's highest waterfall. Its other sections make the total drop of this waterfall 979 metres.

LAKE FACTS

- The Great Lakes in North America were gouged out by glaciers about 2,000 m thick.
- Lake Baikal in Russia is the deepest lake. At its deepest point it is almost 2 km deep.
- Lake Victoria is the largest lake in Africa and the third largest in the world.
- The world's largest underground lake was discovered in a cave in Namibia, Africa, in 1986. It has a surface area of 26,100 sq km.
- Britain's largest lake is Loch Lomond in Scotland. It has a surface area of over 70 sq km and it is more than 30 km from end to end.

How are lakes formed?

Most lakes are in areas once covered by glaciers. A glacier cuts deep valleys as it moves. Earth and boulders carried along by the glacier are deposited when it melts, making a dam. Melting ice from the glacier fills the valley to make a lake. Other lakes are formed in the craters of extinct volcanoes or sometimes when a river changes its course.

Where are the Great Lakes?

The Great Lakes of North America form the largest group of freshwater lakes in the world. The biggest is Lake Superior, with an area of 82,000 square kilometres. There are four other Great Lakes: Huron, Michigan, Erie and Ontario.

What is the world's largest lake?

The Caspian Sea, on the borders of Russia, Azerbaijan, Turkmenistan, Kazakhstan and Iran, is the biggest body of inland water in the world. The sea's area is about 372,000 square kilometres (it is now known to be shrinking) and it is 1200 kilometres long. Its waters are salty, so it is thought of as a sea rather than a lake. A canal links the Caspian with the Black Sea.

◀ **Angel Falls was spotted by an American pilot named Jimmy Angel in 1935.**

ENVIRONMENT AND RESOURCES

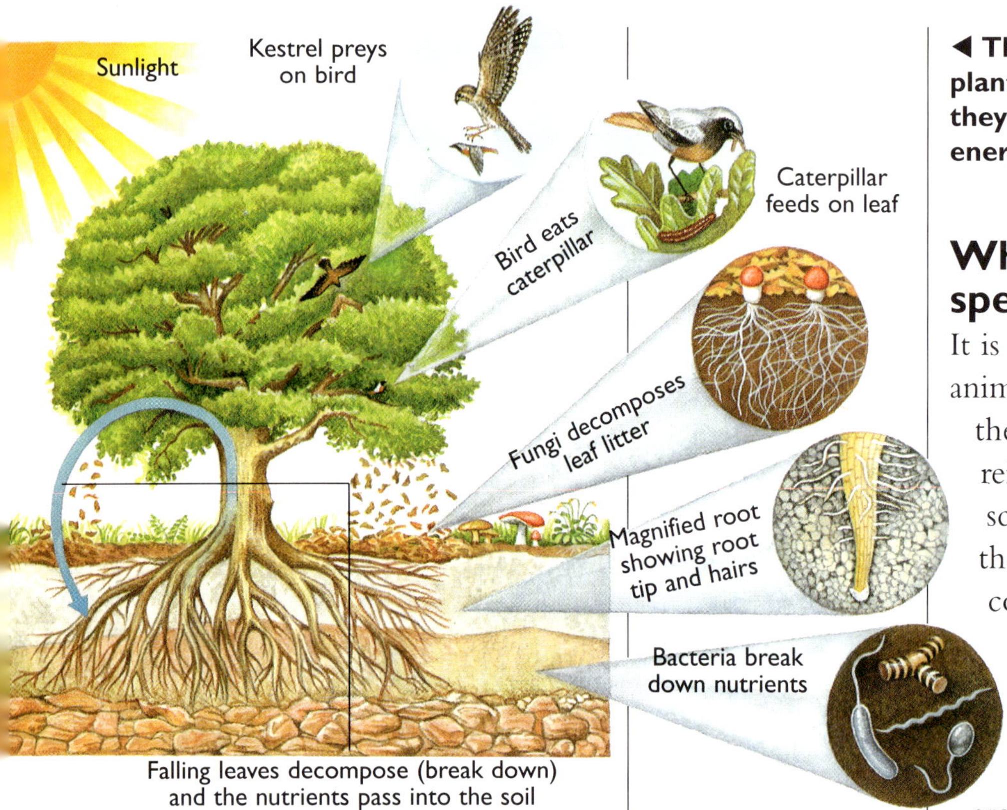

◀ **The Sun's energy is harnessed by plants and passed on to animals when they feed. Bacteria and plants absorb energy from animals' dead bodies.**

Is there a balance of nature?

Plants and animals depend on one another in various ways. All living things depend on their environment. This is the 'balance of nature'. The balance is very delicate since so many living things are involved. Upsetting one part of the structure – by people over-hunting an animal, for instance, or by introducing another animal – can upset the whole. A group of living things (plants and animals) which live together in a particular place is known as an ecosystem.

Why are animal and plant species valuable?

It is a tragedy to lose one species of animal or plant. Once it has gone there is no way that it can be reintroduced. By the year 2050 scientists fear that as many as half the Earth's animal and plant species could be extinct. Yet each species is a storehouse of genetic resources. For example, drugs made from the rosy periwinkle, a plant of the Madagascar forest, are now used to help treat children suffering from leukaemia (a form of cancer). If this plant had died out, its value would never have been known.

▼ **These are all species in danger of dying out. The thylacine, a Tasmanian marsupial, may already be extinct.**

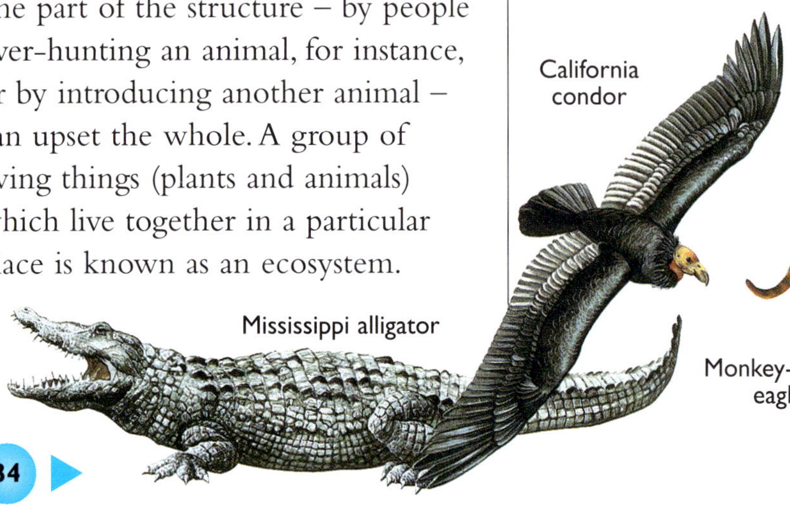

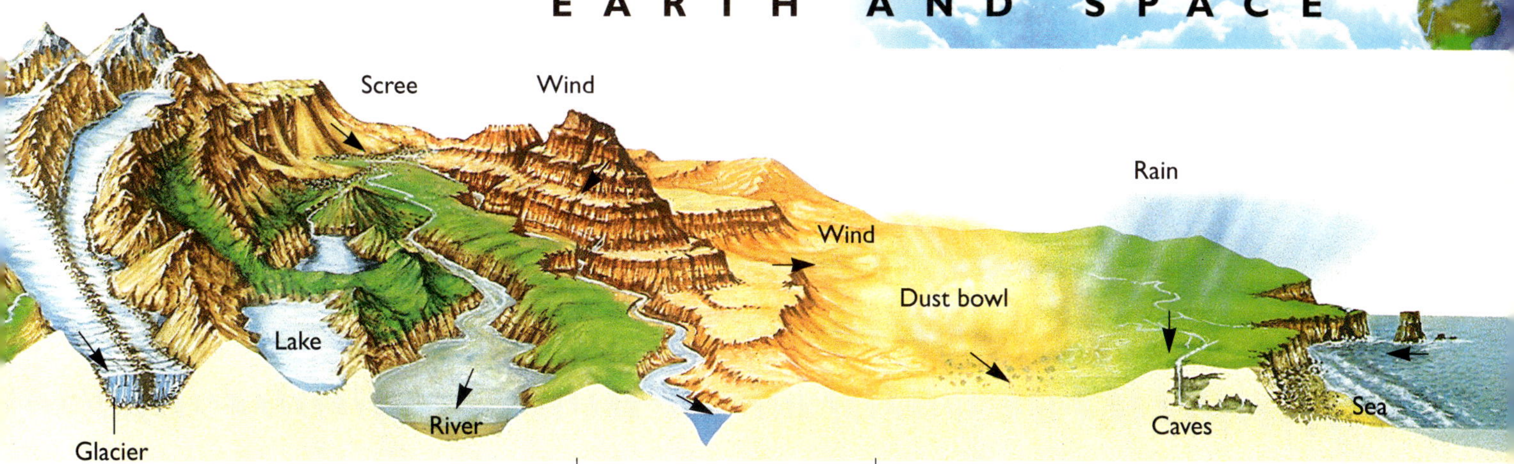

Which environments are richest?

Some environments are very rich in living things. Tropical rainforests have the greatest mix of species. A ten-kilometre-square patch of forest may be home to more than 2,000 plant species, 400 kinds of birds, 150 butterflies, 100 reptiles and 60 amphibians. There are so many insects that no one can count them!

Which was the first national park?

Hunting parks and forests reserved for kings were an ancient form of nature reserve. Animals were protected (except from the royal hunters) and people were kept out. The first true national park set up to protect nature and wildlife for everyone to enjoy was Yellowstone National Park in Wyoming, USA, founded in 1872.

Could life exist without soil?

Much of the Earth's surface is covered with soil. Soil is a mixture of mineral and organic (living) particles, dead plant and animal matter, air and water. Life as we know it depends on soil. Most plants grow in soil, taking food from it. Animals in turn eat plants.

▲ Wind and water are powerful forces of erosion. Rocks and soil are moved from higher levels by glaciers and rivers and then deposited lower down.

NATIONAL PARKS FACTS

- In 1576 a wooded nature reserve was set aside by the Dutch government. This was one of the world's first nature parks.
- Large national parks in Africa include Tsavo (Kenya), Serengeti (Tanzania) and Kruger (South Africa).
- India's first national park was the Corbett National Park, where tigers are now protected.
- Sweden set up Europe's first true national parks in 1909.

National parks could be becoming too popular. If too many people visit them, the wildlife they protect are put under pressure.

What is erosion?

Natural forces affect rock and soil, through erosion and weathering. Rain can wash away fertile topsoil and winds can blow away thin soils, leaving bare rocks on which plants cannot grow. This is erosion in action. Erosion can cause new deserts to be formed. Alternate heating and cooling of rock can crack them into smaller pieces, to be washed away by rain and rivers. Even mountains, over millions of years, are worn away. Rainwater can also react with minerals to dissolve rock. Wearing away of rocks is called weathering.

What keeps soil fertile?

A fertile soil is rich in humus. Humus is a fine organic matter made by microbes, or soil bacteria, as they break down dead plants and animal waste. Soil microbes work best in warm, airy soil, where there is plenty of leaf mould or grass. A fertile soil needs the right amounts of minerals and water. Plants help to keep land fertile. If large ploughed fields are left unplanted in dry weather, the soil becomes dusty. Winds can then blow away the topsoil. Trees and hedges are important in protecting fields from wind erosion.

Why is pollution a problem?

Human beings have always polluted their surroundings, with rubbish or smoke for example. The problem now is that so many more people pollute and spoil our world in many ways. We release gases and smoke into the air. We pour poisons into water. We damage the soil with chemicals. We drop litter, cover fields with concrete and make a lot of noise. Pollution can make people ill and kills wildlife.

What is smog?

Smog is a mixture of pollutants that causes a fog-like haze over a city. It is worst in places with lots of cars or factories close to the city centre. These give off chemical fumes and smoke. Cities with bad smog include Mexico City, Los Angeles, Athens, Beijing, Tehran and Lagos. Breathing smoggy air is said to be as harmful as smoking forty cigarettes a day.

What started warming the Earth?

In the past, the Earth's climate warmed and cooled over millions of years. Since the 1700s, however, people have caused a far more rapid climate change. The Industrial Revolution which began in the 1700s brought factories, railways, fast-growing cities and motor vehicles. Carbon dioxide and other gases have been poured into the atmosphere from burning fuels such as coal and oil in factories, homes and vehicles. This change, brought about by the Industrial Revolution, is warming the Earth and affecting its climate.

▶ Factories and power stations give off waste gases. Chemicals in these gases cause acid rain.

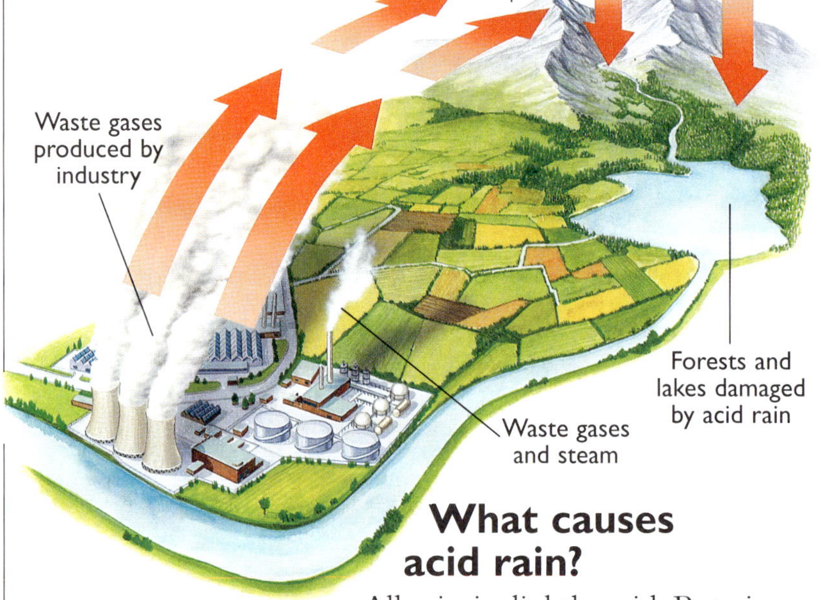

What causes acid rain?

All rain is slightly acid. But air pollution from factories and fuel-burning power stations can increase the amount of chemicals in the air, making rain more acid. This acid rain may fall far away from its source and damage the environment. Trees may die, lakes may become unfit for fish to live in and buildings may be eroded by the chemical action of the acids in the rain.

If the Earth gets too hot, some ice at the Poles could melt. The seas would rise and drown many cities along low-lying coasts.

▶ Los Angeles seen on a day when its smog is severe. Smog is a dark, sulphurous fog containing dust and soot particles. It pollutes the atmosphere of many industrial cities.

What happens to our rubbish?

Most of the rubbish we throw away is dumped into holes in the ground or tipped into the sea. In some countries it is burned in incinerators. Only a small amount of it is recycled, or treated so that the materials in it (paper, glass, metal and plastics, for example) can be reused.

What is recycling?

Recycling means reusing materials such as paper, metal cans and glass jars. It makes good sense. Although saving your old newspapers does not save endangered trees, it does save energy. The paper industry grows trees for paper-making, just as a grain farmer grows wheat. Recycled paper production uses half as much energy as making paper from new wood and only a third as much water. In addition the paper we throw away into dumps rots slowly and gives off methane gas, which contributes to global warming.

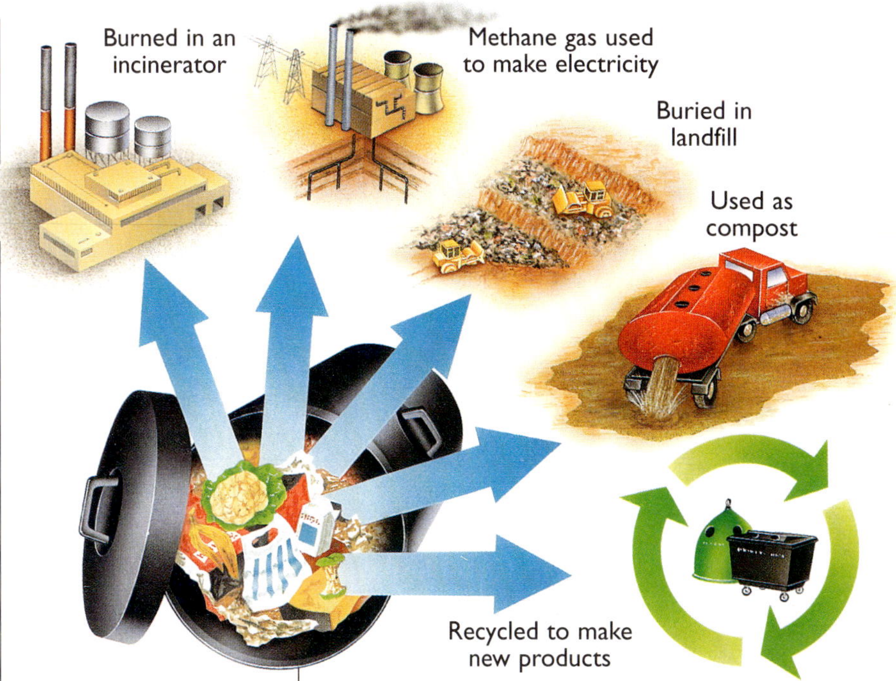

▲ There are many ways to get rid of rubbish. Rotting rubbish gives off methane gas which can be burned to make electricity. Kitchen and garden waste can be made into compost. Other materials can be recycled.

What causes an oil slick?

Oil tankers regularly wash out their tanks before they reload. A tanker accident at sea can form a huge patch or slick. If this slick washes ashore, it fouls beaches and kills seabirds, fish and other animals. Detergents and other chemicals used to clean up oiled beaches may do as much damage as the oil itself.

Can volcanoes affect climate?

The smoke and ash from a volcano pours out into the atmosphere to form clouds. The clouds can blot out the Sun and so cool the Earth. This happened when Mount Pinaturbo erupted in the Philippines in 1991.

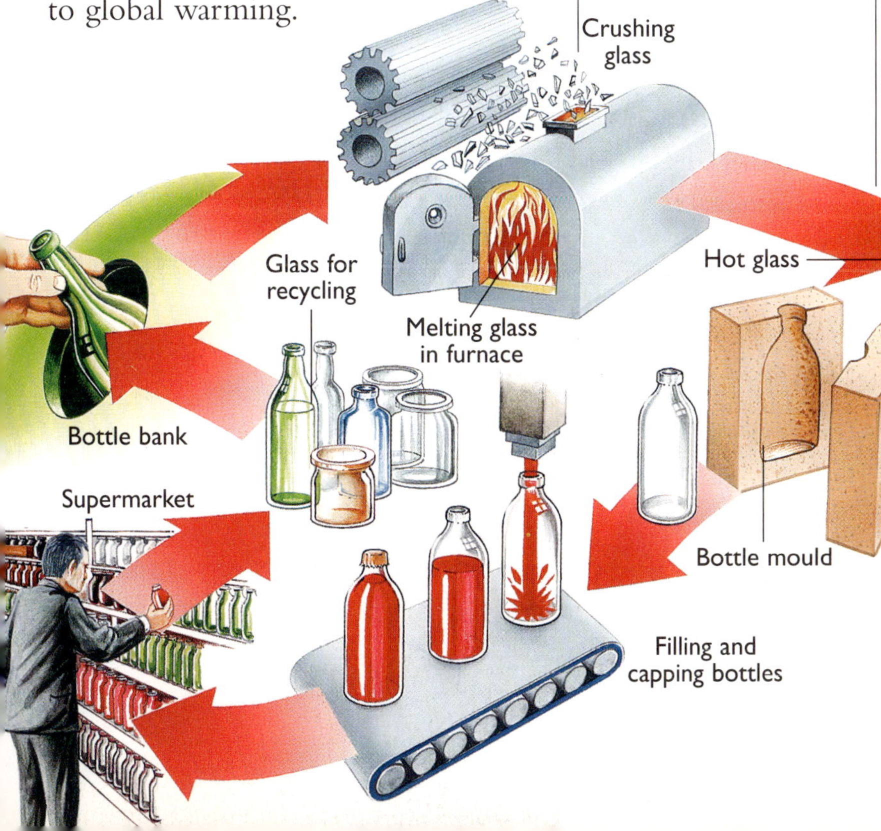

◀ Glass is easy to recycle. Used glass is collected, cleaned, broken into small pieces, and melted. Then it is moulded into new bottles, which are filled for use again.

THE UNIVERSE

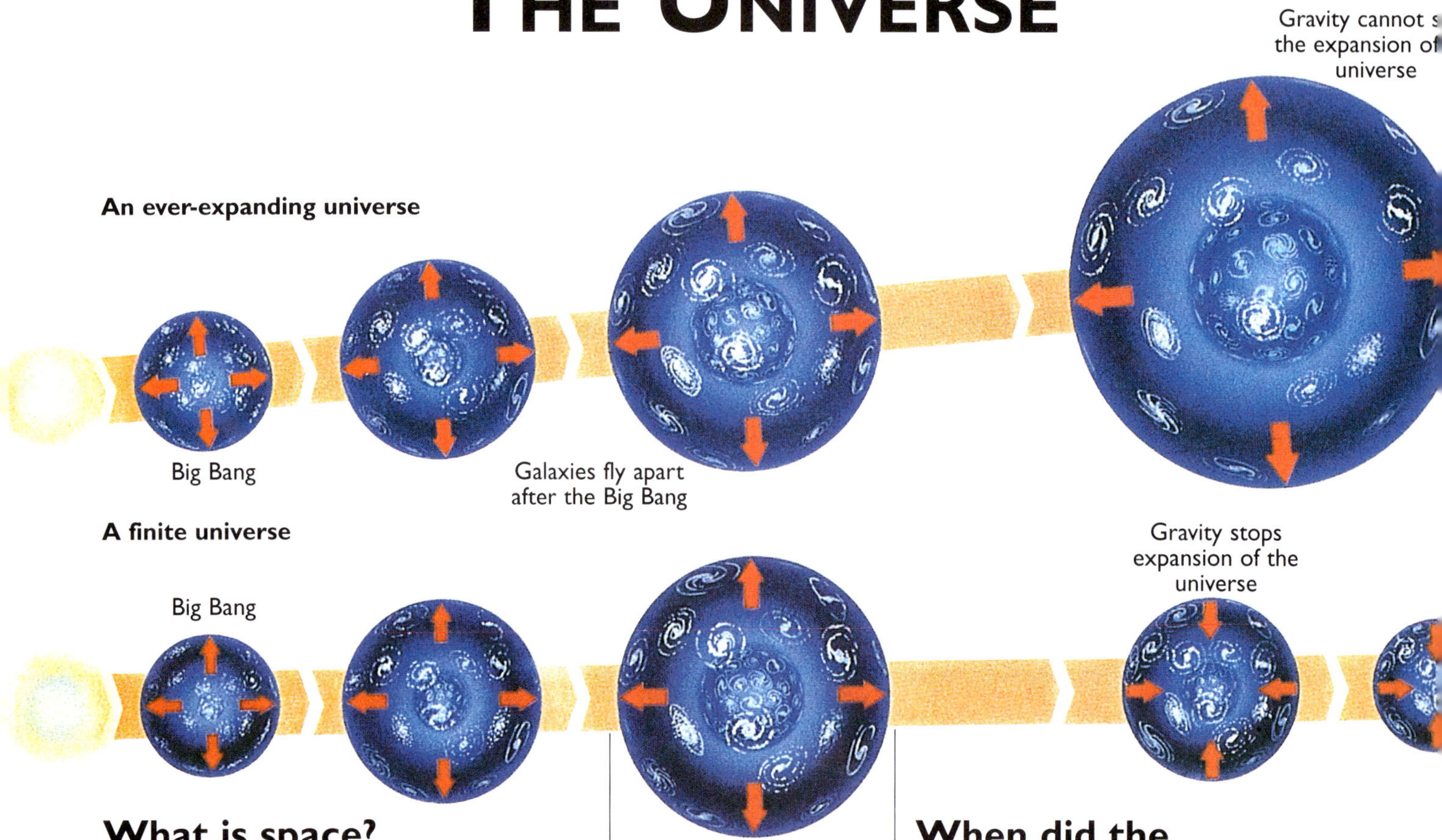

▲ The universe may keep on expanding, galaxies flying apart for evermore. Or it may all rush together in a 'Big Crunch' and start a new universe.

What is space?

Space is nothing – or almost nothing. It is the space that lies between the Earth and the Moon, between the planets of the Solar System, and between the stars. Space is almost empty. It does not contain any air. A piece of space the size of a house would contain a few atoms of gases and perhaps some specks of dust.

What holds the universe together?

The same force that keeps your feet on the ground holds the whole universe together. This is the force of gravity. Gravity extends through space between planets, between stars and between galaxies (groups of stars). It keeps the planets together in the Solar System and holds the stars together in huge galaxies.

To see how the universe is getting bigger, paint some spots on a balloon (for galaxies) and watch them get bigger as you blow it up.

When did the universe form?

A long time ago, all the galaxies in the universe would have been squeezed into a small space. Perhaps a great explosion happened, causing the galaxies to spread out. This explosion, or Big Bang, would have happened about 15 billion years ago.

How big is the universe?

No one knows for sure how big the universe is. There may be parts of the universe beyond the reach of our telescopes. Also, astronomers are not sure that light comes from the most distant objects in the universe in straight lines. The lines could be curved, making the objects closer than they appear to be. However, they could be as much as 15 billion light years away.

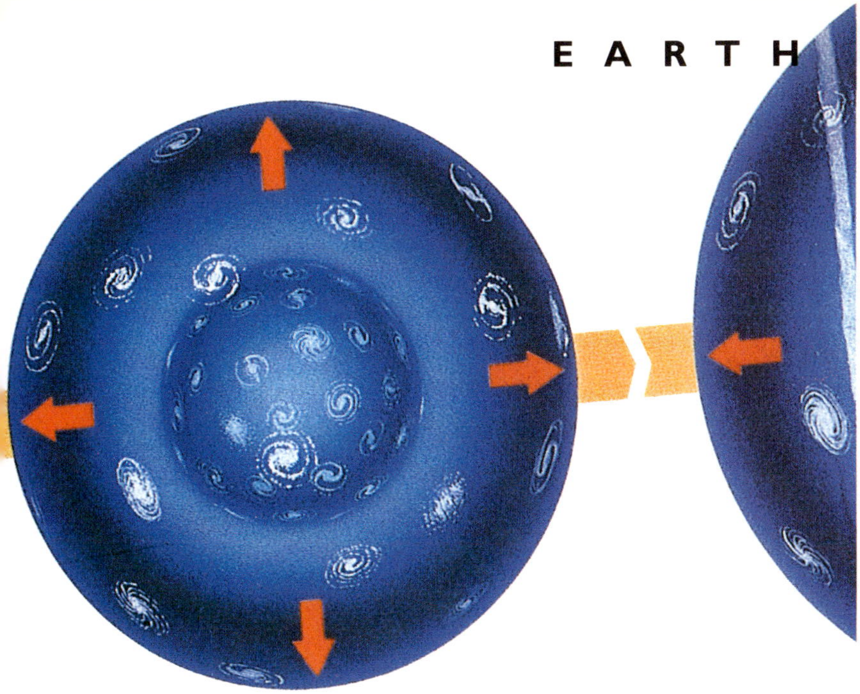

A series of universes
A completely new universe begins

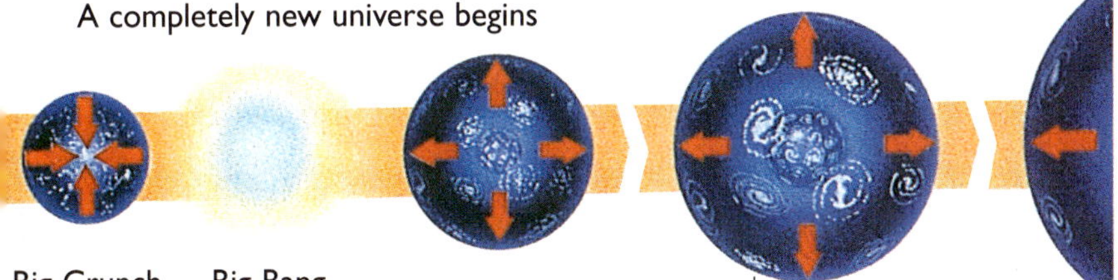

How do we know the universe is getting bigger?

Astronomers can measure the speed with which stars and galaxies are moving. Most of them are moving away from us. The farther away a galaxy is, the faster it appears to be moving away. This means that the universe is getting bigger. No one knows for certain if the universe will ever stop growing.

Where are we in the universe?

The universe is everything that exists – all the planets, moons, stars and galaxies put together. The universe stretches out in all directions. There may be parts of the universe that we cannot see through our telescopes, and so we cannot tell where exactly we are in the universe.

UNIVERSE FACTS

- In 1965, scientists found a very feeble warmth in space. This is all that's left of the fantastic heat given off by the Big Bang.
- Imagine the edge of the universe is a hollow ball the size of the Earth. On this scale, the Milky Way galaxy would be 40 m across. The Earth would be too small to see without a microscope!
- The study of how the universe began is called cosmology.
- Scientists think they have found at least one Earth-sized planet orbiting a distant star. The planet is 30,000 light years away.

What is the difference between a planet and a star?

A star is a huge ball of hot glowing gas, like the Sun. A planet is a world like the Earth. The Sun and stars produce their own light. The planets are lit by light from the Sun. In the night sky, you cannot tell the planets from the stars. They all look like tiny points of light, because they are far away. However, the planets are nearer than the stars. Through a powerful telescope, you can see that the planets are other worlds. The stars are so very distant that they still look like points of light, even through the most powerful telescope. Astronomers think that some stars have planets orbiting around them, just like the Sun.

Which star is nearest to the Earth?

The star Proxima Centauri is the nearest to us, at a distance of 4.2 light years. Next closest are Alpha Centauri (4.3 light years) and Barnard's Star (6 light years).

How do astronomers gaze into the past?

Light reaching us from even the closest stars has taken several years to cross the enormous distances of space. The nearest star is more than four light years away, so the light from it takes four years to reach us. This means we see the star as it looked four years ago. Other stars are millions of light years away. So when astronomers study light from these stars, they are seeing them as they were millions of years ago.

The Sun

How big is the Sun?

The Sun is 1,392,500 kilometres across, 109 times the diameter of the Earth. It weighs 333,000 times as much as the Earth, and its volume is so huge that it could swallow up 1,300,000 Earths. If the Earth were the size of a tennis ball, then the Sun would be as big as a house.

What is the Sun made of?

The Sun is a huge, self-luminous ball of intensely hot gas. Its temperature is so high that it glows white hot, giving out light and heat rays. Most of the gas in the Sun is hydrogen. This is slowly turning into another gas, helium, inside the Sun. As it does so, it produces tremendous amounts of heat. The bright surface of the Sun is called the photosphere.

When did the Sun begin to shine?

The Sun began to shine about 5 billion years ago. It formed from a cloud of gas and dust floating in space. The cloud gradually got smaller and became thicker. As the cloud shrank, the centre heated up. Eventually, it became so hot that it began to glow and the Sun was born. The rest of the cloud formed the Solar System, including planets, moons, asteroids and comets.

▼ If we could cut a slice out of the Sun, we would see layers of hydrogen below the surface. There are sunspots and huge streamers of glowing gas called prominences forming arches of fire.

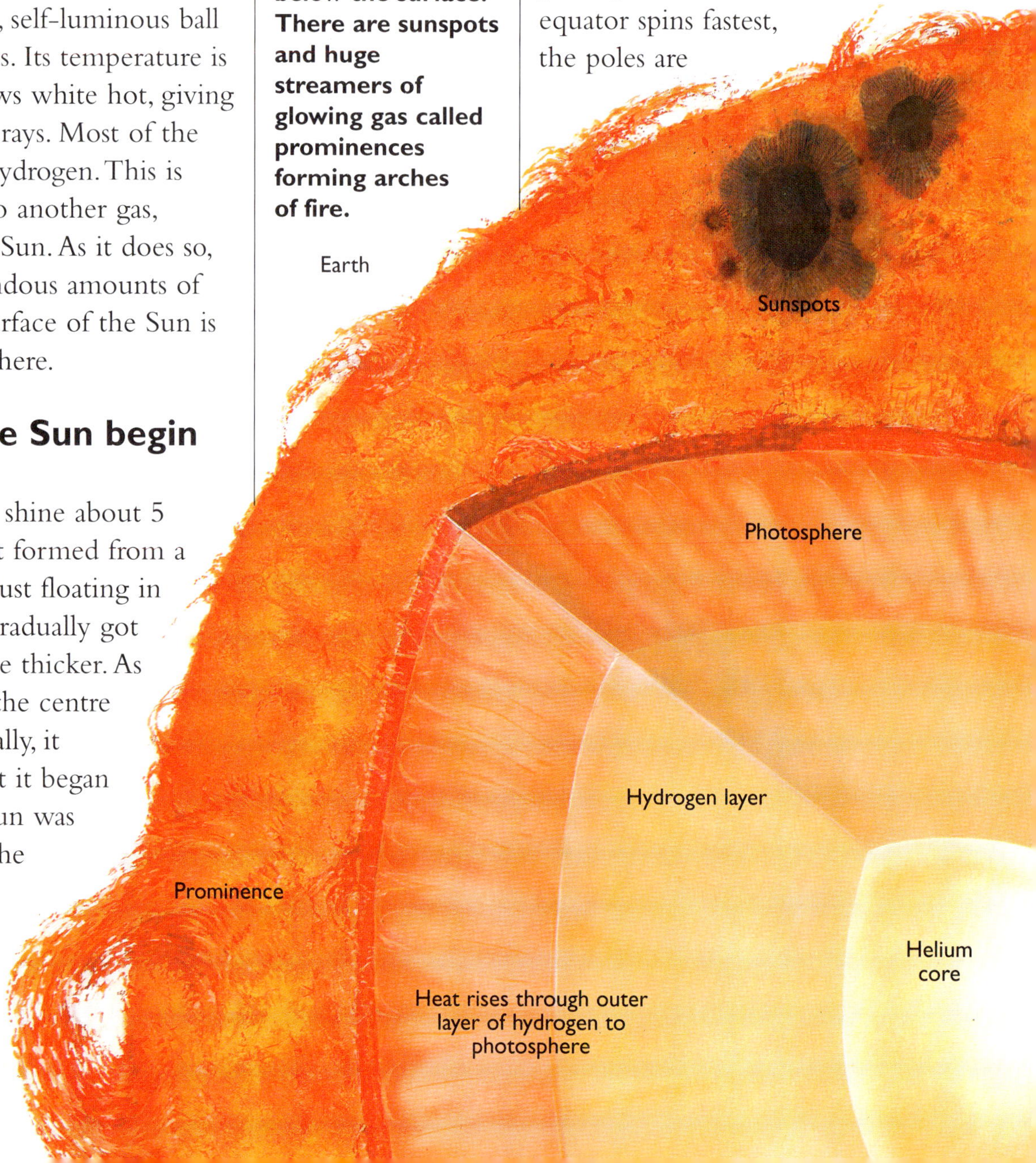

Does the Sun move?

The Sun appears to move across the sky from dawn to dusk. However, this motion is caused by the Earth spinning. The Sun only seems to be moving, and it is we who are moving and not the Sun. Nevertheless, the Sun moves in other ways. It spins as the Earth does, though slowly, but because it is made of gas, different parts spin at different rates – its equator spins fastest, the poles are slowest. Also, as the Earth moves around the Sun with the Moon, so the Sun moves around the centre of the Galaxy taking the Earth and the rest of the Solar System with it.

What happens during an eclipse of the Sun?

The Moon moves in front of the Sun during an eclipse of the Sun. It gets dim outside and the Sun appears to get smaller, like a new moon. In a total eclipse, the Sun disappears for a short time and it becomes dark and cold outside. During an eclipse of the Moon, the Moon seems to get smaller and may disappear. This is because the Earth moves in front of the Sun, and its shadow falls on the Moon.

WARNING

- It is very dangerous to look directly at the Sun.
- A person who looks directly at the Sun through binoculars or a telescope can be blinded for life.
- NEVER look at the Sun in this way. Use binoculars to project an image of the Sun onto a piece of card.

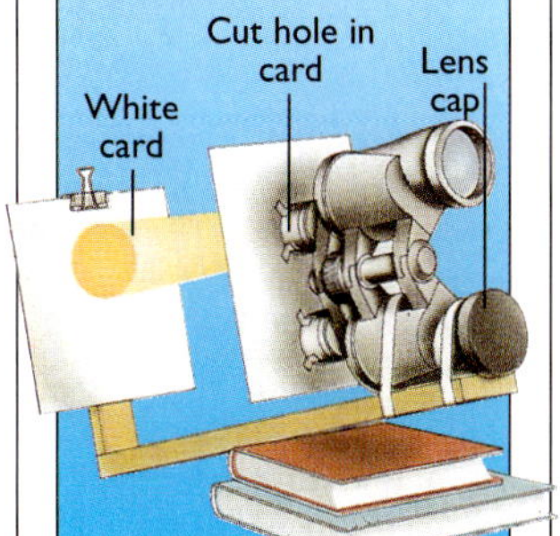

What are sunspots?

Sunspots, looking like darker patches, appear and disappear on the surface of the Sun. Chinese astronomers studied them as early as 300 BC. European astronomers were puzzled by sunspots. As they believed the Sun was a 'perfect sphere' in the heavens, they could not accept that there were any 'imperfections' on its surface.

Where is the Sun hottest?

At the centre. Here, where the nuclear reactions that keep the Sun shining are going on, the temperature is 15 million degrees Celsius. The surface temperature is only 6,000 degrees Celsius, that is, 60 times the temperature of boiling water!

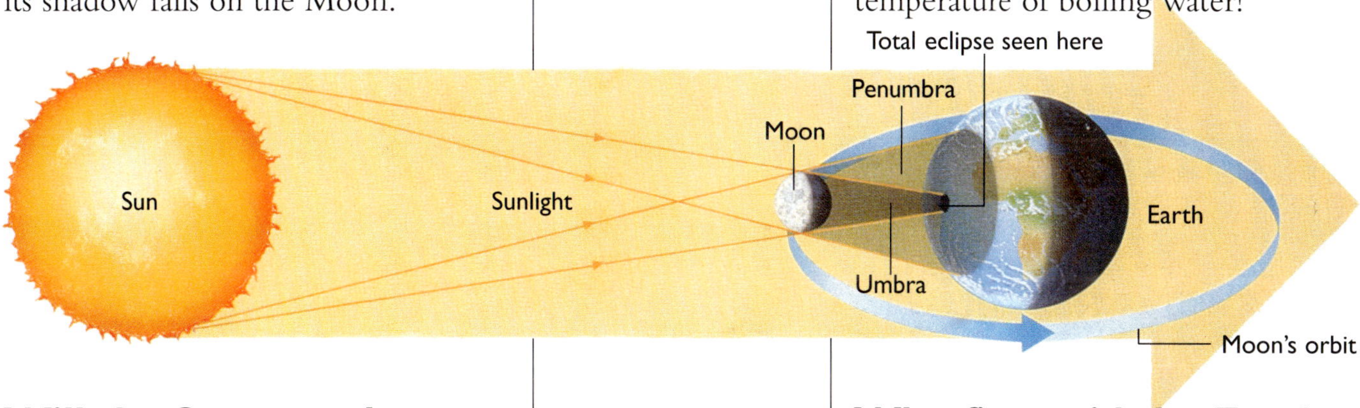

▲ When the Moon passes between the Earth and the Sun, it casts a shadow and causes an eclipse. Within the central shadow, or umbra, the Sun is completely hidden.

Will the Sun grow hotter or colder?

The surface temperature of the Sun is about 6,000 degrees Celsius. The Sun is an 'average' star, in terms of its size and brightness. Billions of years from now, it will swell up to become a 'red giant' perhaps a hundred times its present size. The Earth itself may even be engulfed by the gigantic Sun. In time, the red giant Sun will shrink and become a tiny, very dense star called a 'white dwarf'. As its life ends, it will gradually cool and become invisible.

Who first said the Earth travels around the Sun?

The Polish astronomer Nicolaus Copernicus published a book in 1543 that upset many people's ideas about the universe. Copernicus declared that the old theory that the Earth was the centre of the universe was wrong. In his book he showed a drawing of the Solar System, with the Sun at its centre and the six known planets circling it. Many people were alarmed by these new ideas, but modern astronomy was built on the foundations of Copernicus.

The Moon

How big is the Moon?

The Moon is 3,476 kilometres across – about the same width as Australia. Its total area is less than four times the size of Europe.

Where does the Moon come from?

The Moon formed when the Solar System was formed, at the same time as the Earth. This was about 4.6 billion years ago.

Why is the Moon covered in craters?

There are craters on Earth. They are made by meteorites crashing from space, and also by volcanoes. The same kinds of craters occur on the Moon. The action of the weather smoothes out most of the craters on Earth. However, there is no weather on the Moon so its craters have never changed and never will.

How does the Moon stay up in the sky?

The Moon is pulled by the Earth's gravity, just like anything that falls to the ground. It moves around the Earth in a path, or orbit, that is almost circular. In this way, it keeps about the same distance from the Earth. It is an average of 385,000 kilometres away, or thirty times the diameter of the Earth. If the Earth were an orange, the Moon would be about the size of a cherry 2 metres away.

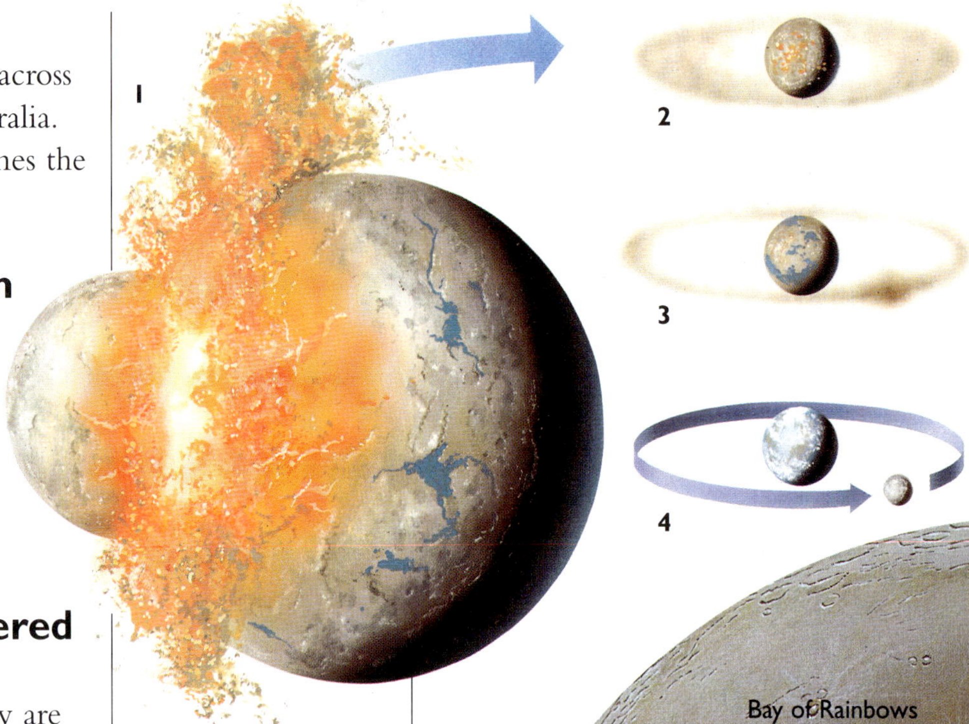

▲ The Moon may have been made by a space collision, when a planet-sized body smashed into the Earth (1). Debris formed a cloud orbiting the Earth (2 and 3) which finally formed the solid Moon (4).

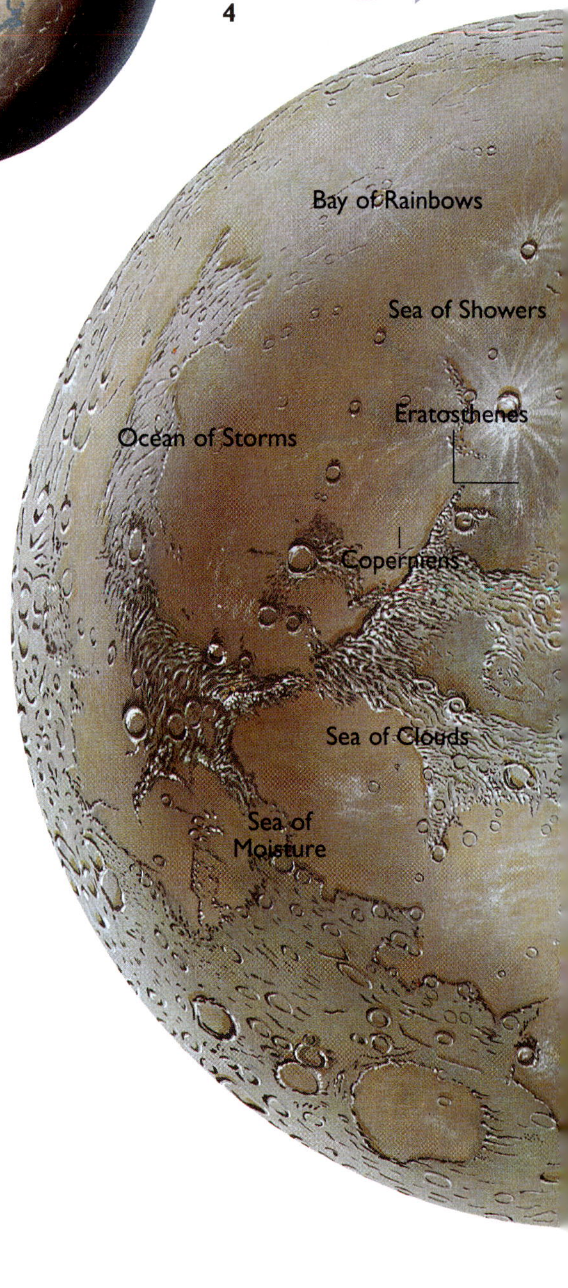

▶ The near side of the Moon, the side we see from Earth, has huge plains, called maria ('seas' in Latin). These plains were formed by floods of volcanic lava. There are also huge craters.

Why does the shape of the Moon change in the sky?

Every four weeks, the Moon goes from a crescent-shaped new moon to a round full moon and back again. These changes are called phases. The Moon does not actually change shape. As it moves around the Earth, different parts become lit up by the Sun. We see only the lit-up parts.

How high could you jump on the Moon?

You could jump higher on the Moon than on Earth because your body would weigh six times less there. This is because the Moon's gravity is one-sixth of the gravity on Earth. However, this doesn't mean that you could jump six times as high as you can on Earth, because you would have to wear a heavy and bulky spacesuit to stay alive.

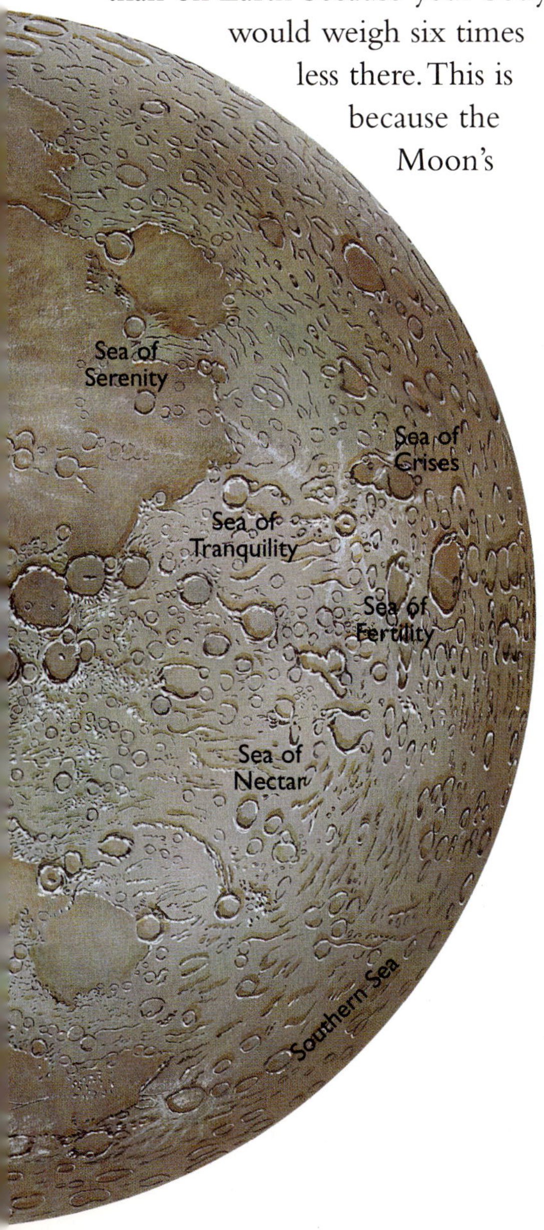

The Moon's gravity isn't as strong as Earth's. You would be about six times lighter on the Moon. So you could jump six times higher – but only without a spacesuit.

MOON FACTS

- Before spacecraft flew around the Moon, no human had ever seen the far side.
- Because the Moon has no wind or weather, footprints left by astronauts will remain undisturbed for ever.
- Craters on the Moon were formed by smaller bodies hitting the surface. The far side of the Moon has far more craters than the near side.
- Moon rock is older than any rock yet found on Earth. The oldest Moon rock found is 300 million years older than any rock found on Earth.
- The Moon is pretty small. It is only 3,476 km across, less than the width of the United States.

Why is the Moon lifeless?

The Moon is only 3,476 kilometres across. Its gravity is too weak to hold down the gases left in its atmosphere after it formed. They floated away into space, leaving the Moon a dead, airless world.

How fast does the Moon spin?

The Moon spins once each time it goes round the Earth. That means it spins once every 29.25 days – the same time it takes to complete one orbit around the Earth.

Can we see all of the Moon?

One side of the Moon is always turned away from the Earth – the dark side of the Moon. As the newly formed Moon cooled, the Earth's gravity pulled at it. This slowed the Moon's spin and raised a bulge on the side nearest the Earth. Because the Moon spins once as it orbits, this same side always faces Earth.

How does the Moon affect the Earth?

The pull of the Moon causes the rise and fall of the ocean tides. The Moon can also black out the Sun's light during an eclipse. When this happens, a black shadow covers part of the Earth, which darkens.

THE PLANETS

How were the planets formed?

The Sun and its planets were formed at about the same time. A whirling cloud of gas and dust collected in space. It grew denser and denser as gravity squeezed the gas and dust together. Most of the cloud formed the Sun. What was left over became the planets.

Who are the planets named after?

All the planets, except for one, are named after gods and goddesses in Greek or Roman legends. The biggest planet, Jupiter, is named after the Roman king of the gods, for example. The exception is our planet, which we call Earth. This is because the other planets were thought to be in heaven, like the gods, and our planet lay beneath, like the earth. Five of the planets can be seen with the unaided eye and were named thousands of years ago. They are Jupiter, Saturn, Mars, Venus and Mercury. Uranus was found in 1781, Neptune in 1846 and Pluto in 1930.

If the Earth were the size of an orange, then the Moon would be the size of a cherry.

What is the difference between a planet and a moon?

A planet is a world that goes around the Sun. A moon is a smaller world that goes around a planet. All except two of the planets have moons. The Earth and Pluto have only one, whereas Jupiter has sixteen. Mercury and Venus have none.

What is the Solar System?

The Solar System is made up of the Sun and all the bodies that go around the Sun. These are the planets and their moons, the asteroids or minor planets, meteoroids and comets. Each

▼The nine planets of the Solar System move in orbits at different distances from the Sun. By far the biggest are the giant planets Jupiter and Saturn. Four planets have rings.

moves in a particular path or orbit around the Sun. The Sun's force of gravity holds all these bodies together in the Solar System because it is bigger than they are.

How many planets are there?

The Sun has nine planets. They are Mercury, which is closest to the Sun, followed by Venus, Earth, Mars, Jupiter, Saturn, Uranus, Neptune and finally Pluto. Pluto is usually the most distant planet, but at the moment it is closer to the Sun than Neptune and will be until 1999.

Which is the smallest planet?

Pluto is the smallest planet. Its diameter is 2,250 kilometres. This is about two-thirds the size of our Moon and only twice the size of the largest asteroid.

▶ Io is a small moon of Jupiter. It has active volcanoes. Jupiter has 15 other known moons.

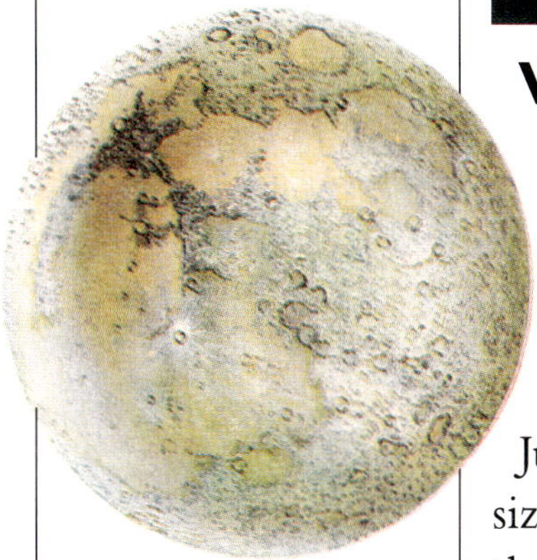

The Moon

Pluto

Which is the biggest planet?

The biggest planet is Jupiter. Its diameter is 142,800 kilometres, more than eleven times the diameter of the Earth. In volume, Jupiter is more than 1,300 times the size of the Earth! Jupiter is so massive that it weighs 2½ times as much as the other eight planets put together.

Which planet has the most moons?

Saturn has at least 18 moons. A moon is a small world going around a planet. It is held in orbit by the planet's gravity.

FACTS ABOUT THE PLANETS

PLANET	Distance from the Sun in km	Diameter at equator in km	Time taken for 1 orbit
■ Mercury	58 million	4,878	88 days
■ Venus	108 million	12,104	224 days
■ Earth	152 million	12,756	365.25 days
■ Mars	228 million	6,794	687 days
■ Jupiter	778 million	142,800	11.9 years
■ Saturn	1,427 million	120,000	29.5 years
■ Uranus	2,870 million	52,000	84 years
■ Neptune	4,497 million	48,400	164.8 years
■ Pluto	5,900 million	2,250	247.7 years

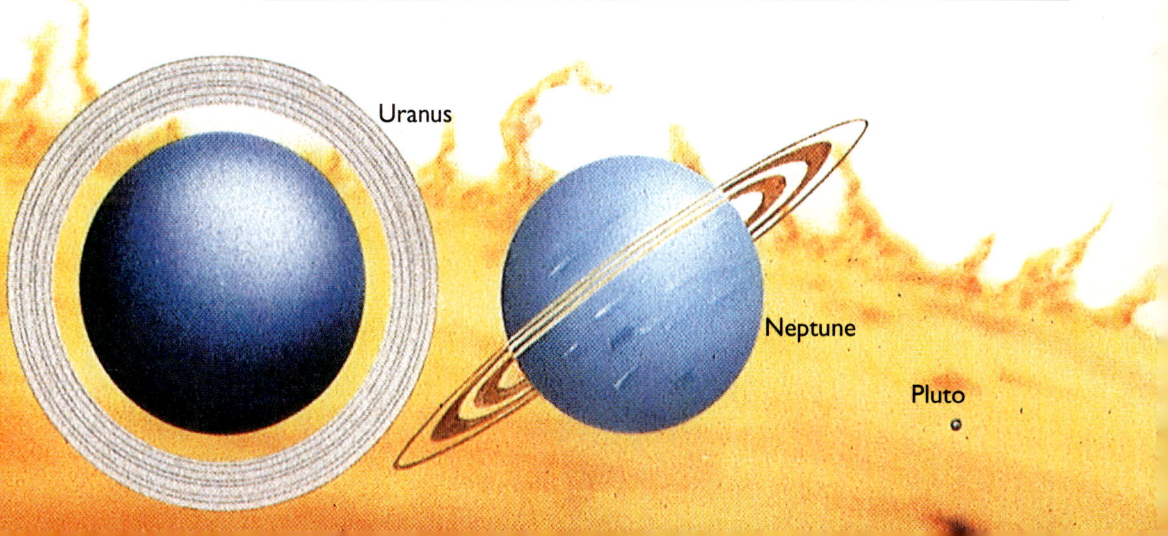

Where does the Solar System end?

The most distant planet, Pluto, is often thought to be at the edge of the Solar System. Its orbit takes it an average distance of 5.9 billion kilometres from the Sun. However, some comets are thought to travel halfway to the nearest star – a distance of about two light years. This would make the Solar System about four light years across, which is nearly 40 million million kilometres.

The word planet comes from the Greek word *planetes*, which means wanderer. The Greeks saw 'wandering' stars in the night sky.

Where are the inner and outer planets?

The inner planets are the four planets nearest to the Sun. They are Mercury, Venus, Earth and Mars, all made of rock and metal. The five other planets – Jupiter, Saturn, Uranus, Neptune and Pluto – are farther away from the Sun and are called the outer planets. These, except Pluto, are gaseous.

▼ The planets and asteroids go around the Sun in oval paths, or ellipses.

What is an orbit?

An orbit is the circular or oval path that something follows as it moves through space. The planets move in orbits around the Sun, and moons travel in orbits around planets. Satellites orbit the Earth. To get into orbit around the Earth, a spacecraft has to fly out into space beyond the atmosphere where it is partly free from the Earth's gravity.

Which planets have rings around them?

Four planets have rings around them – Jupiter, Saturn, Uranus and Neptune. The rings are thin belts of rocks orbiting the planets. Saturn's rings make it the most beautiful planet in the sky.

▼ The four giant planets all have rings. Saturn has the biggest ring system.

Which planet is so hot that lead would melt there?

The hottest planet is not Mercury, the planet nearest the Sun. It is Venus, the second nearest. It is very hot on Venus because, unlike Mercury, Venus has an atmosphere. The atmosphere acts rather like the windows in a greenhouse and helps to heat the surface of the planet. The temperature there is about 475 degrees Celsius, which is hot enough to melt several metals, including tin, lead and zinc. No plants or animals could live on the scorching, rocky surface.

Which planet turns so slowly that one day lasts two years?

Mercury is so near the Sun that the Sun has slowed its rotation. It spins so slowly that one complete day on Mercury – from one sunrise to the next – takes 176 Earth days. This is equal to two of Mercury's years, which are 88 Earth days long. On Mercury, you would have two birthdays every day!

Does a planet have to be bigger than a moon?

A moon is always smaller than the planet around which it moves. A smaller body always orbits around a larger body, because the larger body has a greater force of gravity. However, not all moons are smaller than all planets. Our Moon and six other moons of the outer planets are all bigger than the tiny planet Pluto. But Pluto may once have been a moon of Neptune.

PLANET FACTS

- Mercury holds two records: it is the planet with the longest day and the shortest year.
- Mars has two small rocky moons, Deimos and Phobos.
- There are valleys on Mars that look like dried-up river beds.

▶ Mars is a rocky planet and seems to be without life. It has an ice cap, mountains and craters.

▲ Mercury is the planet closest to the Sun. It is heavily scarred with craters, probably formed many millions of years ago.

What is the Red Planet?

The Red Planet is the fourth planet from the Sun, Mars. When it nears the Earth, it looks like a bright red star in the sky. Mars looks red because its surface is made of red soil and rock. Even its sky is red, because red dust floats in the atmosphere.

Which planet spins faster than any other?

The planet that spins the fastest is also the largest planet – Jupiter. It spins once around every 9 hours 50 minutes, 2½ times as fast as the Earth. A point on Jupiter's equator is moving around the planet's centre at a speed of more than 45,000 kilometres per hour. This is so fast that it makes Jupiter bulge in the middle.

Where is the highest mountain in the Solar System?

There were once volcanoes on Mars. A volcanic mountain, Olympus Mons, rises 23 kilometres above the surface. This is the highest mountain in the Solar System.

Which planet could float on water?

If you could take the planets and place them in a vast ocean of water, then most of them would sink immediately. However, one would float. This planet is Saturn, which is the second largest planet in the Solar System. Because it is made mostly of gas and liquid, it is less dense or lighter than water and would float. All the other planets are more dense.

Are there any living things on other planets?

The Moon, and the planets and their moons, do not have air like our world. They are also very hot or very cold. People could not live there, neither could the animals and plants that live on Earth. Astronauts that went to the Moon did not find life there, nor did the Viking space probes that landed on Mars. In 1996 some scientists became excited when they discovered what they thought might be fossil bacteria on Mars. But other scientists were more doubtful.

It is very unlikely that there are living things anywhere else in the Solar System.

Are there any more planets beyond Pluto?

Astronomers believe that there may be an unknown planet beyond Pluto. They have searched for it with telescopes, but the mystery planet has not been found. If the planet does exist, it could disturb the paths of space probes moving among and beyond the outer planets. In this way, astronomers may discover the planet.

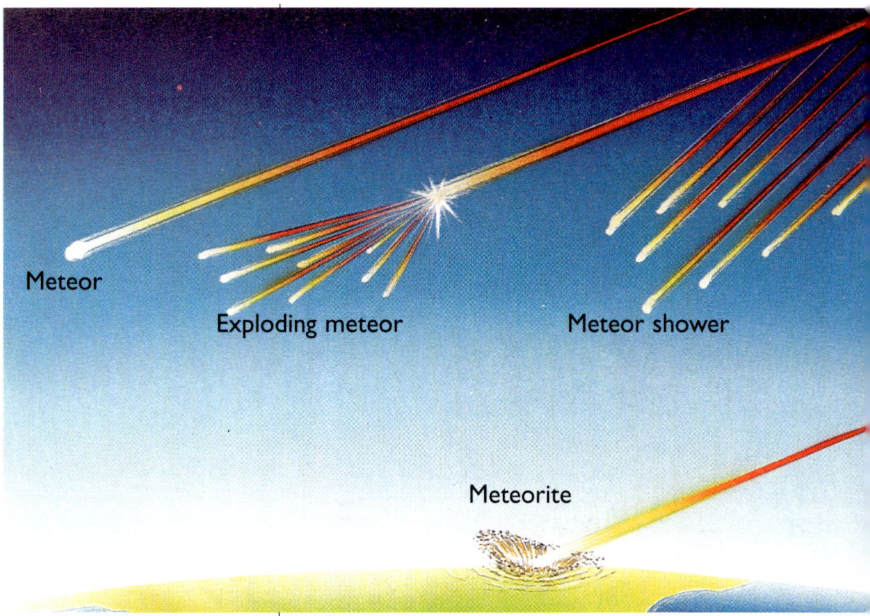

▲ A meteor shower is seen when the Earth passes through a swarm of meteoroids – particles thrown out from the crumbly heart of a comet.

COMET FACTS

- Some comets take thousands of years to go round the Sun once.
- Comet Encke, first seen in 1786, hurries round the Sun in just over three years!
- The most famous comet is named after Edmund Halley (1656–1742), an English scientist.
- Halley believed that comets seen in 1531, 1607 and 1682 were in fact the same one. He predicted it would return in 1758. And Halley's Comet did, on Christmas Day!

What are shooting stars and meteorites?

A shooting star looks like a star that suddenly shoots across the night sky. It lasts only a second or two before disappearing. It is in fact not a star at all but a small particle of rock that strikes the Earth's atmosphere from space. It moves so fast that it heats up as it moves through the air, becoming white hot before burning away. A particle or piece of rock that moves through space is called a meteoroid. If it burns up in the atmosphere, it is called a shooting star or meteor. Some meteoroids are big enough to survive their fiery descent and strike the ground. These are called meteorites.

What is a comet?

A comet is thought to be composed of small rocks and dust particles cemented together by frozen gas and ice. It orbits around the Sun and appears to hang in the sky like the Moon. It is actually moving through space at about the same speed as a planet moves around the Sun.

Are comets dangerous?

We have little reason to fear comets. The Earth has even passed through the tail of Halley's Comet with no apparent damage.

Where are asteroids found?

Asteroids are small worlds that orbit the Sun as planets do. They are also called minor planets. There are thousands of asteroids, most only a few kilometres across. They lie in a huge belt around the Sun between Mars and Jupiter.

Could an asteroid hit the Earth?

Some asteroids move in orbits that can bring them close to the Earth so collisions are possible. Some scientists believe that an asteroid hitting the Earth led to the climate changes that caused the the extinction of the dinosaurs about 65 million years ago.

▶ **Halley's Comet crosses the orbit of the Earth once every 76–77 years. It was last close to us in 1986.**

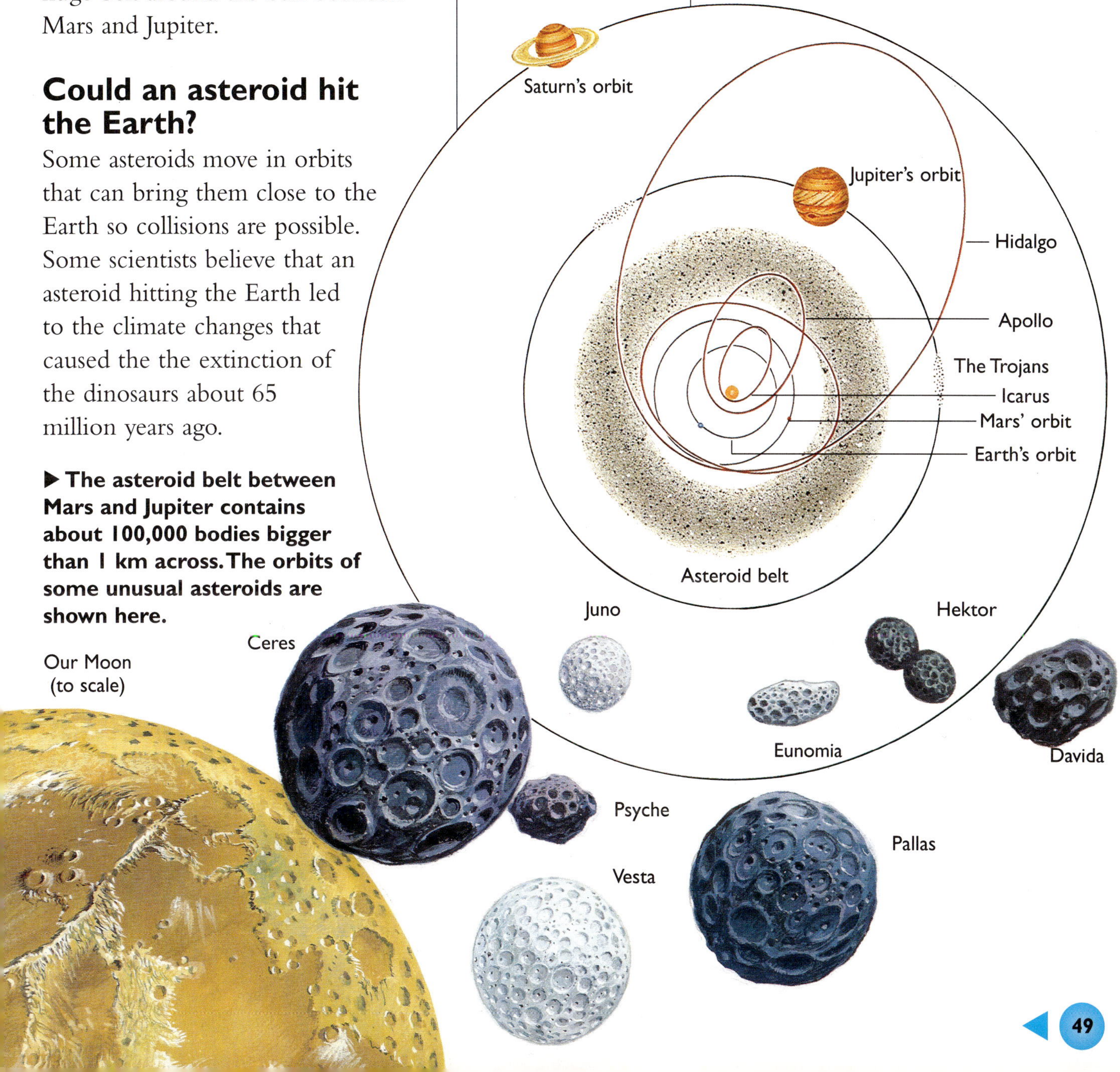

▶ **The asteroid belt between Mars and Jupiter contains about 100,000 bodies bigger than 1 km across. The orbits of some unusual asteroids are shown here.**

STARS AND GALAXIES

Where do stars form?

Stars form in clouds of gas and dust, as the Sun did. Far away in space, there are huge clouds of gas and dust called nebulae. Some nebulae are luminous and shine with light, and it is there that stars are forming. This process is going on right now.

How far away is the nearest star?

The nearest star to the Earth is the Sun. It is 152 million kilometres away, or nearly 12,000 times the diameter of the Earth.

How far away is the most distant star?

Our Sun is one of about 100,000 million stars that make up the galaxy. The most distant stars on the other side of the galaxy to the Sun are about 80,000 light years away. However, there are millions of other galaxies much farther away, each containing millions of stars.

Which is the brightest star?

The brightest star in the sky is the Sun. It outshines all the other stars because it is so near to us. The brightest star in the night sky is Sirius. It actually produces 25 times as much light as the Sun. Other stars are even brighter, and may be as much as a million times more luminous than the Sun. They look fainter than Sirius because they are much farther away.

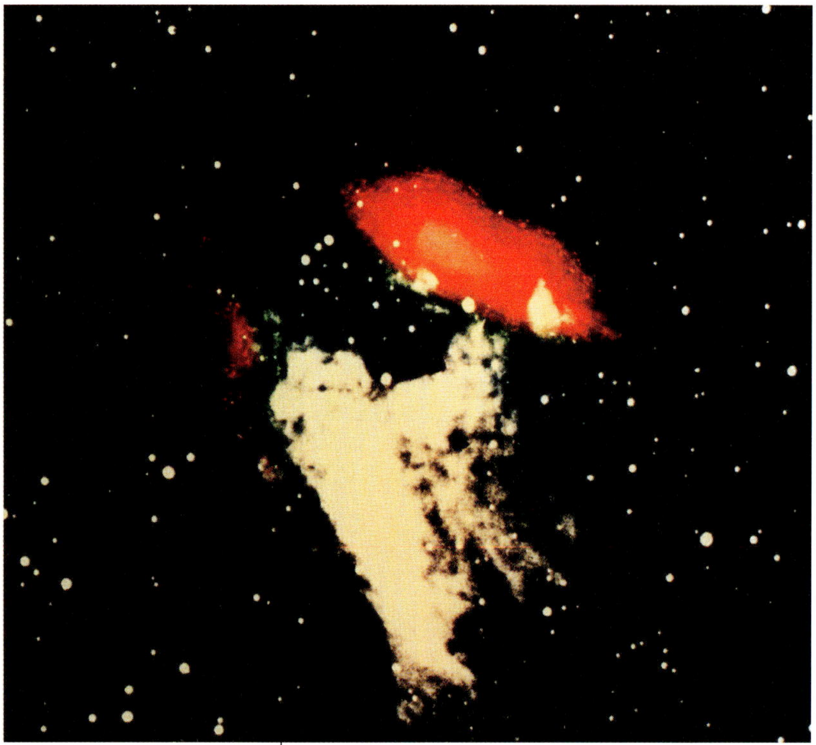

▲ **An infrared photograph of the Swan Nebula, a cloud of young stars and gas in the constellation Sagittarius.**

Did you know that stars are being born all the time? Young stars begin their lives in star-nurseries called clusters.

How many stars are there in the sky?

On a very clear night, far from a town, you could count about 2,000 stars in the sky. From all points on the Earth, about 6,000 stars can be seen in all. With a telescope, many fainter stars reveal themselves. There are millions upon millions of stars in the universe.

Is the Sun an unusual kind of star?

To us on Earth, the Sun looks enormous and very bright. But this is only because we live so close to the Sun. Compared with most stars, it is of average size and brightness and it is not in any way unusual. There are millions of other 'suns', many bigger and much brighter.

What is a supernova?

A supernova is a star that suddenly flares up, becoming millions of times brighter. It gets so bright that it may be seen during the day, but it soon fades. A supernova is a very rare sight, because it is the explosion that marks the end of a large star. The last supernova observed in our galaxy was seen by Kepler in 1604.

Why do the stars twinkle?

The light from a star has to get through the atmosphere before it reaches our eyes. The atmosphere contains moving layers of air. The layers keep on bending the path of the starlight a little, and make the star appear to twinkle. In fact, the stars shine steadily.

▼ Star maps show the constellations of the Northern and Southern Hemispheres. Each major constellation has a name. Some of these are listed in the box (right).

Some Northern Hemisphere constellations

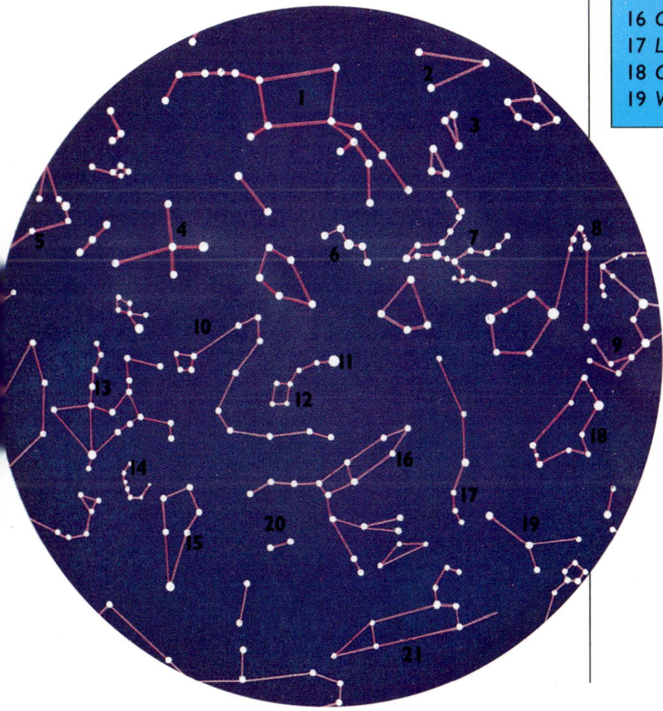

CONSTELLATION FACTS

Northern Hemisphere

1 *Pegasus*, Flying Horse
2 *Pisces*, Fishes
3 *Aries*, Ram
4 *Cygnus*, Swan
5 *Aquila*, Eagle
6 *Cassiopeia*, Lady in Chair
7 *Perseus*, Champion
8 *Taurus*, Bull
9 *Orion*, Hunter
10 *Draco*, Dragon
11 *Polaris*, Pole Star
12 *Ursa Minor*, Little Bear
13 *Hercules*, Hercules
14 *Corona Borealis*, Crown
15 *Bootes*, Herdsman
16 *Ursa Major*, Great Bear
17 *Lynx*, Lynx
18 *Gemini*, Twins
19 *Cancer*, Crab
20 *Canes Venatici*, Hunting Dogs
21 *Leo*, Lion

Southern Hemisphere

1 *Aquarius*, Water-Bearer
2 *Phoenix*, Phoenix
3 *Grus*, Crane
4 *Orion*, Hunter
5 *Lepus*, Hare
6 *Columba*, Dove
7 *Tucana*, Tucan
8 *Sagittarius*, Archer
9 *Volans*, Flying Fish
10 *Triangulum Australe*, Southern Triangle
11 *Ara*, Altar
12 *Scorpius*, Scorpion
13 *Crux*, Cross
14 *Lupus*, Wolf
15 *Hydra*, Water Snake
16 *Corvus*, Crow
17 *Libra*, Scales
18 *Crater*, Cup
19 *Virgo*, Virgin

▲ Very few star patterns look like the things they are named after. Leo, the Lion, is one that does.

What are constellations?

The stars form patterns in the night sky that never change. These patterns are called constellations. Long ago, people gave them names like the Swan, the Scorpion, the Plough and Orion the Hunter because the patterns resembled animals, familiar objects, people or gods. We still use their names for the constellations. Sometimes the names are in Latin. The Swan, for example, is Cygnus.

Some Southern Hemisphere constellations

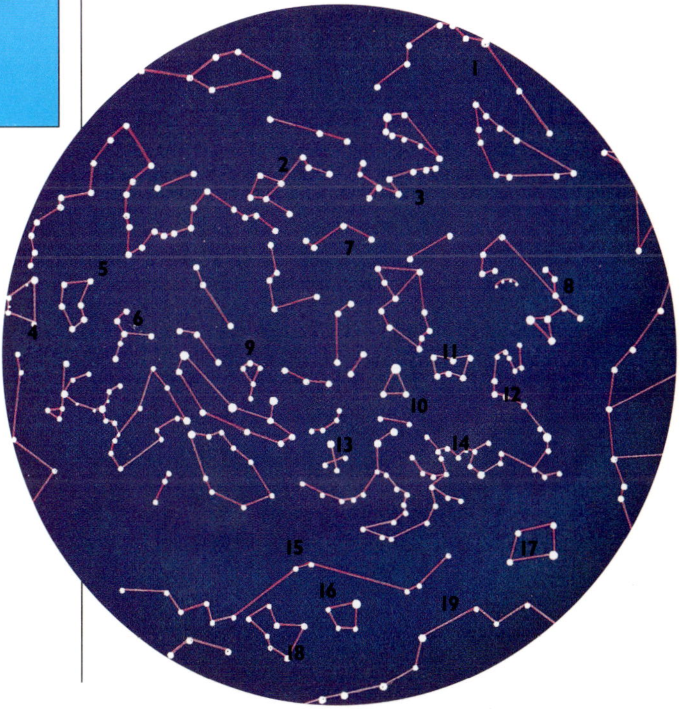

What is the Milky Way?

The Milky Way is the name of the great band of stars that stretches across the night sky. When we look at the Milky Way, we are looking into the vast group of millions of stars that make up our galaxy.

▲ **The Milky Way stretches across the sky like a milky cloud, spinning in space.**

What is a galaxy?

A galaxy is a great group of millions of stars. Our galaxy, the Milky Way, is shaped like a flat disc with spiral arms of stars. It is about 100,000 light years across. There are millions of other galaxies in the universe. They form groups, and even larger superclusters.

Why can stars only be seen at night?

Stars cannot be seen during the day because the Sun is so bright. Its light spreads out over the sky, making it appear blue. The stars are still there in the sky, but our eyes adjust to the bright blue of the sky and cannot make out the fainter stars. At dawn and dusk, when the sunlight is pale, the brightest stars and planets can be seen quite clearly.

What is a quasar?

Quasars are mysterious galaxies that astronomers discovered in 1960. They are sources of light or radio waves and are the most distant objects known.

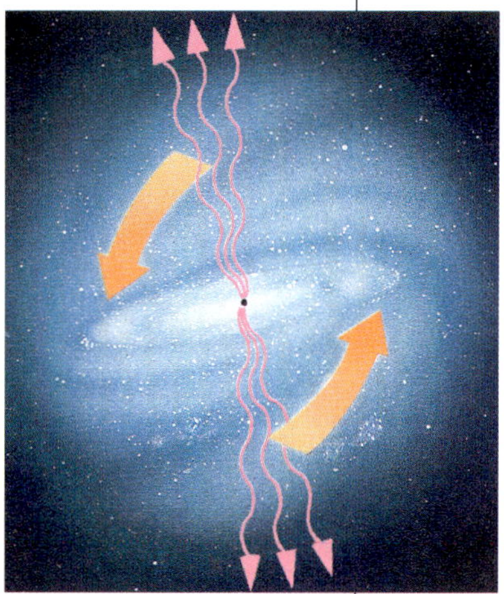

▲ **Quasars are incredibly bright. Perhaps a black hole at the centre of these mysterious distant galaxies is sucking in stars, sending matter spinning around and giving off enormous energy.**

What is the most distant object we can see without a telescope?

The great spiral galaxy of Andromeda can be seen as a faint cloud in space. It is a spiral galaxy, like our own Milky Way, made up of millions of stars. Andromeda is 2.2 million light years away and is the farthest object visible from Earth with the naked eye.

Where are we in our own galaxy?

The Milky Way is made up of many millions of stars, of which our own Sun is just one. If you imagine the Galaxy as a wheel lying on its side, with the hub as its centre, the Sun lies roughly two-thirds of the way out towards the rim.

SPACE EXPLORATION

Who first used a telescope to study the heavens?

The Italian scientist Galileo learned of the invention of the telescope and built one for himself in about 1610. With his telescope, Galileo discovered a universe far larger than anyone had imagined. He could see 'ten times as many stars'. He discovered four of the moons of Jupiter. Turning his telescope on our own Moon, he saw that it had a rough surface, pitted with craters.

▲ Galileo Galilei (1564–1642) was one of the great scientists of his day. He built his own telescopes to study the night sky.

Which was the first planet to be discovered?

The five nearest planets to us – Mercury, Venus, Mars, Jupiter and Saturn – have been known since prehistoric times. In 1781, the British astronomer Sir William Herschel accidentally discovered a new planet while searching the stars with his telescope. It was named Uranus. In fact, Uranus can be seen with the naked eye, but no one had realized that it was a planet.

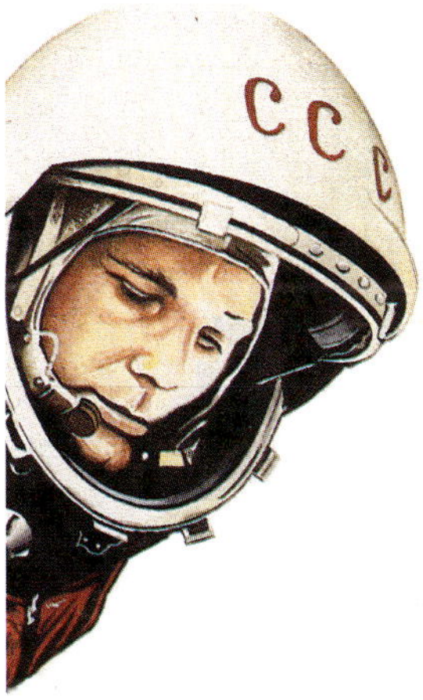

▲ Yuri Gagarin, the world's first cosmonaut.

◀ William Herschel (1738-1822) discovered the planet Uranus through a home-made telescope.

Who took the first photographs of the Moon?

John Draper of the United States took the first astronomical photographs of the Moon, in 1840. This was not long after the invention of photography. Today, astronomers observe distant stars using powerful computers and television cameras.

A photographic plate exposed for several hours can collect the very faint light from a distant star, too far away to be seen through the largest optical telescope.

Who was the first man in space?

A Russian cosmonaut (astronaut) named Yuri Gagarin made the first manned spaceflight. He was launched into space aboard the spacecraft *Vostok 1* on April 12, 1961, and made one orbit of the Earth before landing 1 hour 48 minutes later.

Who first stepped on the Moon?

The American astronaut Neil Armstrong became the first person to set foot on the Moon on July 21, 1969. He was commander of *Apollo 11*. As he descended from the lunar module of the spacecraft and stepped onto the Moon, he said these now famous words: 'That's one small step for man, one giant leap for mankind.' Armstrong was followed a little later by Edwin Aldrin, his fellow astronaut.

When did the first spacecraft go into space?

The first rocket to go beyond the atmosphere into space was an American rocket in 1949. But the first true spacecraft was the first satellite to go into orbit around the Earth. This was the Russian satellite *Sputnik 1*, which was launched into space on October 4, 1957. It had no person or animal aboard. Instead it sent information back to Earth by radio. The second satellite, *Sputnik 2*, carried a dog into space.

How fast does a spacecraft travel?

To reach the Moon or any of the planets, a spacecraft has to be launched away from the Earth at a speed called escape velocity. This is 11 kilometres/second, or 40,000 kilometres/hour – fast enough to go once around the world in an hour. This speed is reached high above the Earth, and the spacecraft then coasts on through space to its destination. If it does not reach escape velocity, the spacecraft will either fall back to Earth or go into orbit.

What do satellites do?

A satellite is any body or object that moves around another. However, most people use the word satellite to mean an artificial object that orbits the Earth. These satellites make scientific observations of space and of the Earth below, sending back pictures that help us to forecast the weather, for example. Satellites also send television programmes and telephone calls from one continent to another.

SPACE FACTS

- *Luna 2* (USSR 1959) crashed into the Moon.
- *Luna 9* (USSR 1966) was the first spacecraft to soft-land on the Moon.
- *Venera 4* (USSR 1967) landed on Venus.
- *Salyut 1* (USSR 1971) was the world's first space station.
- *Vikings 1* and *2* (USA 1976) made the first landings on Mars.
- *Voyager 1* (USA) flew past Jupiter in 1979 and Saturn in 1980.
- *Voyager 2* (USA) flew past Uranus in 1986 and Neptune in 1989.
- *Galileo Probe* (USA) entered Jupiter's atmosphere in 1995.

▼ Shown here are three satellites: *Meteosat*, a weather satellite; *IRAS*, which studied comets; and *Solar Max*, which looked at the Sun.

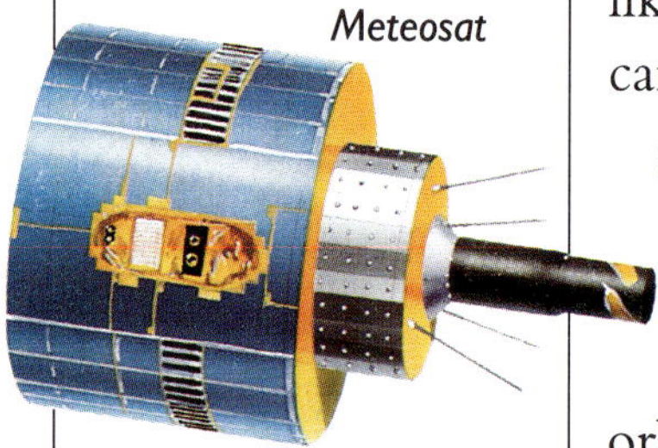

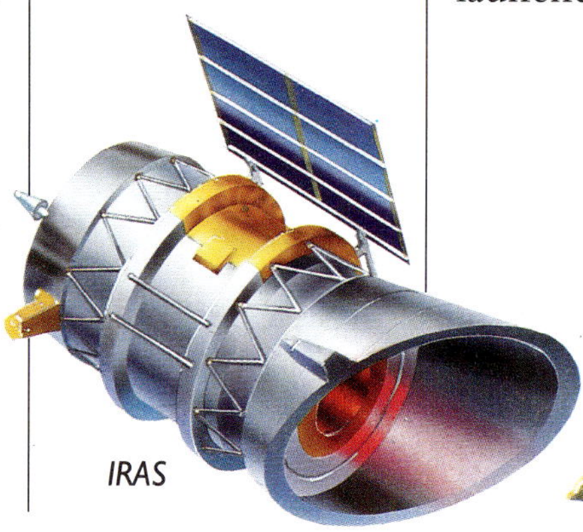

▼ The Space Shuttle can launch satellites from its large cargo bay. It can also carry sections of a space station to be assembled by astronauts in orbit.

What does the Space Shuttle do?

The Space Shuttle is a reusable spacecraft. Unlike all earlier spacecraft, it can be used again and again. It takes off from Earth like a rocket, but lands like an aircraft. The Space Shuttle cannot fly to the Moon or planets. It goes into orbit around the Earth. There, the crew can do scientific work, place satellites in orbit, and visit satellites and space stations in orbit. The first Space Shuttle was launched in 1981.

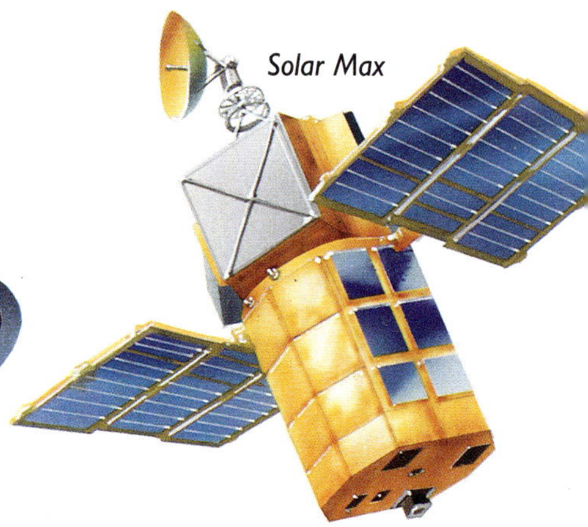

How much would you weigh in space?

If you were to travel in space, you would weigh nothing at all for most of your flight! Only when the engines were firing at the beginning and end of the flight would you have any weight. In between you would float in mid-air in the cabin of the spacecraft. This is because without gravity there is nothing to pull the astronaut to the floor of the cabin.

How can people live in space?

There is nothing in space to keep people alive – no air, no water and no food. Without protection, a person would die in seconds. A spacecraft provides air, water and food for the astronauts. Outside, they must wear spacesuits, which have an air or oxygen supply, drink, camera and computers. The spacesuit also has cooling or heating systems, for it can be very hot or very cold in space.

Astronauts using the toilet in space wear seatbelts. Space toilets don't flush. Everything is sucked away.

▼ A spacesuit is made of layers of plastic. It provides oxygen for the person inside to breathe. It allows the astronaut to work comfortably outside the spacecraft.

15 layers of plastic

What is a space station?

A space station is a laboratory orbiting the Earth. Parts of the station are brought up by rockets and assembled in space. Teams of astronauts and scientists can live in a space station for up to a year.

How many people have stood on the Moon?

In 1969 *Apollo 11* made the historic first manned landing on the Moon. From 1969 to 1972 the Americans sent seven Apollo missions to the Moon. One mission, *Apollo 13*, failed to make a landing but returned safely after an explosion on board the spacecraft. The other six missions all succeeded. In all, 12 astronauts have stood on the Moon.

What was the first real space rocket?

The first rocket which could fly fast enough and high enough to enter space was the German V2 missile. It was first fired in October 1942, flying a distance of 200 kilometres and landing within four kilometres of its target. After World War II the Americans and Russians used captured V2s to help start their spaceflight and missile programmes.

What happens to people in space?

Astronauts have stayed in space for about a year. When they return to Earth, they are a little taller. Because there is less gravity in space, their bones are less squashed together.

EARTH AND SPACE QUIZ

Is the centre of the Earth solid or liquid? *(page 9)*

How old is the Earth...15 billion years, 4.6 billion years, 1 billion years? *(page 10)*

Most of the Earth is covered by water. True or False? *(page 11)*

Which Greek god was thought to ride across the sky in a chariot of flames? *(page 12)*

Does a compass needle always point to the North Pole? *(page 13)*

When were the first reasonably accurate maps drawn? *(page 14)*

What do the contour lines on a map show? *(page 15)*

What was Pangaea? *(page 16)*

Do stalactites grow up or down? *(page 17)*

What spouts hot water and steam every 76 minutes? *(page 18)*

In which country have earthquakes killed the most people? *(page 19)*

In which continent is the Sahara? *(page 20)*

Where is the world's longest coral reef? *(page 21)*

Which are the richest forests on Earth? *(page 22)*

Which is the world's highest mountain? *(page 23)*

Where is the troposphere? *(page 24)*

Which gas makes up most of the air? *(page 25)*

How many sides has a snowflake? *(page 26)*

What are cirrus and cirrocumulus? *(page 27)*

Where is the coldest spot on Earth? *(page 28)*

Which travels fastest: thunder or lightning? *(page 28)*

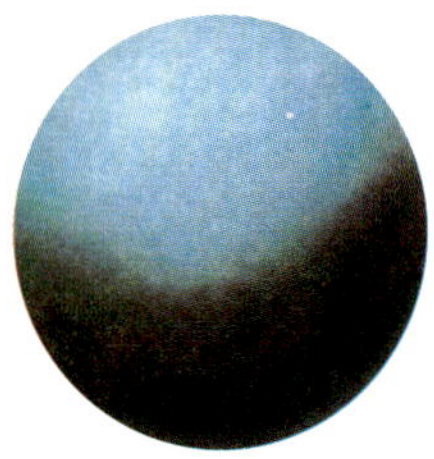

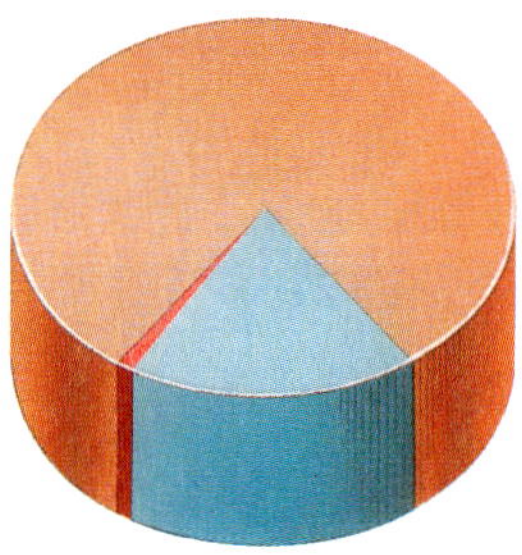

Is it true that hurricanes are Pacific Ocean storms? *(page 29)*

Where does the salt in the sea come from? *(page 31)*

Where would you find an oxbow lake and a meander? *(page 32)*

What is the world's deepest lake? *(page 33)*

What is, or was, a thylacine? *(page 34)*

Why has the Earth begun to warm up since the 1700s? *(page 36)*

How are bottles recycled? *(page 37)*

What keeps your feet on the ground? *(page 38)*

Do planets make their own light? *(page 39)*

How long has the Sun been shining? *(page 40)*

Why should you never look directly at the Sun? *(page 41)*

Is there weather on the Moon? *(page 42)*

What made the craters on the Moon? *(page 42, 43)*

How many planets have no moons? *(page 44)*

Is Pluto bigger or smaller than our Moon? *(page 45)*

What does the word 'planet' mean? *(page 46)*

Where would you have two birthdays on the same day? *(page 47)*

Which is the most famous comet? *(page 48)*

How big are asteroids? *(page 49)*

What is a supernova? *(page 51)*

What shape is the Milky Way? *(page 52)*

What did Galileo see through his telescope? *(page 53)*

When did the first Space Shuttle fly? *(page 54)*

ATOMS

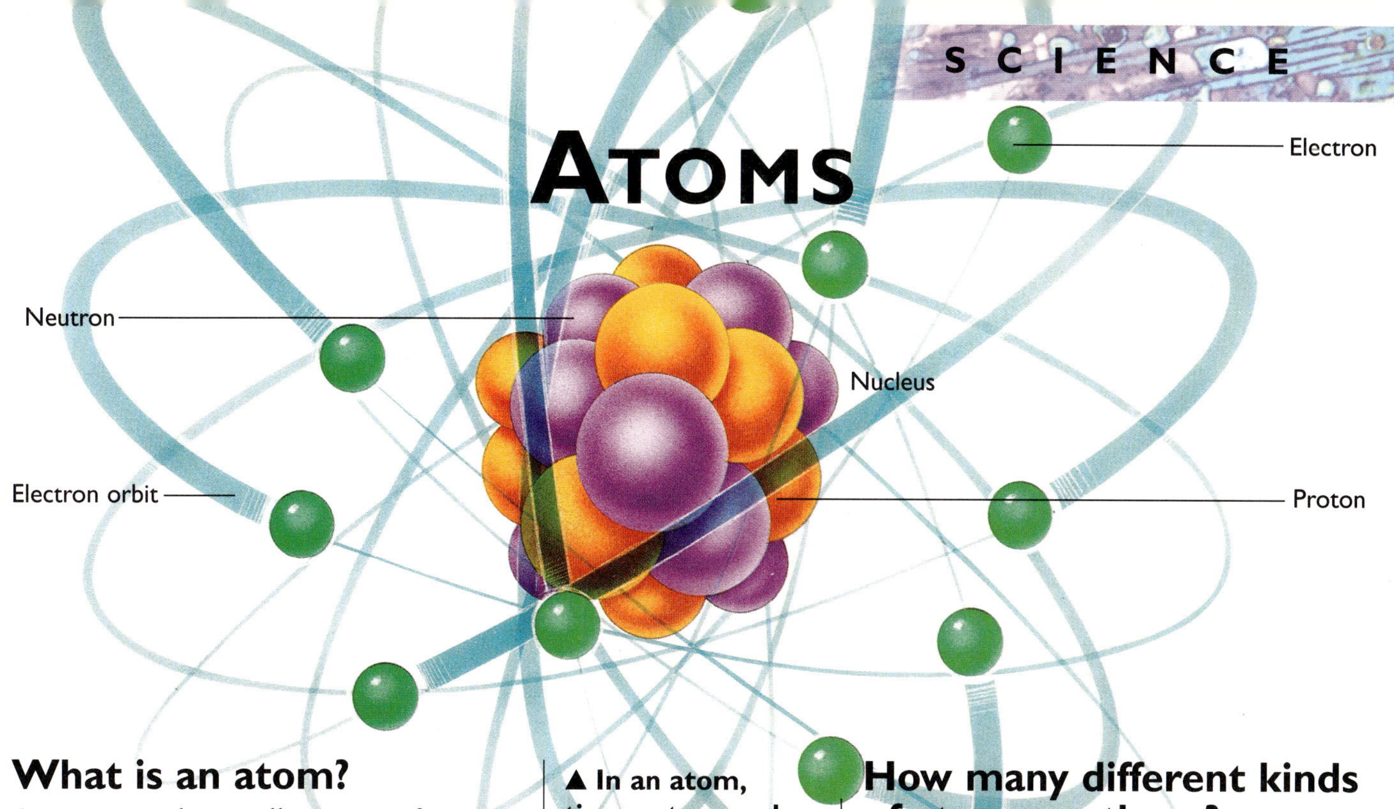

What is an atom?

An atom is the smallest unit of a chemical element – iron or copper, for example – to have its own recognizable identity. Scientists can tell the atoms of one element from those of another by their structure. Atoms are the building blocks of the elements which make up all matter in the universe.

At the centre of an atom is its nucleus, which is made up of tiny particles called protons and neutrons. Orbiting the nucleus are other particles called electrons, held in place by electrical charges. The arrangement of protons, neutrons and electrons is different for each kind of atom.

How big is an atom?

Atoms are too small to be seen with the naked eye. But scientists using high-powered electron microscopes have photographed atoms. They look like fuzzy white dots.

The nucleus is ten thousand times smaller than the atom itself. Electrons are smaller still.

▲ In an atom, tiny protons and neutrons make up the centre or nucleus. The particles orbiting the nucleus are called electrons.

▼ Atoms are very small. If an atom were as big as your fingernail, your hand could pick up the Earth!

How many different kinds of atom are there?

There are 92 different chemical elements found in nature. Therefore there are 92 different kinds of atom forming these separate elements. A few other elements and atoms have been made by scientists in the laboratory. An atom of uranium is two hundred times heavier than an atom of hydrogen, but in fact all atoms are roughly the same size. There are about two million atoms in the thickness of this page.

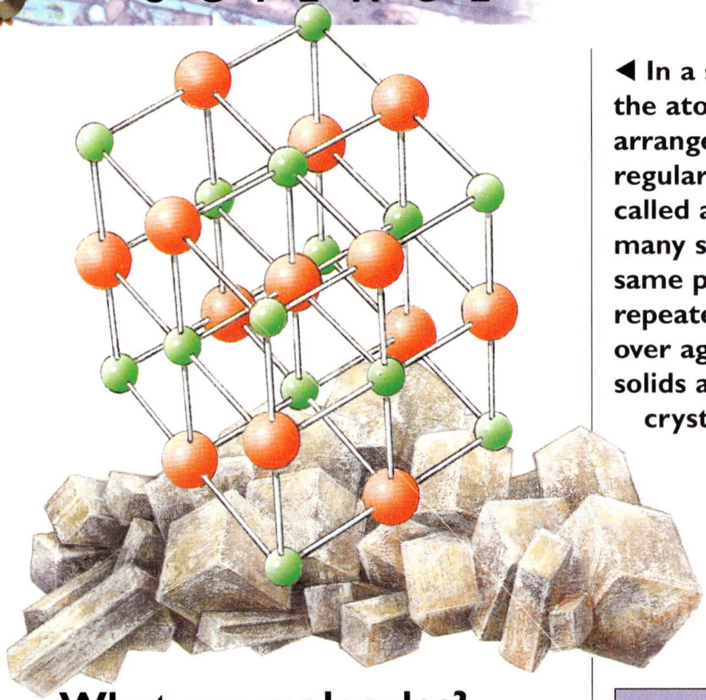

◀ **In a solid, the atoms are arranged in a regular shape called a lattice. In many solids, the same pattern is repeated over and over again. Such solids are called crystals.**

What are molecules?

A molecule is the smallest part of a substance that retains the nature of the substance. Take paper, for example. The thickness of each page of this book is roughly 100,000 paper molecules. If each paper molecule were broken up, it would no longer be paper, just a random group of atoms. Every molecule of a substance is made of exactly the same number of atoms linked together in exactly the same pattern.

Molecules are tiny. There are at least as many molecules in a teaspoon of water as there are teaspoonsful of water in the Atlantic Ocean.

Who first tried to weigh atoms?

The British chemist John Dalton (1766-1844) worked out that a molecule of water always contains the same proportions of oxygen and hydrogen. He thought oxygen atoms must be heavier than hydrogen atoms. In fact an oxygen atom weighs 16 times more than an hydrogen atom.

ATOM FACTS

- In the 400s BC, the Greek scientist Democritus gave the name 'atom' to what he thought was the smallest particle of matter.
- In 1818 Jons Berzelius, a Swedish chemist, classified 45 different substances by their atomic weights.
- Berzelius also suggested naming elements by using the first letter or letters of their names, for example O = oxygen.
- Atoms are incredibly light. There are about 600 billion trillion hydrogen atoms in a gram!
- Electrons whizz around at amazing speed. They constantly change positions as they orbit the nucleus, making billions of trips in just one millionth of a second.

Who discovered electrons?

Electrons were discovered in 1895 by Sir Joseph John Thomson, a British scientist. Thomson worked in the Cavendish Laboratory at Cambridge University and was investigating the rays produced when an electric current passed through a vacuum. For this discovery he received the Nobel Prize for Physics in 1906.

Sir Joseph John Thomson

Who first split the atom?

Until the early 1900s, nobody knew how the atom was arranged. Sir Joseph John Thomson thought that the atom looked something like a plum pudding, with electrons scattered around like currants. Ernest Rutherford, in 1911, and Niels Bohr, in 1913, put forward different ideas.

Rutherford, a New Zealander, discovered the nucleus of the atom and proved that the electrons were very light. Bohr, a Danish physicist, devised the 'sun and planets' model of particles orbiting the nucleus of the atom. This theory is accepted by most scientists today.

Rutherford did what the Ancient Greeks thought impossible. He split the atom, and in so doing changed one substance into another. He bombarded atoms of nitrogen gas with alpha particles. This changed them into oxygen and hydrogen atoms. Rutherford first split the atom in 1919, while working at Cambridge University in Britain.

Why does splitting the atom release so much energy?

The great scientist Albert Einstein devised a famous formula to explain why, when an atom is split by a neutron, the mass of all the pieces is actually less than the mass of the original atom plus the neutron. Einstein's formula was $E = mc^2$. It can be explained as follows: E = energy released; m = mass lost; c^2 = the speed of light squared. The energy released in a nuclear reaction is equal to the mass lost multiplied by c^2. And c^2 is huge, for light travels at 300,000 kilometres a second! Even if the mass m is tiny, the energy E will be very great. The value of c^2 is 300,000 multiplied by 300,000!

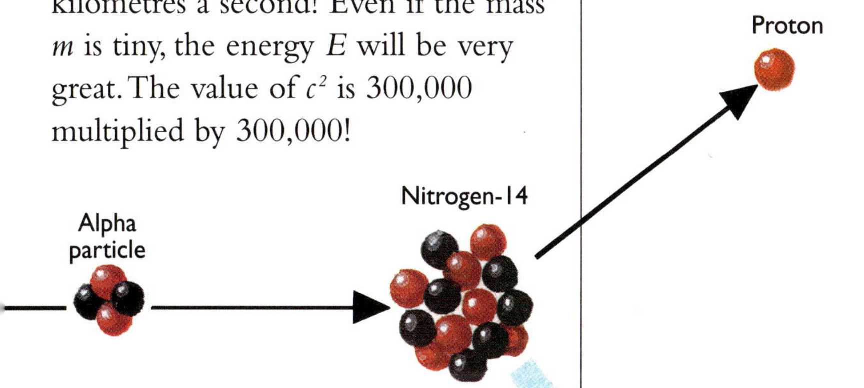

▼ In 1919 the scientist Ernest Rutherford managed to split the atom. He changed nitrogen into oxygen by bombarding it with alpha particles. This important advance led the way to nuclear power.

What is radioactivity?

A few of the heaviest atoms, being unstable by nature, can break down and change into other atoms. As this breakdown, or decay, takes place, radiation is given off. The French scientist Henri Becquerel discovered radioactivity in uranium in 1896. Radioactivity occurs in nature. It also happens when the atom is split by scientists. Radioactive rays are dangerous to health because they can affect the normal working of the cells in the body. This causes radiation sickness and can lead to serious illnesses such as cancer and leukaemia.

Why is nuclear energy so named?

The word 'nuclear' comes from 'nucleus', the core of the atom. When there is a change in the nucleus of an atom, energy is released. This is called nuclear energy. It is found naturally in the Sun and stars as well as on Earth. Scientists can also produce this energy in a nuclear power station or a nuclear weapon.

What is the difference between nuclear fission and nuclear fusion?

Both of these are kinds of nuclear reaction. In fission a heavy nucleus (usually uranium) splits. In fusion, light nuclei fuse, or come together. Fusion produces a thermonuclear reaction and is the most powerful source of energy known. Nuclear fission is used in nuclear power stations and in atomic bombs. Fusion is used in hydrogen bombs and may one day be harnessed to provide unlimited power, using a hydrogen-like fuel called deuterium found in seawater.

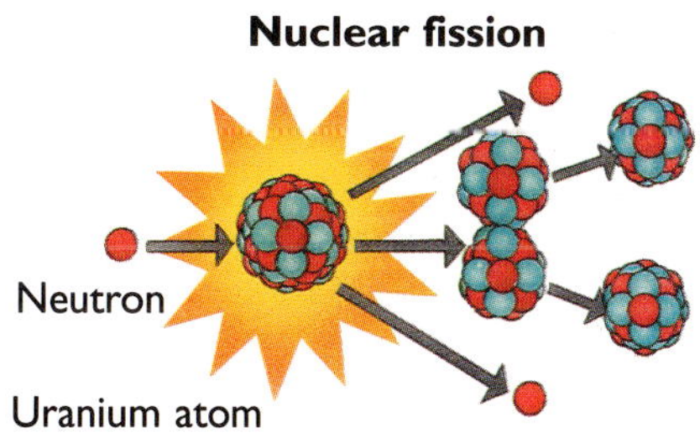

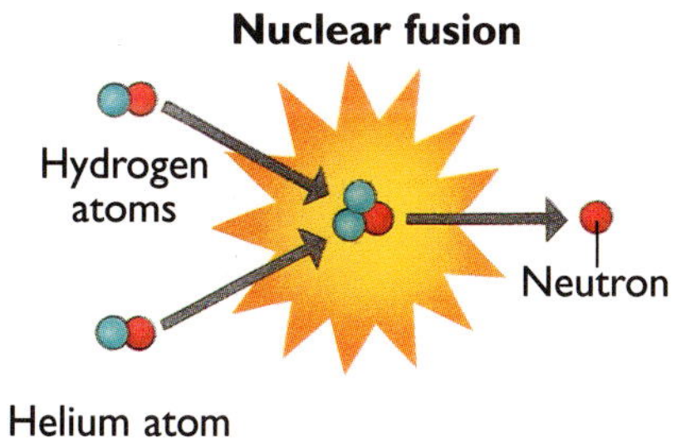

▶ In nuclear fission, a neutron splits an atom, starting a chain reaction. In nuclear fusion, light nuclei join together, forming an atom and a neutron.

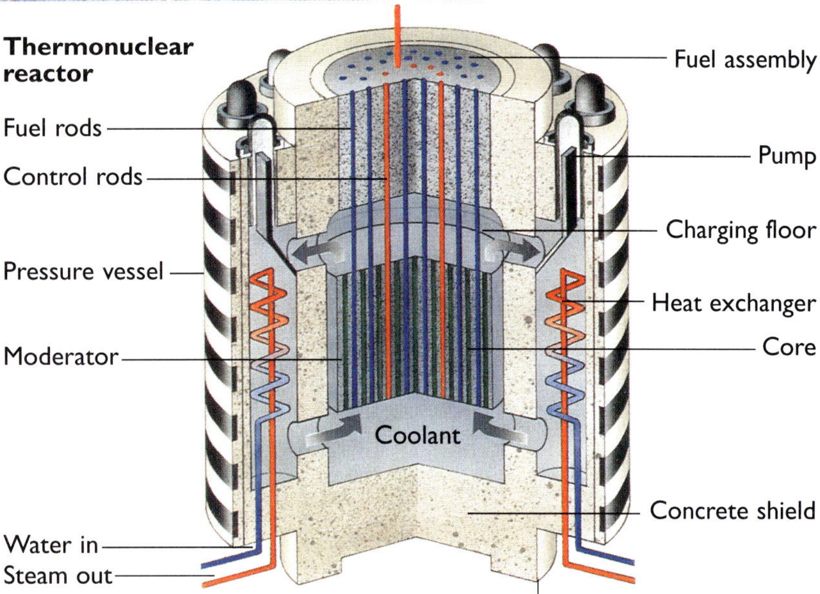

▲ **The core of a thermonuclear reactor contains the uranium fuel rods. Heat from fission of the fuel converts water into steam for driving turbine generators to make electricity.**

How does a reactor make electricity?

A nuclear power station works in the same way as an ordinary coal- or oil-burning power station, by heating water to make steam to drive turbines. The heat to make the steam comes from the enormous energy released by a chain reaction inside the station's reactor.

What happened at Chernobyl?

In April 1986 there was a serious accident at the Chernobyl nuclear power station in Ukraine (then part of the USSR). A reactor exploded and radioactivity poisoned plants and animals. Some people died. Many others were moved to new homes away from the area. The reactor was sealed in concrete for ever.

A recent X-ray device is called a body scanner or CAT scanner. It rotates round the patient's body, sending out a pencil-thin beam of X-rays. A computer screen shows the result – a whole slice of the body.

What is an isotope?

Nearly all elements have atoms of two or more different weights. Atoms that belong to the same element, yet have different weights, are called isotopes. For example, hydrogen has three isotopes which are called protium, deuterium and tritium.

Some radioactive isotopes are useful in industry and medicine. For instance, the radiation from the isotope cobalt 60 is used instead of X-rays to take photographs through metals and so detect cracks and other faults. Radioactive isotope scanning is used by doctors to study the workings of people's organs.

Why can nuclear submarines stay at sea for such a long time?

A nuclear submarine is driven by turbine engines which use steam heated by a nuclear reactor. The reactor uses so little fuel the submarine seldom has to return to port to refuel. The world's first nuclear-powered submarine was the US Navy's *Nautilus* (1955). A lump of uranium fuel the size of an electric light bulb provided enough energy to drive the submarine 100,000 kilometres. In 1960 *USS Triton* circled the world under water in three months without refuelling.

▶ **The reactor of a nuclear submarine heats water to make the steam that drives the submarine's turbine engines.**

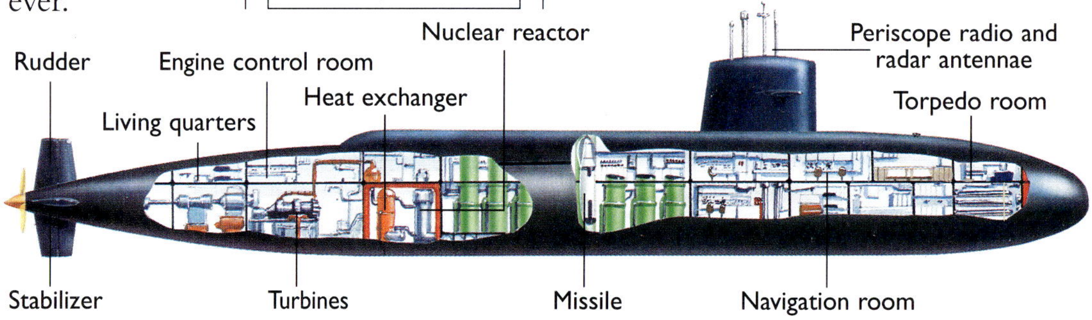

Elements and Matter

What is an element?

An element is a substance made up of only one kind of atom. All the atoms in an element have the same atomic number, and it is impossible to break up an element into parts that have different chemical properties.

There are 92 elements found in nature. Others can be made only in the laboratory during atomic reactions. In all, 109 elements have been officially found, though scientists claim to have discovered two more.

The most common element in the Earth's crust is oxygen (about 50 percent by weight). Next comes silicon (about 28 percent by weight). Each element has a symbol that stands for its name; for example, He (helium), Cu (copper), Zn (zinc), Fe (iron). This makes it easier when writing out long chemical formulas.

▶ Flame tests can identify chemical elements. Platinum wire dipped in compounds of these elements produce a different colour when heated by a Bunsen burner.

▼ The periodic table shows all the elements in order of atomic number. Elements of atoms with similar structures and properties are logically grouped together. The main groups are non-metals, alkali metals, transition metals and the inner transition series metals.

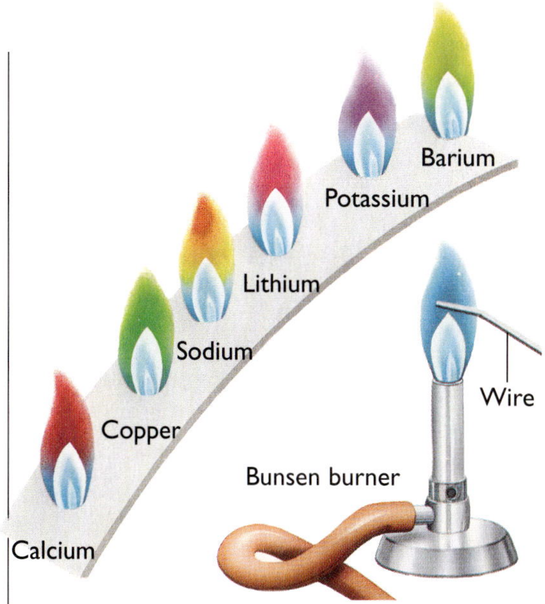

What is a mineral?

Gold, silver and mercury are examples of pure elements, but most chemical elements react with other elements so readily that they are not found singly on Earth. Instead, they combine (join) with one another as minerals. Some 3,000 minerals are known.

Alkali metals — Transition metals — Non-metals — Inner transition series

																	2 Helium He
3 Lithium Li	4 Beryllium Be								1 Hydrogen H			5 Boron B	6 Carbon C	7 Nitrogen N	8 Oxygen O	9 Fluorine F	10 Neon Ne
11 Sodium Na	12 Magnesium Mg											13 Aluminium Al	14 Silicon Si	15 Phosphorus P	16 Sulphur S	17 Chlorine Cl	18 Argon Ar
19 Potassium K	20 Calcium Ca	21 Scandium Sc	22 Titanium Ti	23 Vanadium V	24 Chromium Cr	25 Manganese Mn	26 Iron Fe	27 Cobalt Co	28 Nickel Ni	29 Copper Cu	30 Zinc Zn	31 Gallium Ga	32 Germanium Ge	33 Arsenic As	34 Selenium Se	35 Bromine Br	36 Krypton Kr
37 Rubidium Rb	38 Strontium Sr	39 Yttrium Y	40 Zirconium Zr	41 Niobium Nb	42 Molybdenum Mo	43 Technetium Tc	44 Ruthenium Ru	45 Rhodium Rh	46 Palladium Pd	47 Silver Ag	48 Cadmium Cd	49 Indium In	50 Tin Sn	51 Antimony Sb	52 Tellurium Te	53 Iodine I	54 Xenon Xe
55 Caesium Cs	56 Barium Ba	57-71 Lanthanide series	72 Hafnium Hf	73 Tantalum Ta	74 Tungsten W	75 Rhenium Re	76 Osmium Os	77 Iridium Ir	78 Platinum Pt	79 Gold Au	80 Mercury Hg	81 Thallium Tl	82 Lead Pb	83 Bismuth Bi	84 Polonium Po	85 Astatine At	86 Radon Rn
87 Francium Fc	88 Radium Ra	89-103 Actinide series	104 Rutherfordium Rf	105 Element 105	106 Element 106	107 Element 107	108 Element 108	109 Element 109									

57 Lathanum La	58 Cerium Ce	59 Praesodmium Pm	60 Neodymium Nd	61 Promethleum Pm	62 Samarium Sm	63 Europium Eu	64 Gadolinium Gd	65 Terbium Tb	66 Dysprosium Dy	67 Holmium Ho	68 Erbium Er	69 Thulium Tm	70 Ytterbium Yb	71 Lutetium Lu
89 Actinium Ac	90 Thorium Th	91 Protactinium Pa	92 Uranium U	93 Neptunium Np	94 Plutonium Pu	95 Americium Am	96 Curium Cm	97 Berkelium Bk	98 Californium Cf	99 Einsteinium Es	100 Fermium Fm	101 Mendelevium Md	102 Nobelium No	103 Lawrencium Lr

What are the three states of matter?

The three states in which matter exists are solid, liquid and gas. Solids have both shape and volume; their molecules are held together tightly. Liquids have volume too, but no shape; their molecules are held together less tightly, so that a liquid will flow into a container. Gases have neither volume nor shape; their molecules are free to move about and a gas will fill any container which encloses it.

When you dry your hair, warm air blown from the dryer turns the water on your hair to water vapour, which is absorbed by the air. Washing on a line dries this way too.

Can matter change its state?

Many substances change state quite easily, when heated or cooled. Water is a liquid at normal temperature but changes to a gas (water vapour) when heated. When water is cooled, it becomes a solid (ice). When ice is heated, it changes first to water and then to water vapour (steam).

▲ If you pour hot water (liquid) onto ice (solid), you see water vapour (gas) rising. Water is the only compound that is liquid in its natural form.

What is evaporation?

When a liquid is heated, it will change to a vapour. The steam coming from a boiling kettle is water vapour, a gas. The same thing happens when hot sun shines on a wet road: water vapour can be seen rising. This is evaporation. Evaporation can be used to extract salt from salty water. Boiling causes the water to evaporate as vapour and solid salt crystals are left behind.

Why does a balloon burst when you squeeze it?

If you blow up a balloon, and then squeeze it, the volume of air inside is reduced, and its pressure increases. Eventually the pressure of air inside becomes so great that the balloon bursts. This is a practical demonstration of one aspect of gases' behaviour discovered in 1662 by the scientist Robert Boyle.

How are crystals formed?

Crystals are solids found in nature in an almost endless variety of sizes and shapes. Most solid matter, including nearly all minerals and metals, are crystalline. You can watch crystals form in a sugar solution. If you add sugar to water, the sugar dissolves to make a sugar and water solution. If you heat the solution to boiling point, the water will begin to evaporate. The remaining solution will contain more and more sugar. Eventually, the water that is left will be 'saturated' with sugar and the sugar will begin to form crystals.

▶ These long coloured streamers are crystals growing in a solution of sodium silicate (water glass).

What is a chemical reaction?

When two or more substances are put together, they may mix, as when you mix sand and water in a bucket, but remain separate substances. However, if a chemical reaction takes place, they may undergo a chemical change and become a different kind of substance. For example, when zinc is added to hydrochloric acid, a reaction occurs. The products are hydrogen gas and zinc chloride.

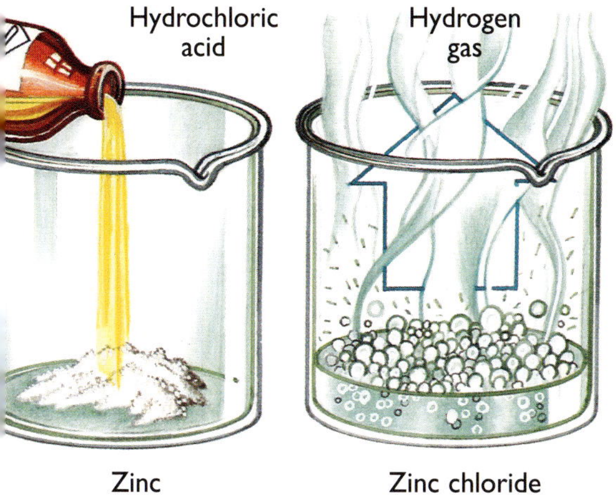

◀ **Zinc is a metal. Hydrochloric acid is a liquid. When zinc and hydrochloric acid are mixed, the acid reacts with the metal to form a new compound, zinc chloride.**

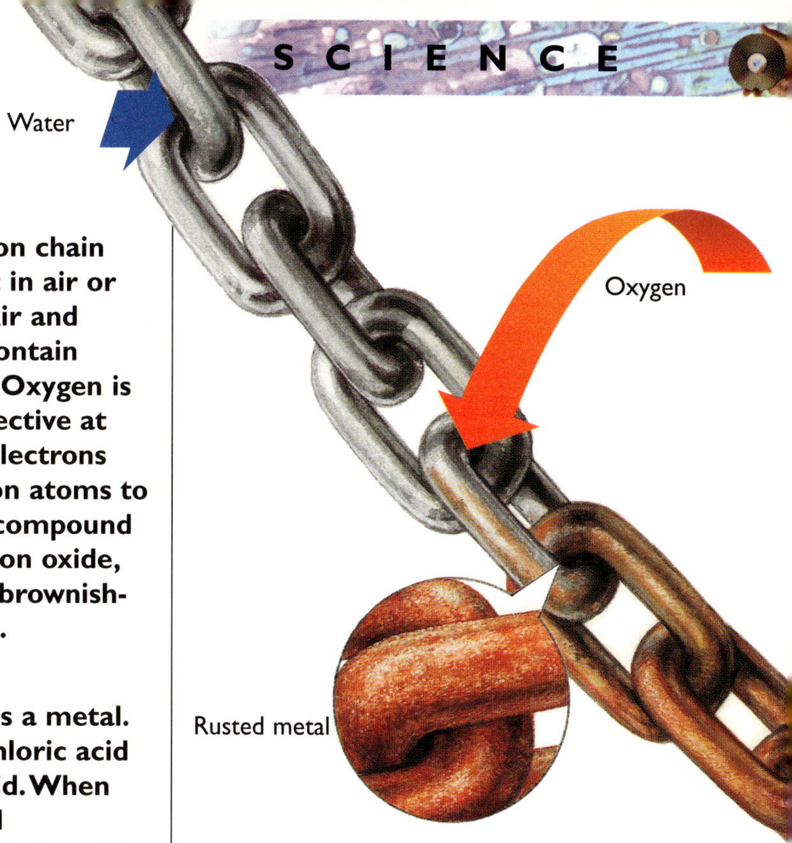

▶ **An iron chain will rust in air or water. Air and water contain oxygen. Oxygen is very effective at taking electrons from iron atoms to form a compound called iron oxide, seen as brownish-red rust.**

What is a compound?

A compound is a substance made up of two or more elements which cannot be separated by physical means. For example, water is a compound of hydrogen and oxygen. Each water molecule is made up of two hydrogen atoms joined to one oxygen atom by invisible forces called bonds.

Why does iron go rusty?

When a piece of unpainted iron or steel is left outside in the damp air, it soon goes rusty. Rust can eat into the surface of metal objects, such as car bodies. Rust is an example of a chemical reaction, or combination, between the iron in the car bodywork and the oxygen in the air. This reaction is called oxidation and produces iron oxide, or rust. A coating of paint, or of a non-rusting metal such as chrome, prevents rust by stopping oxygen reaching the iron.

Salt speeds up rusting. You can test this by putting pieces of wire wool in two tubes. Fill one tube with plain tap water. Mix salt and water in the other. See which piece of wire wool rusts first. Try the same experiment with boiled water. Boiling removes air from the water. What happens to the wire wool?

What did Lavoisier discover?

Antoine Lavoisier, who lived from 1743 to 1794, was a French scientist and one of the founders of modern chemistry. His most important discovery was that matter cannot be destroyed during a chemical reaction, even though it may change its appearance. This is one of the basic laws of science: the law of conservation of mass. It means that the amount of matter produced by a chemical reaction must always be the same as the amount that took part in the reaction. Lavoisier was executed on the guillotine during the French Revolution.

Why are there so many carbon compounds?

Carbon is the only element whose atoms are able to join together to form chains, rings and other more complicated bonds. This means that there is a huge number of organic (carbon) compounds; nearly four million are known.

What are diamonds made of?

Diamond is a form of carbon. It is the hardest substance known. Natural, uncut diamonds look dull and have little lustre. The brilliant gems that are so valuable are made by careful cutting and polishing.

▼ Carbon occurs in three forms. In diamond, the carbon atoms are arranged in a regular framework called a lattice. In graphite, the atoms are in layers. Amorphous carbon has no regular structure.

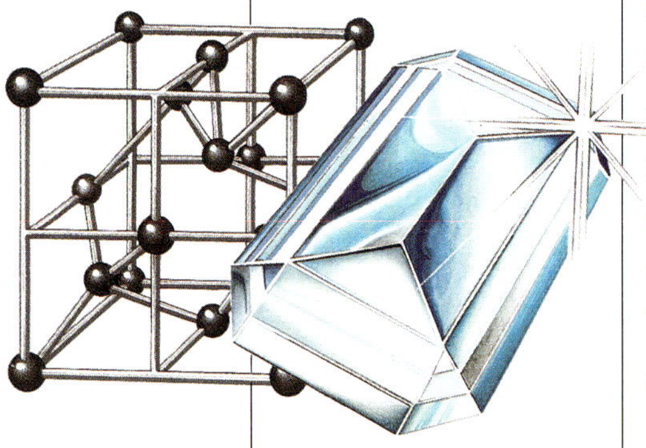

What is an acid?

An acid is a chemical compound containing hydrogen and at least one other element. For example, sulphuric acid (formula H_2SO_4) is made up of hydrogen (H), sulphur (S) and oxygen (O). Acids are normally found as liquids.

Certain acids, known as organic acids, are found in food plants. For instance, citric acids are found in lemons and oranges, and malic acid is found in apples, plums and rhubarb.

Why are some acids dangerous?

In concentrated form, some acids are so strong that they burn skin and even dissolve metals. When diluted with water, they are less harmful.

ACID FACTS

- Some acids can eat through glass, and so must be kept in special containers.
- The human body produces weak hydrochloric acid to aid the breakdown of foods during digestion.
- Sulphuric acid is probably the most important chemical compound. It has dozens of uses, including making fertilizers and drugs.
- When World War I began in 1914, lots of nitric acid was needed to make explosives such as nitroglycerine. German chemist Fritz Haber invented a new way to make nitric acid by heating ammonia and air.

How can you test for acid?

A simple test for an acid is to dip a piece of blue litmus paper into the liquid. Litmus paper is stained with a blue dye from a fungus which turns red in acid. If acid is present, the litmus paper will turn red.

What is a base?

A base is a substance which reacts with an acid to form a salt plus water. Most bases are the oxides or hydroxides of metals: in other words they are the products of reactions with oxygen or hydrogen. One of the most easily remembered chemical rules concerns acids and bases. It is this: Acid + Base = Salt + Water. When this happens, the acid and base are said to *neutralize* one another.

What is a metal?

Elements can be divided into two basic groups: metals and non-metals. Metals can be made to shine or have a lustre, they conduct heat and electricity easily and they are 'malleable' – they can be beaten into shape or pulled out into wire. More than 70 of the known elements are metals.

What is an alloy?

An alloy is a mixture of metals or of metal and another substance. Copper, for example, is a pure metal. When copper and tin (another pure metal) are mixed together by heating them until they melt, they make an alloy called bronze – the earliest known alloy. Copper and zinc together make brass. Steel is an alloy of iron and carbon.

Which metal most easily conducts heat and electricity?

Silver has the highest conductivity of all known metals. It is also valued for its beautiful appearance. Because it is easily worked, and has a bright, light-reflecting finish, it has been used since ancient times for making jewellery, coins and ornaments.

Which is the most abundant metal on Earth?

The metal found most plentifully in the Earth's crust is aluminium, which makes up about 8 percent of the crust. It is found not as a pure metal but as an ore called bauxite.

Which metals give colour to fireworks?

Strontium burns with a red light, copper green, sodium yellow, barium green and magnesium a brilliant white light.

What is the air around us mostly made of?

About 78 percent (by volume) is nitrogen, about 21 percent is oxygen. Carbon dioxide, water vapour, helium and other gases make up the rest.

Heat never stays still. It is always moving. When you stir a hot drink, heat energy moves from the drink into the spoon. That's why the spoon gets hot.

▶ A fire extinguisher smothers a fire with carbon dioxide gas. Without oxygen, the fire dies.

◀ People who make fireworks know that certain metals will give off different colours when the fireworks are burned.

▲ A modern airship is filled with helium gas. Helium is not as light as hydrogen, but it is safer because it does not burn.

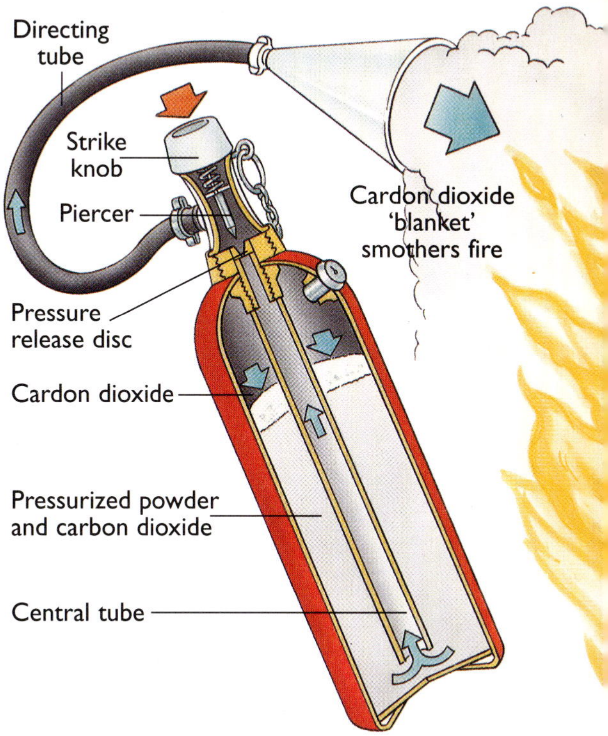

Why will carbon dioxide put out fires?

Carbon dioxide gas will not support combustion. Pure carbon dioxide is also heavier than air. If sprayed on a fire from a fire extinguisher it forms a blanket, cutting off the oxygen which would otherwise feed the flames.

Which gas is most suited for use in balloons and airships?

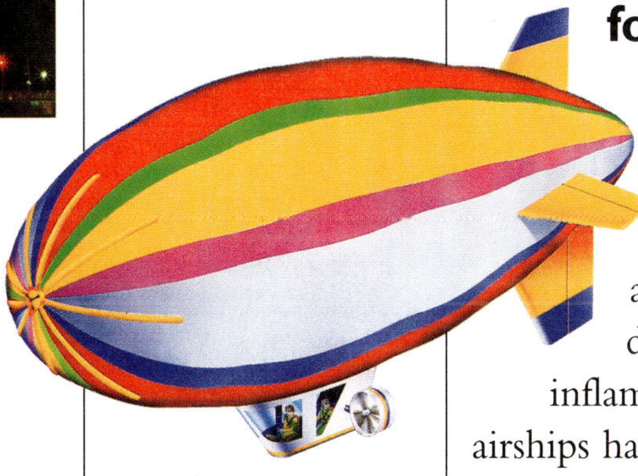

Hydrogen is the lightest gas and was used in early balloons and airships. But it has the great disadvantage of being highly inflammable and several large airships have exploded with great loss of life. Helium is second to hydrogen in lightness. Because helium does not catch fire, it is much safer and is used in modern lighter-than-air craft. The two gases helium and hydrogen make up most of the matter in the Sun and other stars.

Electricity, Magnetism and Electronics

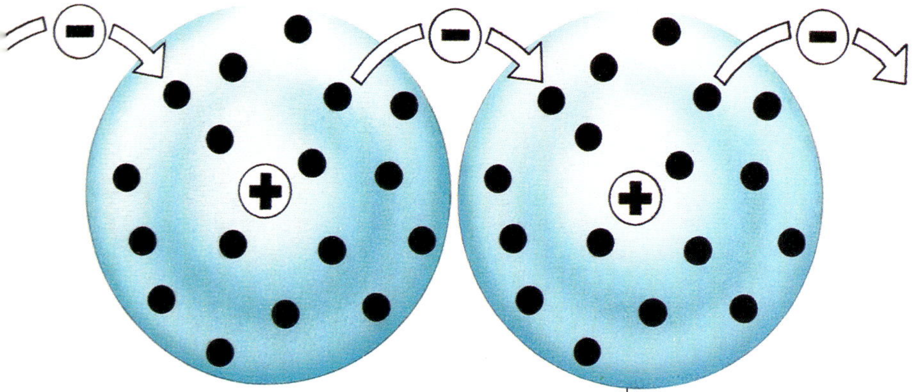

▲ **The positively charged (+) protons of an atom attract negatively charged (–) electrons. Electricity flows when electrons are free to move from one atom to another.**

What is electricity?

Electricity is a form of energy. It is produced when electrons, tiny atomic particles, move from one atom to another. Although scientists had known that this mysterious energy existed, its workings were not understood until the secrets of the atom began to be revealed about a century ago.

Without electricity, our lives would be very different. We would have no radios or televisions, no telephones, no computers. Our streets and homes would be lit by oil or gas lamps and we would have none of the gadgets that we take for granted today.

Who proved that lightning was electric?

In 1752, the American scientist Benjamin Franklin determined to find out if electricity and lightning were connected. He carried out a very dangerous experiment. He took a kite and attached to it a metal rod. Then he tied the end of the kite string to a door key and went out into a thunderstorm. When he flew the kite into a thundercloud, he saw sparks flash and felt a shock as electricity from the cloud passed from the kite down the string to the key. Never try this experiment yourself!

After this, Franklin made and tested the first lightning conductor. Today, all tall buildings are fitted with lightning conductors, which attract lightning more readily than the buildings. The connecting cable safely carries the electricity to the ground, preventing damage to the building.

▼ **In Franklin's experiment, lightning sent an electric charge down the kite string to a key, producing a spark.**

◀ **Rub a balloon against a wool or nylon jumper. This makes static electricity build up on the balloon's skin. Hold the balloon against a wall and it should cling there.**

How can objects be electrically charged?

All matter is made up of atoms. Normally, each atom has the same number of electrons and protons (see page 57). The positive charge of the protons and the negative charge of the electrons cancel each other out. But if this balance is upset, the object becomes electrically charged. For example, if a balloon is rubbed with cloth, electrons pass from the cloth to the balloon. The balloon becomes negatively charged, and the cloth having lost electrons, becomes positively charged. Unlike charges always attract each other, so the cloth clings to the balloon.

What is a conductor?

A conductor is a material through which electricity can pass. Electricity travels more easily through some materials than others. Metals are good conductors of electricity. Lightning conductors are made of copper, which conducts electricity easily.

About 100 years ago, few people had electricity in their homes. The first electrical gadgets were dangerous, and servants sometimes risked their lives using them.

▶ **Rubber is a good insulator. It has few free electrons and so does not conduct electricity well. Plastic, ceramics and glass, also poor conductors, are used as insulators in electrical equipment.**

What are superconductors?

When made very cold, certain substances have almost no resistance to electricity; they become superconductors. This was first observed in 1911 using mercury. More than 25 other metals, including copper and various alloys, behave in the same way. Superconducting coils that allow current to flow practically non-stop are used in particle accelerators. New materials that superconduct at room temperature are being developed.

What is an insulator?

An insulator is a material that will not conduct electricity. Good insulators are diamond, glass, paper, plastic, rubber and many gases. That is why the wires inside an electrical cable are enclosed in a rubber or plastic sheath. The plug on the end of the wire is also made of rubber or plastic. The insulating material protects us from getting a shock when we touch the cable or the plug because it does not conduct electricity easily.

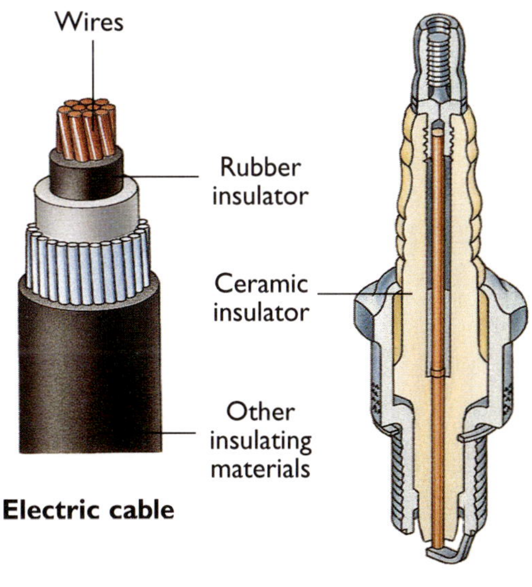

How does electricity travel?

If you put six dominoes in a line, flat and end to end, you can do an experiment to see how electricity moves along a wire. Each domino must touch the next one. Draw back the lead domino and tap it sharply against the next in line. Watch what happens. Each domino moves just a little, except for the end one, which shoots away. The electrons in a wire move in the same way. When one end is 'pushed' by an electrical force, each electron in the wire moves just a little, but together they send a fast and powerful signal along the wire.

▲ Electricity is carried from power stations through cables.

What is an electrical circuit?

In order to flow, a current must be able to find its way around a circuit. For example, if you connect a wire from one terminal of a bell to a battery, you must also connect another wire from the second terminal back to the battery. The circuit is now complete and the bell will work.

Who made the first battery?

Alessandro Volta (1745–1827) was an Italian scientist interested in electricity. In 1799, Volta used zinc and copper discs separated by damp paper to make a 'cell' that produced an electrical current. By standing several cells in a pile, he discovered that he could produce a stronger current. Volta improved his 'voltaic pile' by using acid or salt solution instead of water to moisten the paper. He had made the first battery.

What is a dry battery?

A dry battery is the kind you use in a flashlight. It has a zinc case (negative), and inside is a chemical paste surrounding a carbon rod (positive). So it is not really dry at all; the paste has enough moisture to allow the cell to work. Nickel-cadmium batteries, used in razors, are dry batteries that can be recharged.

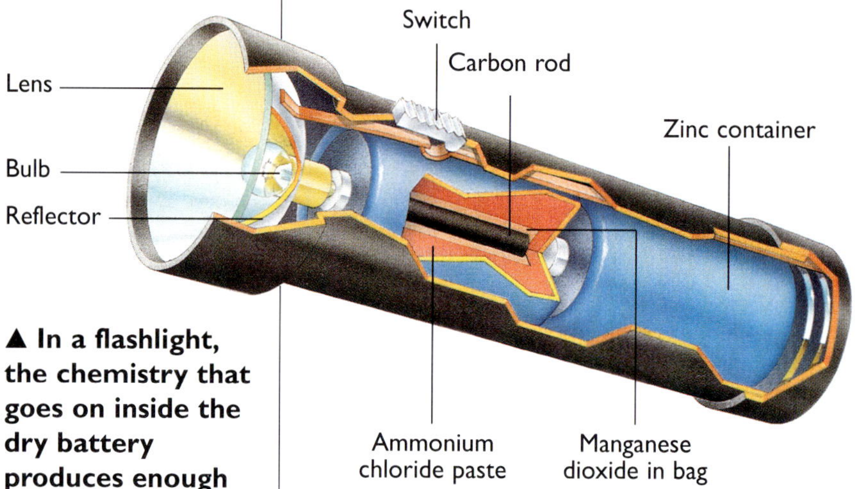

▲ In a flashlight, the chemistry that goes on inside the dry battery produces enough electricity to light up a small bulb. The reflector and lens spread the light given by the bulb.

What is a magnet?

A magnet is a piece of metal with the power to attract other substances. Iron and steel make good magnets. A magnet has two poles, north and south, near to its ends. Unlike poles (north and south) attract each other, just as opposite (+) and (–) electrodes do. Like poles (north and north, south and south) repel each other. Try putting two bar magnets together and watch what happens. Can you tell which are the magnets' like poles?

How did a lodestone point the way?

In ancient times people discovered that the lodestone (an ore now known as magnetite) could attract small pieces of iron. If a bar made from lodestone was spun, it always swung to face north. This strange behaviour made the lodestone valuable as a direction-finder – the first magnetic compass. The Chinese are said to have used lodestone compasses as early as 2000 BC.

Who discovered electromagnetism?

In 1820 a Dane, Hans Christian Oersted, discovered the magnetic effect. He was working with a battery and an electrical circuit, when he noticed that every time he brought a wire through which current was flowing near a magnetic compass, the compass needle jumped. When he disconnected the wire from the battery, the compass needle jumped again. Oersted's discovery that magnetism and electricity were closely connected, and that one could produce the other, was of immense scientific importance.

What does a magnetic field look like?

To see a magnetic field, you need some iron filings, a piece of thin card and a magnet. Sprinkle the filings on the card. Place the magnet underneath and tap the card gently. The filings will form a pattern. The field (and pattern) is strongest around the poles of the magnets.

▲ A lodestone is a lump of naturally magnetic rock. Its scientific name is magnetite. Lodestones were thought to be magical in ancient times because they could pick up iron nails and other iron objects.

DID YOU KNOW?

- Magnetism was named by the Greeks, after a place called Magnesia where lodestones were discovered.
- The Ancient Chinese are said to have used lodestones as compasses as early as 2000 BC.
- If you cut a magnet in half, each half becomes a new magnet, with its own north and south poles.

▼ Iron filings sprinkled on paper over a magnet, show the pattern of the magnetic field.

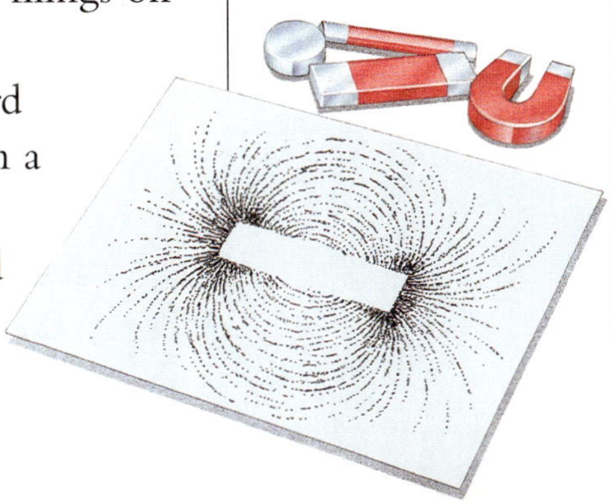

How does a simple dynamo work?

A dynamo is a generator that turns mechanical energy into electrical energy. It has an armature (a coil able to spin on its axis) positioned between the poles of a magnet. When the armature turns, a current flows in the coil each time it crosses the force field of the magnet.

An electric motor works in the opposite way to a dynamo. It turns electrical energy into mechanical energy. When current is passed through the coil, the armature rotates and keeps moving for as long as the current continues to flow.

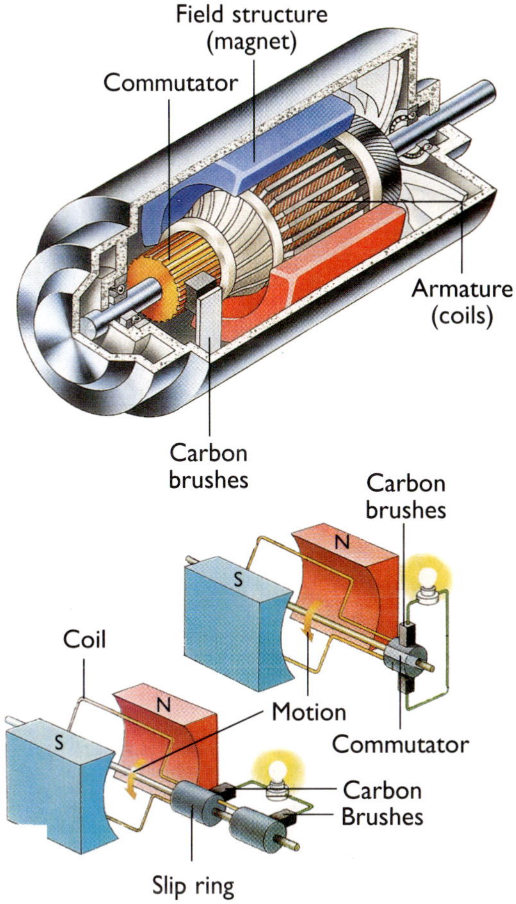

▲ Dynamos (top) are generators that turn mechanical motion into electric current. Both alternating current (bottom left), and direct current (bottom right) can be produced.

Where does our electricity come from?

The electricity that we use is made by giant generators, or dynamos, in power stations. A thermal power station converts heat into electricity by burning fuel to boil water to produce steam. The steam drives turbine generators. The fuel may be oil, coal or nuclear fuel (uranium). A second kind of power station uses the energy of moving water to drive the generators and is called a hydroelectric power station.

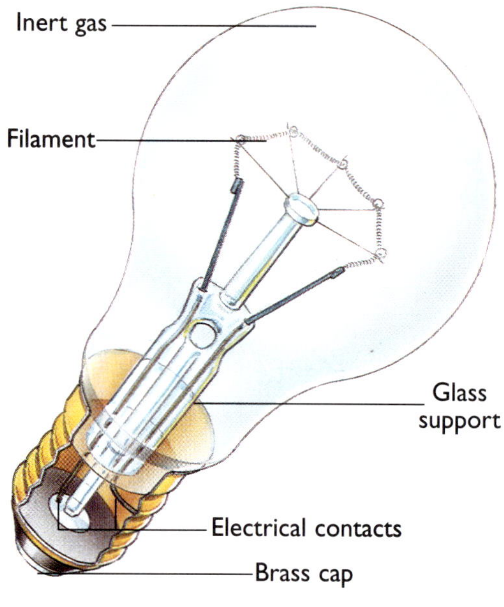

▶ In a light bulb, current flows through the filament. The filament has a high electrical resistance and gets so hot that it glows brightly.

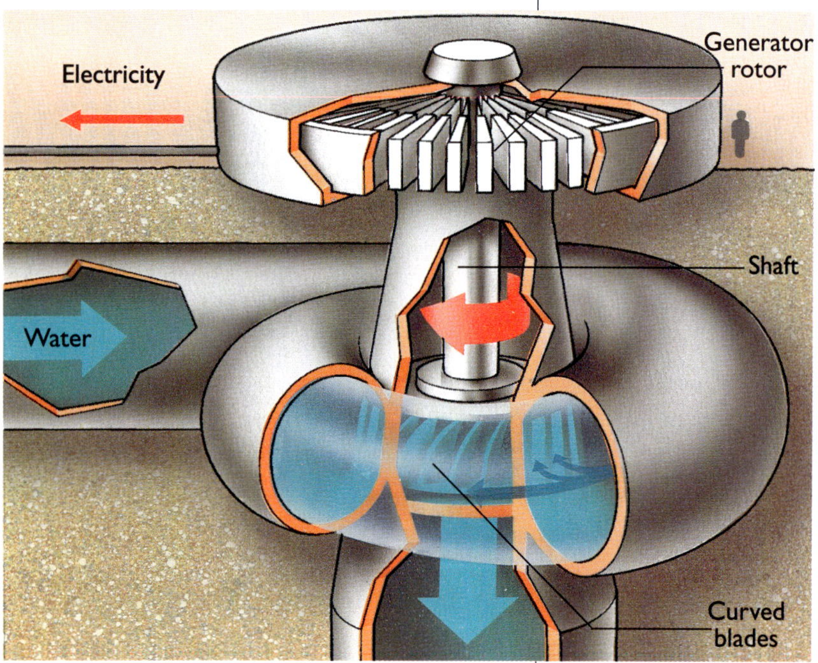

▲ A hydroelectric turbogenerator converts the energy of flowing water into electrical energy. The water drives turbines which turn the shaft of a generator rotor.

What makes a light bulb glow?

The thin wire, or filament, inside a light bulb resists the flow of current through it. When electricity is passed through the bulb, the filament becomes hot and glows brightly. To prevent the filament burning away completely, the glass bulb is filled with a mixture of inert gases (usually argon and nitrogen). The filament in most light bulbs is made of tungsten.

How does a fuse act as a safety device?

A fuse cuts off the electricity supply in a circuit when something goes wrong. Inside the fuse is a thin wire, able to carry a safe amount of current but no more. If an electrical appliance overheats it will start to use more electricity. The thin wire in the fuse (usually in the plug) heats up and melts. This breaks the circuit and cuts off the electricity.

How do 'electronic eyes' work?

When light strikes certain substances, an electrical effect is produced. This electricity is called photoelectricity. The 'magic eye' that automatically opens a door as you approach, or operates a burglar alarm, is worked by photoelectricity. A beam of light shines on a photoelectric cell. When the beam is interrupted (by someone walking through it) the cell activates an electrical circuit. The circuit may start a motor to open a door or (in a burglar alarm) set off a bell.

What is an integrated circuit?

An integrated circuit is a complicated arrangement of transistors and other components on a single piece, or chip, of semiconductor material. The first one was made in 1958. Making circuits smaller and smaller allows an incredible amount of electronic power to be contained in a tiny space. Hundreds of electronic components can be fitted into an integrated circuit the size of a letter in this sentence.

◀ **Printed circuit boards are found in all sorts of things including computers, cars and washing machines. The circuit board links components such as microchips, diodes, capacitors and transistors.**

Why do microchips work so quickly?

Inside a microchip, the components are crammed together into a very tiny space. Electrical charges can move between them in almost no time at all, so the chip does its work at amazing speed.

What was the first electronic computer?

A huge machine called ENIAC, completed in 1946 in the United States, was the world's first electronic computer that could do many mathematical tasks. The name ENIAC is short for Electronic Numerical Integrator And Calculator.

USEFUL TERMS

Bit: Binary digit; a numeral in binary notation (0 or 1).

Byte: Space in a computer's memory occupied by one letter or numeral.

Data: Information processed by a computer.

Hardware: Physical parts of a computer system.

Network: Several computers connected, e.g. by a modem (telephone).

Software: Programs for a computer.

How does a computer use its memory?

A computer has four main parts. It has a central processing unit or 'brain'. It has an input unit that feeds in data (usually linked to a keyboard), and an output unit that produces finished work (for example, as a printout on paper). The fourth and vital part is the memory unit, where the computer stores the information it needs to carry out its work. The computer stores this data as electrical charges on magnetic disks.

How do bar codes work?

In a supermarket, the checkout assistant 'reads' each item in your trolley electronically by scanning the pattern of black and white stripes marked on the package. This pattern is the bar code, containing information which is passed automatically to a main computer, recording each item sold.

▲ **Bar codes are put onto many of the goods we buy. The bar code provides an up-to-date stock record and price.**

LIGHT AND SOUND

What is light?

No one really knows what light is made of. In the 1600s Sir Isaac Newton thought light was made up of bullet-like particles which he called corpuscles. The Dutch scientist Christiaan Huygens thought light was made up of pulses, or waves, travelling through space. Modern science has found some truth in both theories. Light certainly does travel in waves, but it also behaves as if it were made of particles. Scientists now call these light particles photons.

Light is a form of energy, similar to heat. It is the only type of energy we can see. Light comes from a star such as the Sun and travels through space. Stars shine as a result of their immense nuclear energy.

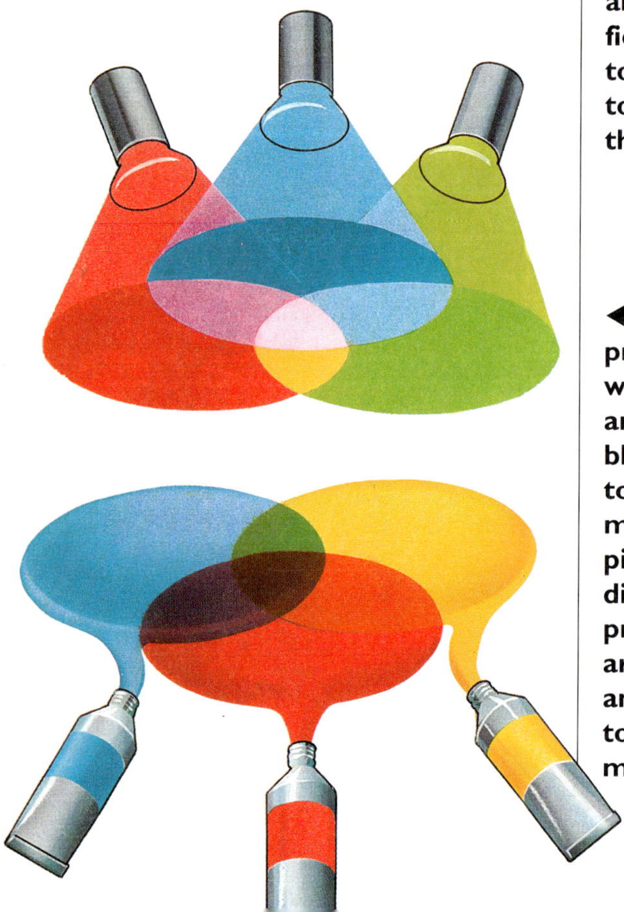

◀ **The three primary colours when mixing light are red, green and blue. Added together, they make white. Paint pigments mix differently. Their primary colours are yellow, blue and red. Mixed together, they make brown.**

The shortest light waves that we can see are blue or violet. The longest light waves we can see are red. There are other waves, shorter and longer, that we cannot see but some animals can. A bee sees colours beyond violet, but it sees red objects as black.

How fast does light travel?

Light travels at enormous speed, at roughly 300,000 kilometres a second (186,000 miles a second). At this speed, the light from the Sun still takes more than eight minutes to reach the Earth. The speed of light was first measured accurately in 1676, by Olaf Roemer of Denmark. Nothing travels faster than light.

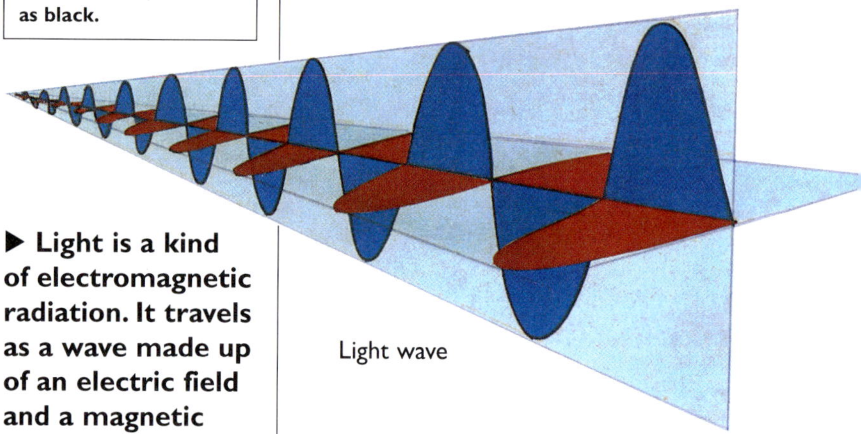

▶ **Light is a kind of electromagnetic radiation. It travels as a wave made up of an electric field and a magnetic field at right angles to each other and to the direction of the wave's travel.**

What are light waves?

If you throw a pebble into a pool, it sends out ripples of waves. Light also travels in waves. In 1873 the British scientist James Clerk Maxwell discovered the wave-structure of light after 20 years' research. He showed that light is made up of vibrating waves of electrical and magnetic fields. The vibrations take place at right angles to the direction of the wave's motion, and to each other. Maxwell was the first to suggest that light was a form of electromagnetic radiation. He went on to state that other kinds of rays must also exist, invisible to the eye.

What makes light bend?

Light is bent when it is bounced back from a surface, such as a mirror. This bending is called reflection. Light is also bent when it travels from one transparent surface to another. This bending is called refraction. It explains why a pencil standing half in and half out of water looks broken.

What makes the colours of the rainbow?

The rainbow is nature's spectrum. Falling drops of rain behave like tiny prisms. They break up white sunlight into the colours of the spectrum.

The first person to show that white light is a mixture of colours was Sir Isaac Newton. Between 1665 and 1666, he carried out experiments in a darkened room. He put a glass prism in a beam of sunlight streaming through a small hole in the wall, and saw it split into the colours of the rainbow: red, orange, yellow, green, blue, indigo and violet. When he placed a second prism in the coloured beam, he saw the light rays bend back and become white again.

▼ When light passes through a glass prism, it splits into the colours of the rainbow: red, orange, yellow, green, blue, indigo and violet. This is known as the spectrum.

▶ When you look in a mirror, your left side looks to be on your left. If you were looking at another person, their left side would be to your right. Light always travels in straight lines. So the mirror reflects light rays from your left side straight back to you on the left.

LENSES AND MIRRORS FACTS

- The first mirrors were made of highly polished metal, such as bronze.
- Making glass mirrors, by coating one side of the glass with silver to make it reflect light, was not perfected until the 1600s.
- A lens that is thinner in the middle than at the edges is said to be concave.
- A lens that is thicker in the middle than at the edges is convex.
- A concave lens spreads light passing through it and makes objects looks smaller. A convex lens narrows the light and makes things look bigger.
- The Arabs knew of the magnifying glass about the year 1000. The first spectacles were made soon after this.

Why do mirrors reflect our images?

Everything reflects light, even the pages of this book. But most surfaces are rough, so the light is diffused, or spread in all directions. We can see the pages of this book from wherever we stand in the room. A mirror's smooth, shiny surface reflects light much more accurately as parallel rays so giving a clear image.

Who invented the telescope?

Lenses are glass or plastic discs that bend light to make objects look larger or smaller. In about 1600 a Dutch spectacle-maker named Hans Lippershey put two lenses together and looked through them at the weather vane on a distant church. He was startled to see how large the weather vane appeared. He had made the first telescope. Soon telescopes were being made all over Europe.

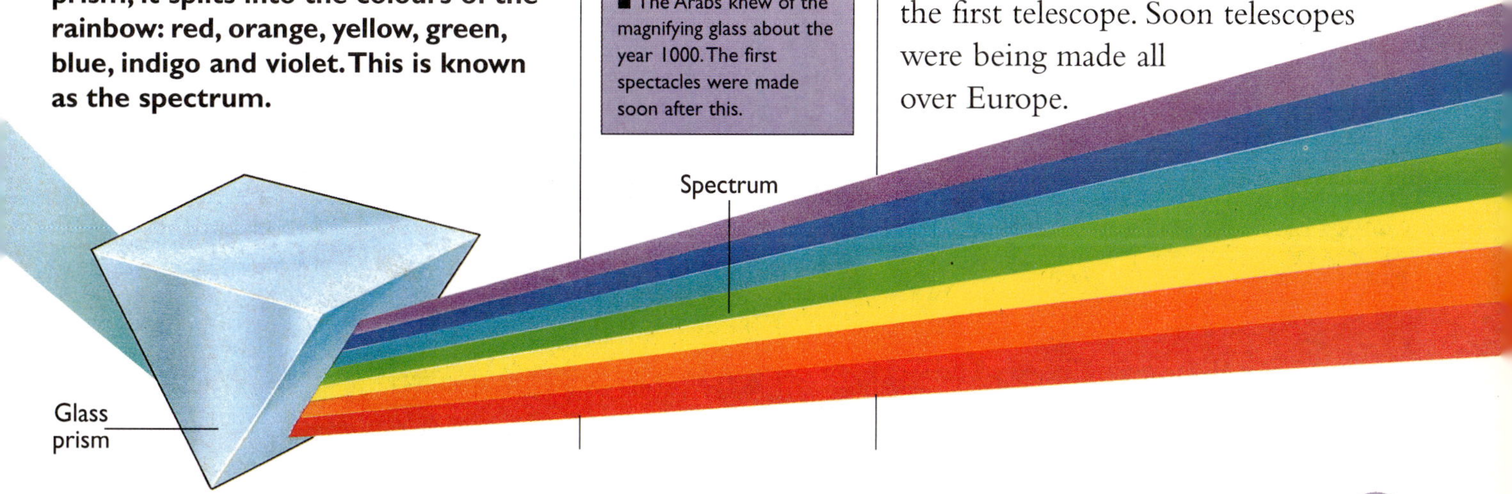

How does a periscope work?

A simple periscope can be made with two flat mirrors, set at an angle of 45°. Light is reflected from the top mirror down to the lower one. In this way, it is possible to see an object over a wall, or above water even when you are in a submerged submarine.

Who invented the microscope?

The microscope was invented in the early 1600s, and there are several claimants for its invention, among them Zacharias Janssen of Holland. What is surprising is that lenses had been known and made in Europe for more than 300 years before this invention, but no one had thought of combining them to make either a microscope or a telescope.

What are the most powerful microscopes?

The best optical microscope cannot magnify an object more than two thousand times. An electron microscope can magnify more than a million times. Electromagnetic fields are the microscope's 'lenses'. A hot wire filament sends a stream of electrons in a beam to hit the object to be examined. The denser areas of the object stop some electrons passing through. The rest travel on and hit a television screen or a photographic plate. The result is a 'shadow picture' of the object.

▶ In the late 1800s, it took so long to take a photo that people needed a back-rest to help them sit still. Eyes looked blurred if the sitter blinked.

Submarines have periscopes so people inside can see what is going on above water while the submarine stays hidden. Submarines often cruise with just the periscope showing. But the world's longest periscope is on land. It is 27 metres long and is used at a laboratory in the United States so that scientists can study nuclear reactors without being exposed to dangerous radiation.

When was the first photograph taken?

The earliest known photograph was taken by the French scientist Joseph Niepce in 1826. It was made on an asphalt-coated pewter plate, and shows a view from a window. The exposure took eight hours.

In the 1830s and 1840s two new photographic processes were developed. They were the daguerreotype of the Frenchman L.J.M. Daguerre and the calotype of the Englishman W.H. Fox Talbot. The daguerreotype used a silver-copper plate instead of glass. It took a minute to expose the plate. In 1888 the American George Eastman invented the Kodak camera, which used roll film instead of plates.

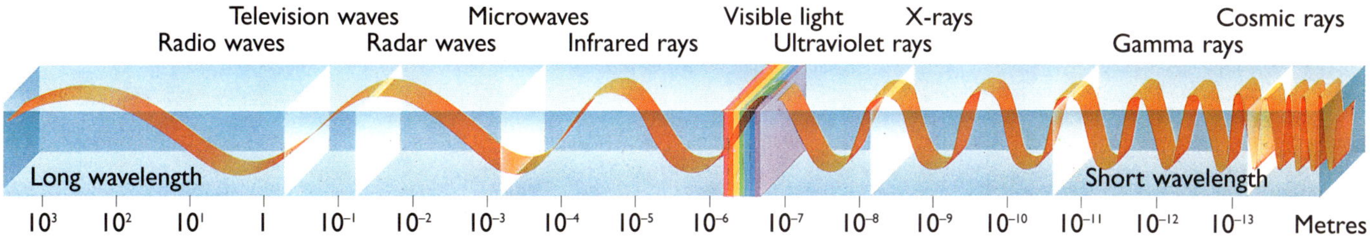

Are there rays that we cannot see?

In the 1870s James Clerk Maxwell predicted other forms of radiation beyond the visible spectrum – in other words, ones we cannot see. The electromagnetic spectrum is a band of radiation of which light is just one part. The rays travel through space in waves of varying lengths. We can see light rays, but other parts of the spectrum are invisible to the eye. At the red end of the visible light spectrum are infrared, microwaves, radar, television and radio waves. At the other (violet) end of the spectrum are ultraviolet, X-rays, gamma rays and cosmic rays.

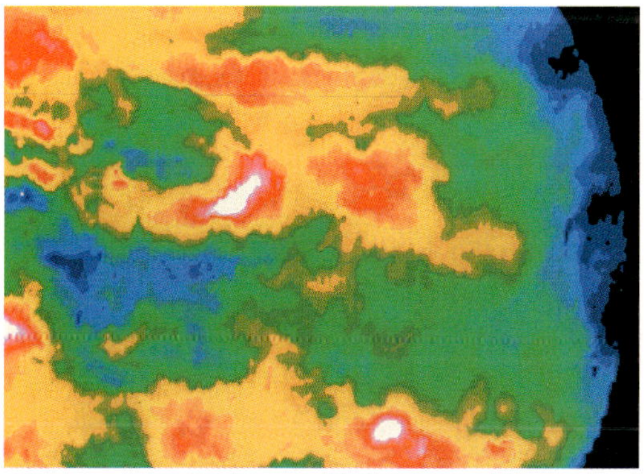

What can infrared photography show up?

We feel infrared rays when we sit in front of an electric fire and feel the 'radiant' heat from its bars. More than half of the Sun's energy comes to us in the form of infrared rays. Infrared photography from space can detect tiny temperature changes on Earth.

▲ The electromagnetic spectrum ranges from long wavelength radio waves through light waves to short wavelength gamma rays. All electromagnetic waves travel at the speed of light.

Because dense cloud covers Venus, radar had to be used to map the planet's surface. In 1990 the *Magellan* spacecraft sent back a radar picture of Venus, revealing its active volcanoes and craters.

◄ A near infrared map of the cloud cover over Venus, taken by the *Magellan* space probe in 1990. Infrared photos of the Earth can reveal diseased crops in fields, and track warm and cold water currents in the oceans.

Who discovered X-rays?

The German scientist Wilhelm Roentgen discovered X-rays by accident in 1895. He was experimenting with a cathode ray tube and noticed that crystals in the same room glowed when the tube was switched on. Even when he moved the crystals to the next room, they still glowed. Roentgen realized that invisible rays were causing the glow. The rays could even penetrate solid walls. He called them X-rays (X = unknown).

How was radar invented?

Radar was invented in the 1930s. It worked by transmitting a radio beam from the ground. Any object crossing the beam (such as an aircraft) produced an 'echo', and this could be received on the ground and used to work out the height and position of the aircraft.

How did the laser get its name?

The first laser was made in 1960 by an American scientist, Theodore H. Maiman. Its name comes from a set of initials that stand for Light Amplification by Stimulated Emission of Radiation. A laser produces a powerful beam of light, so powerful it can burn a hole through metal. Unlike the light from a torch, a laser beam spreads hardly at all.

What is a hologram?

The Greek word *holos* means 'whole'. A hologram is a 'whole picture', or a three-dimensional picture. A hologram is made by illuminating an object with laser light. The three-dimensional picture is viewed by shining a laser of the same colour or wavelength through the hologram. The principle of the hologram was worked out by the Hungarian-born physicist Dennis Gabor in 1948, but making holograms was not possible before the invention of the laser.

Dennis Gabor

Bank and credit cards contain holograms to make the card design more difficult for forgers to copy. Holograms are used to make jewellery and in advertising displays. They can also detect faults in lenses, tyres, and aircraft wings.

How can light be used to send telephone calls?

In a telephone, sounds are changed into electrical signals and sent through wires. In 1966 scientists succeeded in using lasers to carry telephone calls by changing the electrical signals into light-pulses. Instead of wires, they used optical fibres – very long, thin glass rods. The light-pulses travel inside the rods, kept in by the mirror-like sheath. At the end of the cable the pulses are changed back into sounds.

▼ A single optical fibre can carry hundreds of telephone conversations as pulses moving along strands of glass.

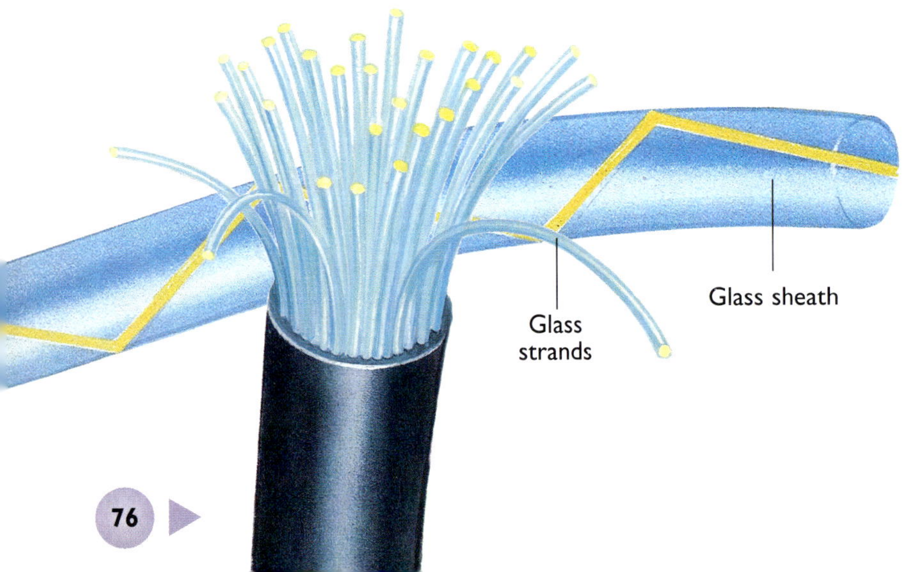

▶ The loudness of sound is how strong it seems when the soundwaves hit our ears. Loudness is measured in decibels. Noises louder than about 140 decibels can cause pain!

What causes sound?

Sounds can be very different – the roar of a jet engine, the music of an orchestra, the song of a bird – but all sounds are made in a similar way. When an object vibrates (moves backwards and forwards), it produces sound.

Sound is a form of energy. Like light, it travels in waves. But sound needs something to travel through. Sound cannot travel in a vacuum such as space.

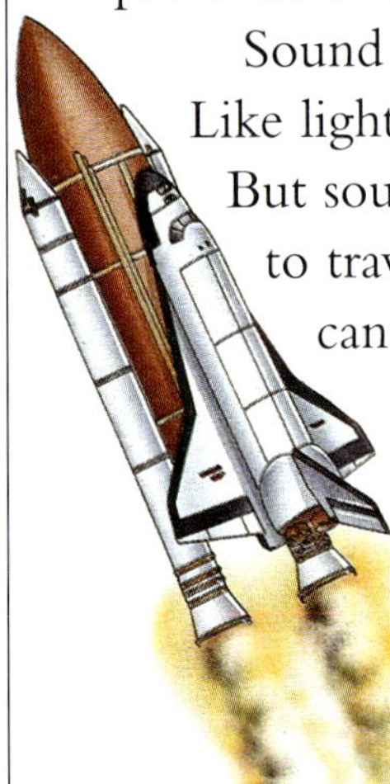

Rocket lift-off
150–190 decibels

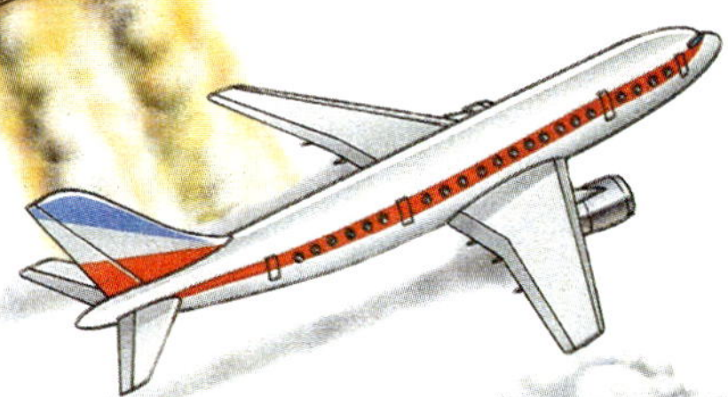

Jet lift-off
120–140 decibels

Thunder
95–115 decibels

Motorbike
70–90 decibels

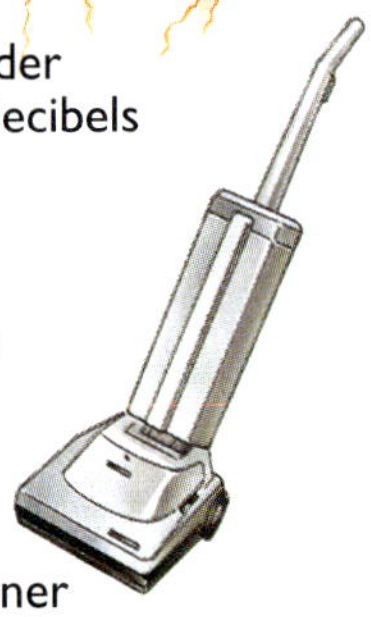

Vacuum cleaner
60–80 decibels

Orchestra
50–70 decibels

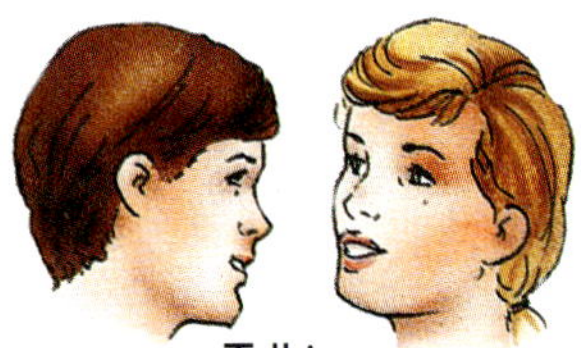

Talking
30–60 decibels

Whispering
20–30 decibels

Falling leaves
20 decibels

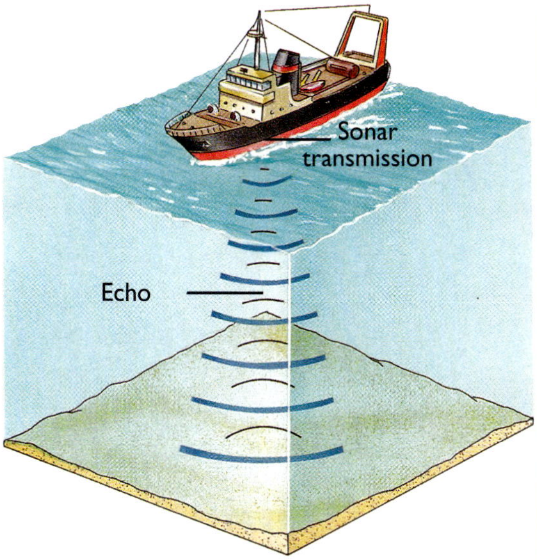

◀ **Ships use sonar to tell how deep the sea bed is. The echoes bounce back from the bottom. Using this method, a survey ship can chart the sea bed.**

What causes an echo?

Have you ever stood inside an old cathedral and heard your voice echoing from the thick, stone walls? The same thing happens inside a cave, or where there are cliffs or high walls. The echo is caused by the sound waves bouncing off the hard wall. The sound is reflected back to your ear and you hear an echo of your voice.

Ships use echo-sounders, devices that send out pulses of sound, to tell how deep the water is. This technique is known as sonar, which is short for SOund Navigation And Ranging.

Why is the Moon a silent world?

You can hear sounds underwater. In fact, sound travels faster through water than through air. Sound can also travel through metal, such as steel. But no sound can travel across the airless surface of the Moon. The astronauts who explored the Moon talked to one another by radio. There were no other sounds, not even when they hit a rock with a hammer. It is impossible for sound to travel through the vacuum of outer space.

▼ **A sound's frequency is the number of vibrations per second, and is measured in Hertz (Hz). We can hear sounds between about 16 Hz and 20,000 Hz. Some animals emit and receive frequencies far beyond those we can hear.**

Is there really a sound barrier?

Before the late 1940s no aircraft had flown faster than sound. People wondered if there was a mysterious 'sound barrier', but the invention of jet planes proved it could be broken. Jets flew faster than sound without being shaken apart and without harm to their pilots. Today the supersonic airliner Concorde regularly carries passengers across the Atlantic at twice the speed of sound.

Are there sounds we cannot hear?

Human ears are most sensitive to sounds at around 2,000 Hertz (Hz). The lowest sound we can hear is about 16 Hz and the highest is about 20,000 Hz. Dogs can hear higher-pitched sounds. Some dog owners use whistles that make a sound too high for them to hear, but which is heard perfectly well by their pet.

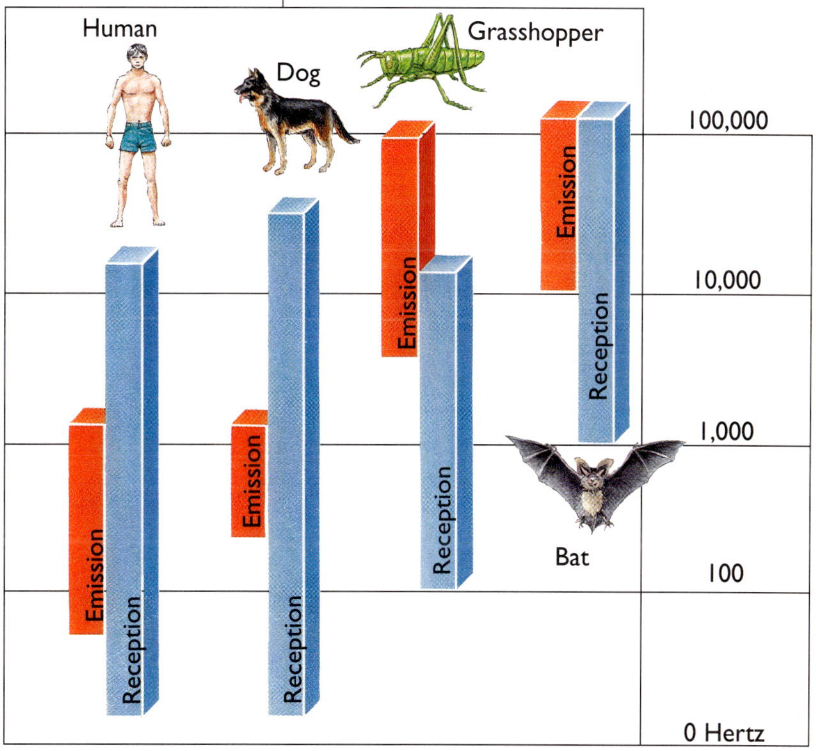

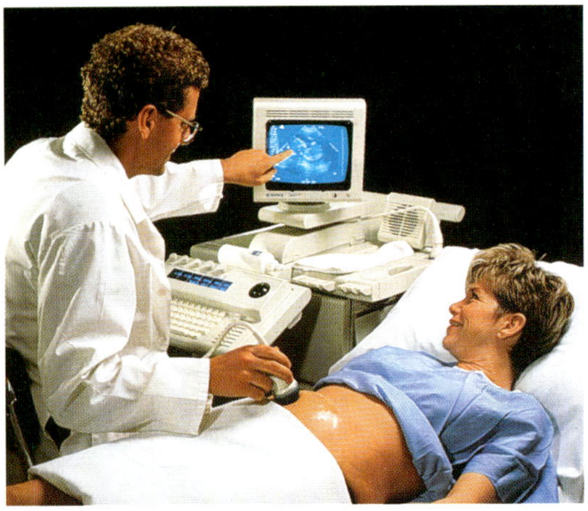

◀ An ultrasound scanner shows how an unborn baby is developing inside the womb of a pregnant woman.

How do doctors examine unborn babies with the help of sound waves?

Ultrasonic waves penetrate flesh and other soft body parts, just like X-rays, and they can be used to produce pictures of the inside of the body. Because the sound waves have no harmful effects, doctors use ultrasonic scanners to examine pregnant women. The scan shows if the unborn baby in the womb is healthy and growing properly.

When were sounds first recorded?

The first sound recording was made by the American inventor Thomas Alva Edison in 1877 on a machine he called the phonograph. Sounds were picked up by a vibrating membrane, and the vibrations made a needle cut spiral grooves on a cylinder covered with tinfoil. When a second needle was moved along the grooves, the sounds were reproduced by means of another vibrating membrane and amplified through a horn.

▼ Edison's phonograph of 1877 recorded sounds as grooves cut into a foil-covered cylinder. Flat records were invented in 1887.

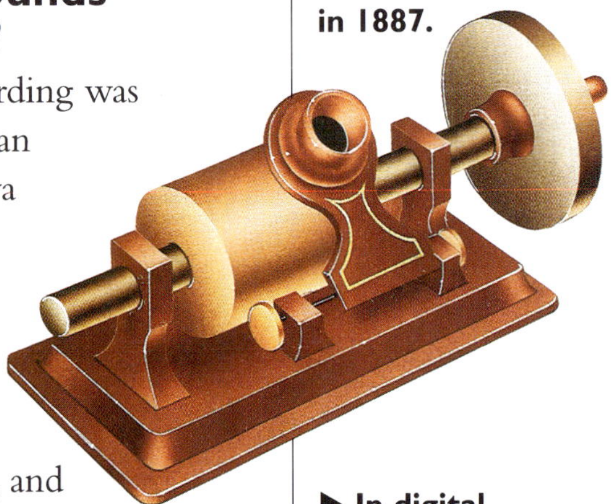

◀ The 'tape recorder' invented by Valdemar Poulsen did not look much like a modern portable stereo. The sound was stored on metal wire, not on plastic tape.

When was recording tape first used?

The first experiments with sound recording on tape were made in 1898 by the Danish inventor Valdemar Poulsen, using magnetized metal wire. In the 1930s paper tapes were developed and reel-to-reel tape recorders appeared in the 1940s. Today's cassette players use plastic tape coated with magnetic material.

What is digital recording?

In older recording systems, the electrical signals are stored as a continuous wave pattern. These build up a replica or analogue of the original sounds. In digital recording, as used on music CDs, the sound waves are converted into electrical pulses which are coded as a series of numbers (digits) in binary form. Digital recordings give more accurate reproduction, because they store much more information about the sounds being recorded.

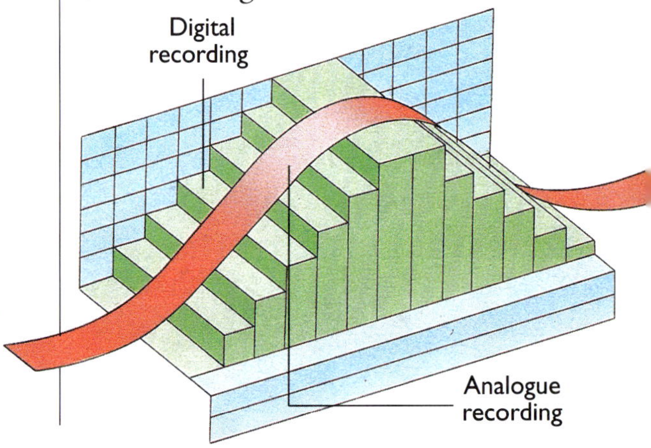

▶ In digital recording the signals are changed into off-on electrical pulses. Analogue recording builds up a continuous sound 'image'.

Energy and Motion

What is energy?

Energy is the ability to do work. When you walk upstairs, or even when you are resting, your body is working, and uses energy. The spring inside a clockwork motor provides the energy to drive the mechanism. A torch battery provides the energy needed to light up the bulb. The Sun's energy enables plants to grow. In fact, all living things depend on the Sun for their energy. Energy can neither be created nor destroyed.

Where does energy come from?

Energy comes from matter. Everything in the universe is made up of matter, so in some form energy is found everywhere. Even the tiniest atomic particles can be changed into energy. Matter can be changed into energy and energy can be changed into matter.

Are there different kinds of energy?

Energy that is stored up is called potential energy. Water stored behind a dam, an archer's bow drawn and ready to fire, both of these are examples of potential energy. Falling water and an arrow shot from a bow each have kinetic energy. Potential and kinetic energy are both forms of mechanical energy. There are other kinds of energy too: thermal or heat energy, chemical energy, nuclear energy and radiant energy.

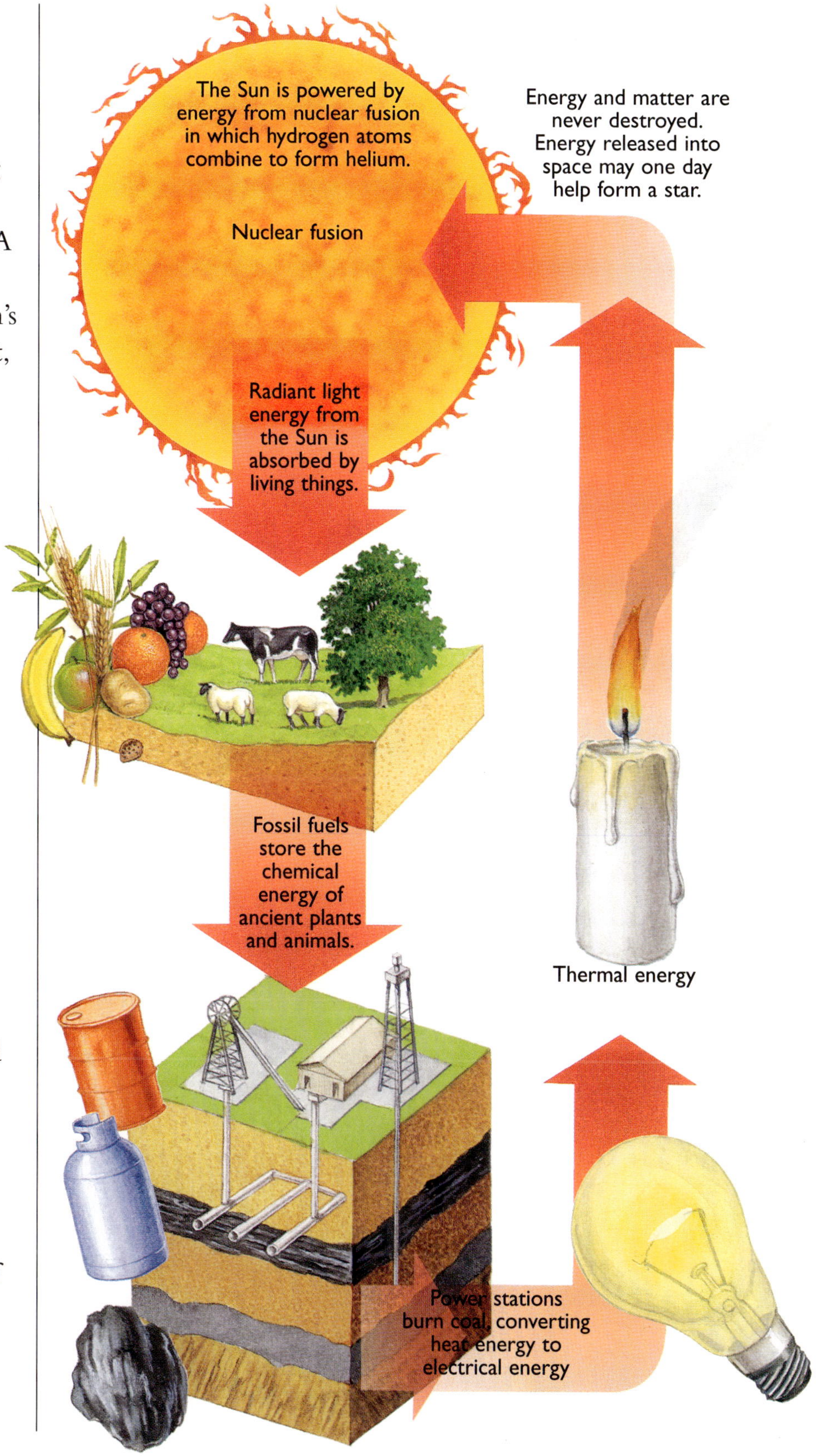

What are fossil fuels?

Much of the energy we use at home and at work comes from the burning of so-called fossil fuels such as coal, oil and gas. These fuels were formed millions of years ago from the remains of plants and animals.

Why do things become hot?

Heat is the transfer of energy from one substance to another. If you rub a piece of cloth with your hand, the cloth will begin to feel warmer. The rubbing has produced heat, as a result of friction.

How can heat travel?

Heat travels in several ways. The heat you feel when you hold a saucepan handle is carried by conduction. The heat energy inside an electric kettle is carried by convection. An electric fire with a shiny reflector sends out heat waves by radiation. Substances that carry heat well are called good conductors of heat. Metals are the best conductors – that is why we use metal cooking pots.

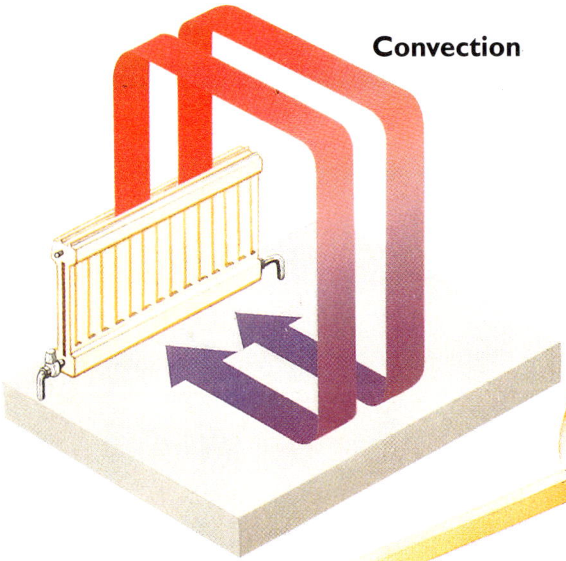

Convection

In the Celsius or Centigrade scale, the boiling point of water is 100 degrees. Scientists use another scale, the Kelvin scale, in which the boiling point of water is 373 degrees. On this scale, water freezes at 273 degrees.

▼The air above a warm radiator (left) rises and cool air moves in creating a convection current. Heat from a match (centre) sets molecules of air moving, causing heat rays. As a metal spoon gets hot (right), molecules at the heated end move faster and collide with their neighbours, setting them moving.

Radiation

Who invented the Celsius scale for measuring temperature?

The earliest scale for measuring temperature was invented by a Dutchman called Gabriel Fahrenheit in the early 1700s. This scale, named after him, has the freezing point of water at 32 degrees, and the boiling point at 212 degrees. In 1742 a Swede named Anders Celsius suggested a scale in which the freezing point of water would be fixed as 0 degrees.

What is the coldest anything can be?

When a substance is warmed, its molecules move about faster. When it is cooled, they move more slowly. The coldest that anything can get is when its molecules stop moving. This is at a temperature of minus 273 degrees Celsius (–273°C), or 'absolute zero'. Scientists have not yet achieved zero, but they have managed temperatures close to it.

Conduction

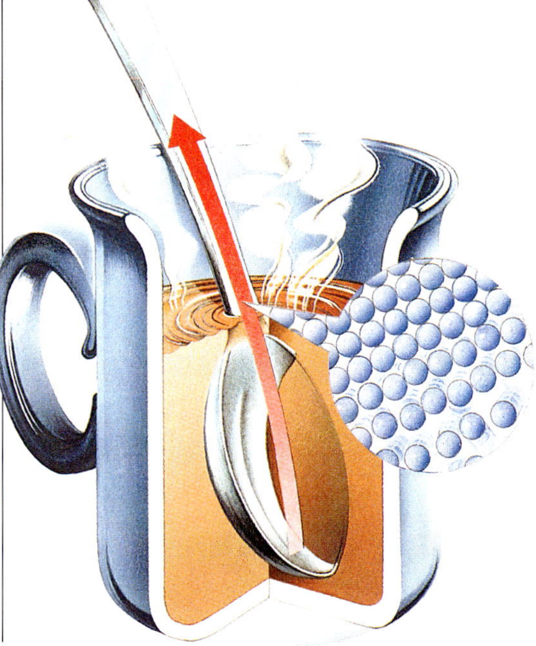

◀ **The ice in an iceberg is less dense than the surrounding water, so it floats. Water expands (and so becomes less dense) when it becomes colder than 4°C.**

Why does an iceberg float?

Unlike most liquids, water expands (gets bigger) when it freezes and becomes less dense as a result. An ice cube will therefore float in a glass of water and not sink. This fact explains why huge icebergs float and also why rivers do not freeze solid in winter. Ice forms as a floating layer on top, and this layer stops further freezing beneath. If the ice sank to the bottom, the river would quickly freeze solid.

What are the oldest known machines?

A machine is a device for doing work, and the oldest known machines are the simplest: the wedge, the lever and the inclined plane. These were used by Stone Age people 100,000 years ago. Their inventors are unknown. The wheel was a later discovery, and was not in common use until about 5,000 years ago.

ICE FACTS

- Salt water freezes at a lower temperature than fresh water.
- The thickest ice in the world covers the Antarctic continent to a depth of 4,800 m.
- Only the tip of an iceberg shows above water. About 80 percent of an iceberg (or even more) is hidden beneath the water's surface.
- The largest icebergs break off the Antarctic ice cap. The biggest was 320 km long and 97 km wide.

How does a lever work?

The lever is a simple machine that moves objects. The commonest kind is called a first-class lever. The object to be moved is known as the load, and the force needed to move it is call the effort. The lever needs a pivot, or fulcrum. Using a branch as a lever and resting it on a small rock (the fulcrum), it is possible to lift a much heavier weight. When Stone Age people discovered this, they had invented one of the basic machines: the lever.

▼ **Three simple machines, the crowbar, hammer and wheelbarrow, are used on building sites. The crowbar is a lever. So is the wheelbarrow. The hammer acts as a lever too. The fulcrum is the worker's shoulder joints and the load is the hammer head.**

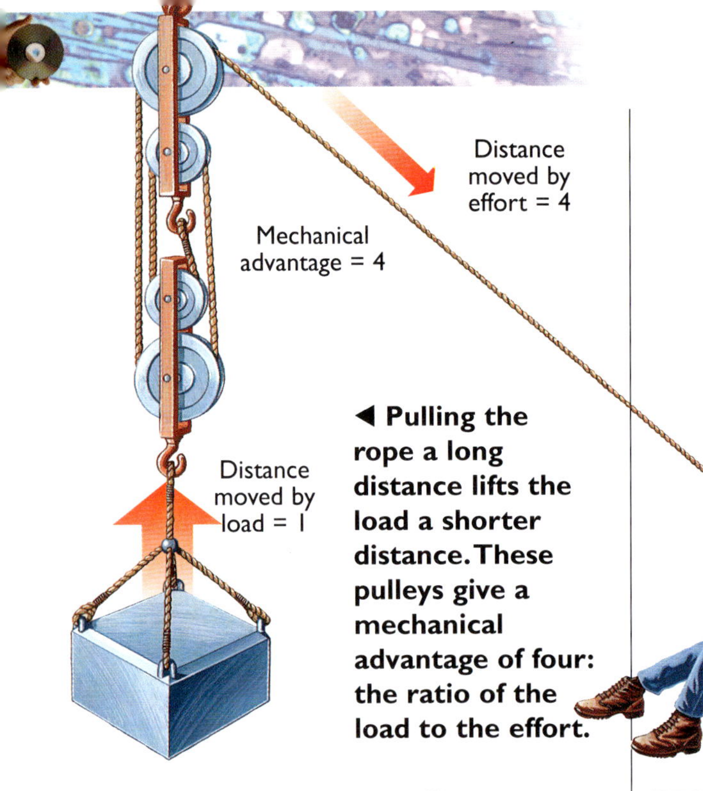

◀ **Pulling the rope a long distance lifts the load a shorter distance. These pulleys give a mechanical advantage of four: the ratio of the load to the effort.**

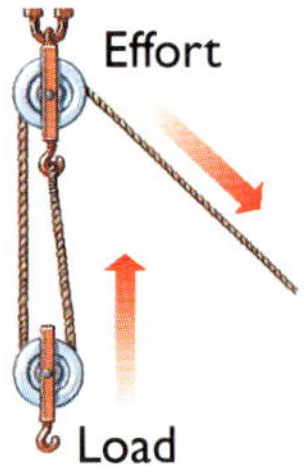

How do more pulleys make less work?

A pulley is a useful machine for changing the direction of a force. For example, by pulling downwards on a rope running over a pulley wheel, you can lift a load upwards. The more pulleys there are, with one continuous rope running through them, the greater the mechanical advantage and so the greater the load that can be lifted with the same effort.

When were building cranes first used?

The Romans introduced the crane, a machine for lifting loads using the principle of the pulley. Their cranes were worked by treadmills. Slaves trudging inside the treadmill produced the effort needed to lift the load of building stone.

More than 2,000 years ago King Hieron of Syracuse challenged Archimedes to show what simple machines could do. The Greek scientist built a system of pulleys. Unaided, he lifted a ship out of the water and onto the land!

▼ **Inertia in action. A car stays still or moves steadily in a straight line unless it is stopped by another force – such as the brick wall in this picture.**

How do gears work?

A gear is a wheel with teeth along its rim. The teeth fit, or mesh, with teeth on other wheels. As one wheel turns, so do the others. Gear wheels can be used to change the direction of a movement, and also to increase the speed and power of a machine. A big wheel with forty teeth, for example, will turn at a quarter the speed of a wheel with ten teeth, if they are connected. But it will have four times as much power. A car in low gear moves slowly, but has more power for starting and going uphill.

What is inertia?

To start an object moving, a force is needed. When you kick a ball, the ball begins to move. It keeps moving until some other force stops it. The ball has inertia. It rolls on until stopped by another force (your foot perhaps, or a wall, or the friction of the ground). All moving objects have inertia: they try to keep moving until a force opposes them. Have you ever been standing on a bus when it pulled up suddenly? People are thrown forwards, because of the inertia affecting their bodies.

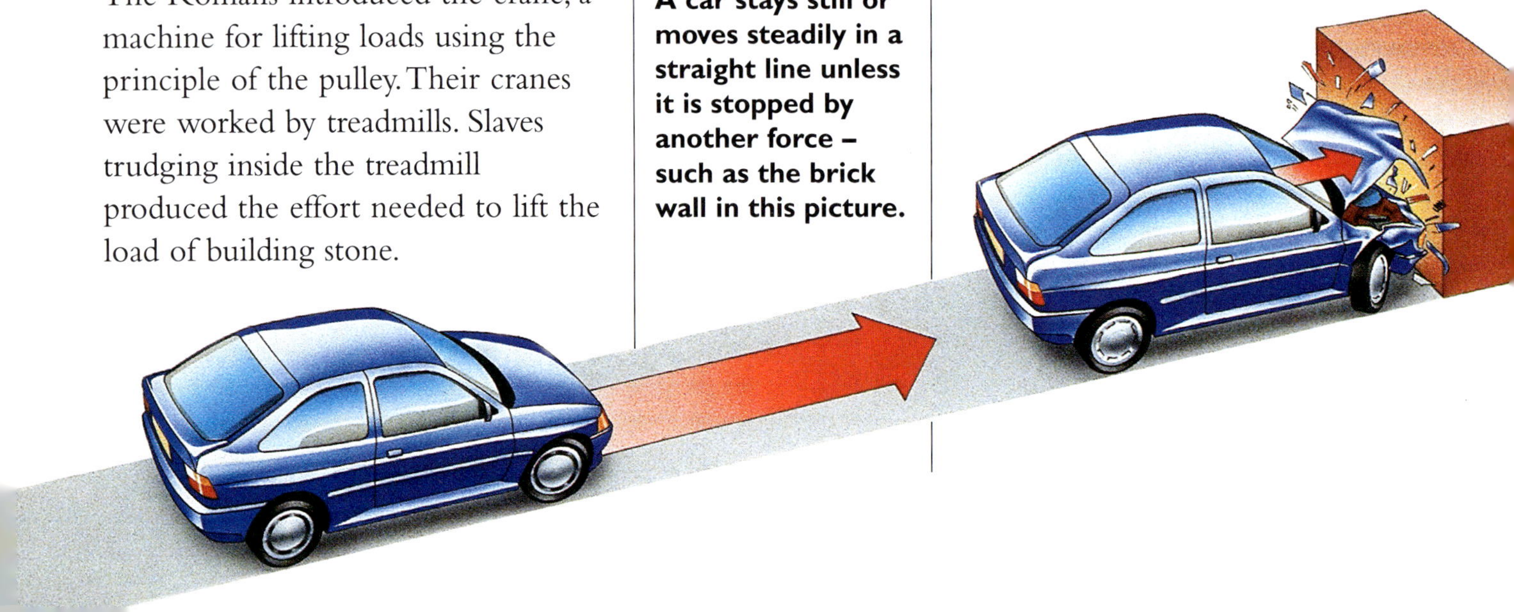

Why does a pendulum swing?

You can make a simple pendulum by fastening a weight to the end of a length of cord. Hold the cord so that the weight hangs vertically. When you give the pendulum a push, it swings away from you. The force of your push gives it motion. When it reaches the lowest point of its swing, the pendulum does not stop but swings on, this time upwards. Inertia keeps it going until a stronger force (gravity) halts it and the pendulum swings back down towards the vertical again.

The Italian scientist Galileo Galilei (1564–1642) made many discoveries. One of them was that the time it takes for a pendulum to swing (known as its period) depends not on its weight, but on its length. Galileo is said to have made this discovery after watching a chandelier swinging.

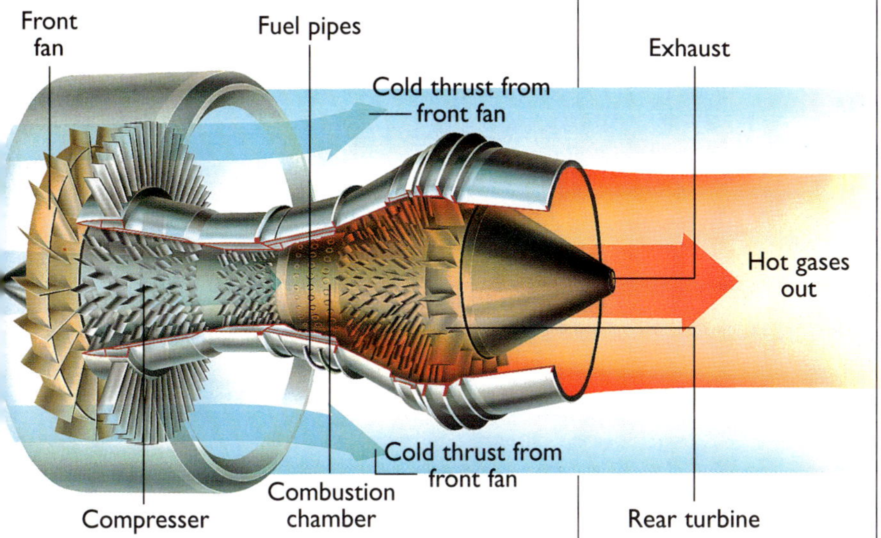

▲ A jet engine sucks in air with a fan. The air is compressed and forced into the combustion chamber where fuel is sprayed in and burns. Hot, expanding gases spin a rear turbine that drives the compressor and the fan. Finally, gases shoot out of the exhaust, producing thrust.

How does a jet engine work?

A jet engine is an action-reaction engine. It shoots out a mass of hot gas, and the force of this gas pushing in one direction produces another equally strong force in the opposite direction. For every action (here the hot gas shooting out backwards), there is an equal and opposite reaction (the jet plane flying forwards). Sir Isaac Newton knew this, long before jet planes. This was his Third Law of Motion.

How can an iron ship float?

A hollow object has low density because it is mostly filled with air. Even an iron ship will float in water because of the air inside. However, if the vessel is holed, water pours in and pushes the air out. The overall density of the ship becomes greater than that of water and the ship sinks.

How can objects float in air?

Air is fluid, like water, but it has such a low density that few objects will float in it. Hydrogen gas is lighter than air, so a balloon filled with hydrogen is less dense than air and will rise upwards. Eventually, it will reach a height where the air is so thin that the hydrogen no longer has a lower density, and can rise no higher.

Why do things fall to Earth?

Gravity is a force which pulls us, and everything else, towards the Earth. Gravity is what makes rain fall downwards and not upwards. Gravity explains why if you throw a ball into the air, it will fall back to Earth again.

Gravity is one of many forces which act on objects on Earth. A plane flying through the atmosphere is thrust forward by its engines, but held in place above the ground by air pressure under its wings acting against the pull of gravity.

The planet Earth exerts a gravitational force on everything. But much smaller bodies also produce a similar effect. Between any two objects there is a gravitational force.

Why do the planets keep moving in their orbits?

The planets have been moving ever since the formation of the Solar System. They were given their starting 'push' then, millions of years ago, and have kept moving around the Sun ever since. The Sun's massive gravitational force holds the planets in orbit around it. They keep moving because there is no force in the Solar System powerful enough to stop them and no friction force opposing them.

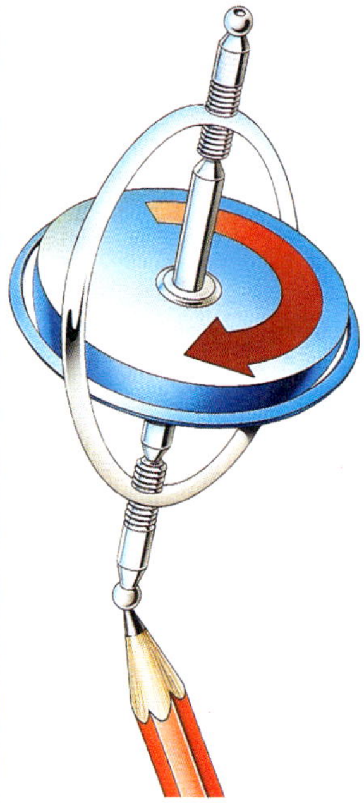

▲ A toy gyroscope will balance so long as it keeps spinning fast enough. The wheel's axle points continuously in the direction it is first set at.

How can a gyroscope balance on a pencil point?

A gyroscope looks like a spinning-top inside a wheel-like frame. Once set spinning, it will not alter its direction. If balanced on a pencil point, it will not fall off so long as it keeps spinning. The pull of gravity (which tries to upset the gyroscope) is countered by another force called precession, found in spinning bodies. This makes the gyroscope move around the point of the pencil as if it were in orbit.

How much would you weigh on the Moon?

The weight of an object is the force of gravity acting upon it. Weight is really measured in newtons (the newton is a unit for measuring force). Mass is measured in kilograms (or pounds). The mass of an object never changes, but if you travelled to the Moon, you would weigh less than on Earth, because the Moon has only one-sixth of the Earth's gravity.

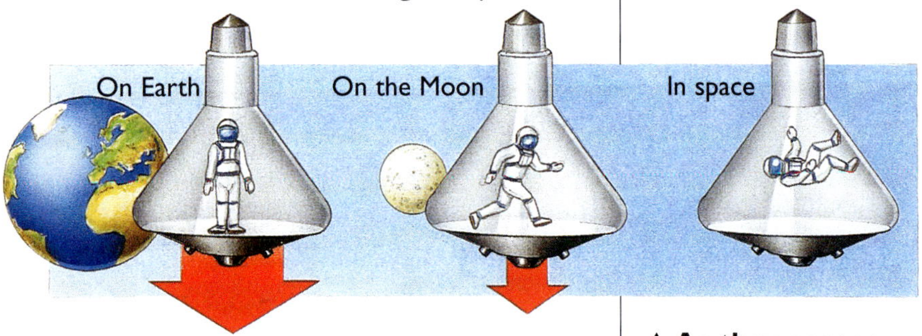

▲ As they escape Earth's gravity, astronauts become weightless. On the Moon, there is very little gravity so an astronaut can bounce around. In space, an astronaut floats.

What is it like to be weightless?

People inside a spacecraft orbiting the Earth float about inside, as if swimming in air. There is no gravity from Earth to pull them down. If an astronaut lets go of a tool, it drifts about instead of falling to the ground. Imagine eating food from a plate!

What causes friction?

Friction is produced when two surfaces rub against each other. Even a smooth-looking surface is actually covered with tiny holes and bumps, as can be seen by looking through a microscope. The rubbing together produces heat. This is why a match struck on a matchbox bursts into flame. There is friction between even the most insubstantial surfaces such as air and water.

Why don't trains have rubber tyres like cars and trucks?

Running a vehicle on rails is actually more efficient than running it on a road. This is because a solid wheel, like that of a train creates less friction than an air-filled tyre (as on a car), since a solid wheel does not flatten out under pressure. So it is easier to pull a heavy load along a train track than along a road. But without some friction to 'stick' the wheels to the rails, a train's wheels would spin helplessly and not grip at all.

Space and Time

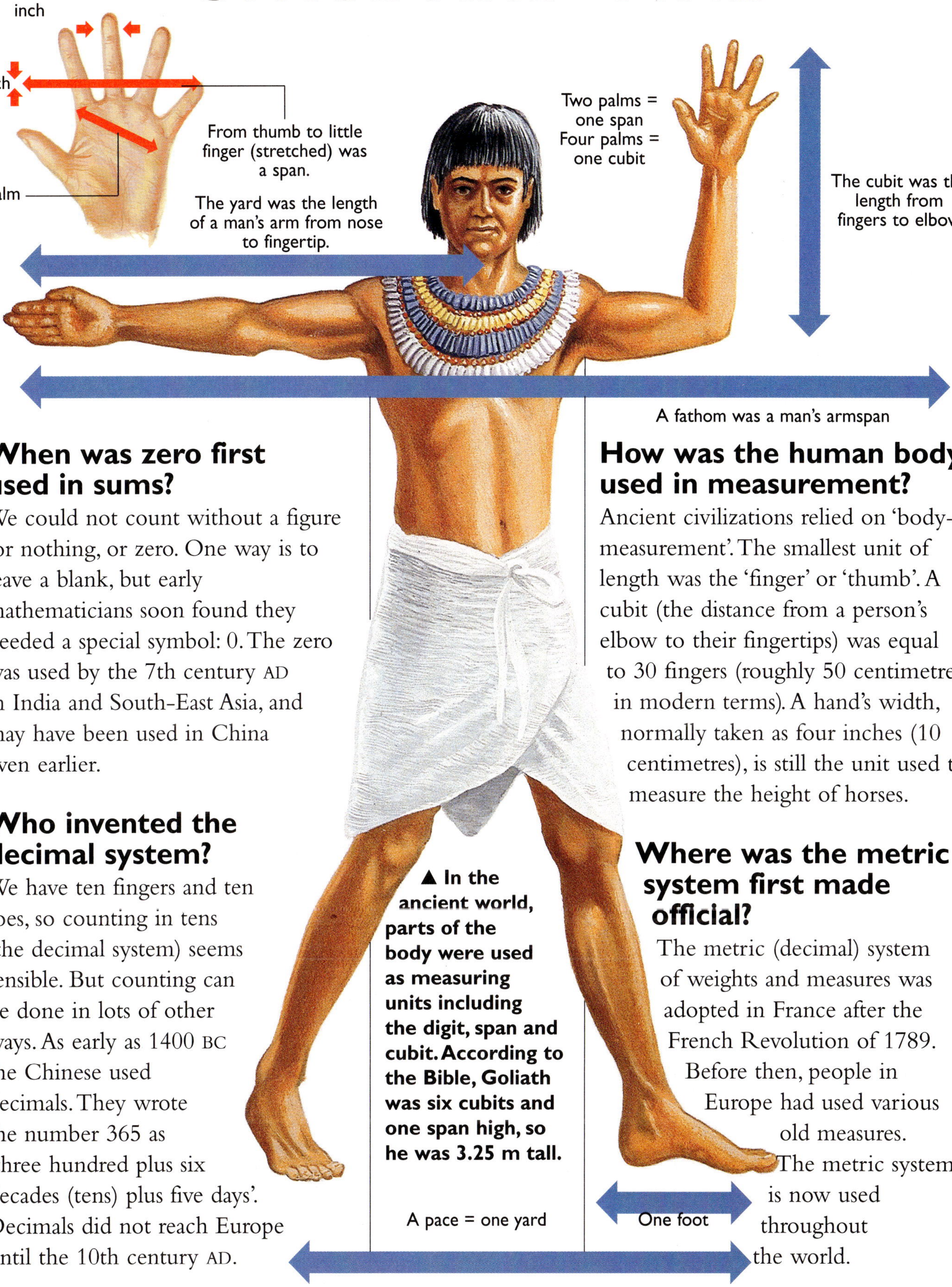

▲ **In the ancient world, parts of the body were used as measuring units including the digit, span and cubit. According to the Bible, Goliath was six cubits and one span high, so he was 3.25 m tall.**

When was zero first used in sums?

We could not count without a figure for nothing, or zero. One way is to leave a blank, but early mathematicians soon found they needed a special symbol: 0. The zero was used by the 7th century AD in India and South-East Asia, and may have been used in China even earlier.

Who invented the decimal system?

We have ten fingers and ten toes, so counting in tens (the decimal system) seems sensible. But counting can be done in lots of other ways. As early as 1400 BC the Chinese used decimals. They wrote the number 365 as 'three hundred plus six decades (tens) plus five days'. Decimals did not reach Europe until the 10th century AD.

How was the human body used in measurement?

Ancient civilizations relied on 'body-measurement'. The smallest unit of length was the 'finger' or 'thumb'. A cubit (the distance from a person's elbow to their fingertips) was equal to 30 fingers (roughly 50 centimetres in modern terms). A hand's width, normally taken as four inches (10 centimetres), is still the unit used to measure the height of horses.

Where was the metric system first made official?

The metric (decimal) system of weights and measures was adopted in France after the French Revolution of 1789. Before then, people in Europe had used various old measures. The metric system is now used throughout the world.

What is geometry?

Geometry is the branch of mathematics that has to do with the study of shapes and sizes. The name comes from Greek words meaning 'Earth measurement', and it was by using geometry that Greek mathematicians first calculated the size of the Earth. Every advance in science has been aided by geometry, for without it we could not make accurate measurements. In about 300 BC the Greek mathematician Euclid wrote a book called *Elements* in which he brought together many geometrical discoveries made by the Greeks. Euclid's textbook has inspired mathematicians ever since.

How often can you expect to throw a six when playing dice?

Mathematicians have long sought ways of solving problems involving unpredictable factors, such as the fall of dice. The Frenchman Blaise Pascal worked out the basic 'laws of probability' in 1642, using dice. The simplest problem is this: a die has six sides, each with a different value. When you throw it, each side has an equal chance of falling uppermost. The probability that one side will do so is therefore 1 in 6.

The probability of throwing a number greater than two

Probability of throwing greater than two is therefore four out of six

MATHS FACTS

- As long ago as 3000 BC, the Egyptians used geometry for land surveys and for building.
- Arabs invented algebra in the 9th century AD.
- Negative numbers, such as -1, -2, -3 and so on, were unknown in Europe until the 1500s, though the Chinese used them long before.
- The acre is still used as a field measurement by many farmers. In the Middle Ages, an English acre was the area of land an ox could plough in a day – 22 furrows (lengths) or 'furlongs'.
- The 17th-century French mathematician Pierre Fermat had a secret test for finding prime numbers. He could give almost instant answers.
- There is an endless number of prime numbers. There are more than 660,000 between 1 and 10 million.

Euclid thought 6 was a 'perfect' number. 1, 2 and 3 divide exactly into 6. Added together, they make 6. Euclid knew of three more perfect numbers: 28, 496 and 8,128. After that, perfect numbers get very big indeed!

Where did Arabic numerals come from?

The Arabic numerals we use today were first used in India and reached Europe about the year AD 1000. A book written in 1202 by an Italian mathematician named Leonardo Fibonacci did much to persuade Europe's scientists that they must use Arabic numerals in order for the science of mathematics to progress.

Who first proved that the angles of a triangle always add up to 180 degrees?

The Ancient Greeks were fascinated by geometry. They knew that a circle is made up of 360 degrees, a number probably chosen by the Babylonians. No matter what its shape, a triangle has angles that always add up to 180 degrees. This was first proved by Euclid about 300 BC.

Why do mathematicians hunt for prime numbers?

A prime number is one that can be divided only by itself and 1. For example, 12 is not a prime number because it can be divided by 1, 2, 3, 4 and 6. On the other hand, 11 is: it can be divided only by 1 and 11. What mystifies mathematicians about prime numbers is that they can find no pattern. A Greek named Eratosthenes worked out a slow, but effective, method of finding prime numbers. That was in the 3rd century BC.

◀ If you roll a die, what is the chance of rolling a number higher than 2? Four of the six possible numbers are greater than 2, so the probability of rolling one of them is 4/6 or 2/3.

▲ **Hundreds of years ago, the Aztec people of Mexico made a calendar. It was a huge stone shaped like the Sun. Signs for the days were carved around the edge.**

Who counted in suns and nights?

People have measured time in a number of ways. Early people counted the days (from sunrise to sunset). But not all used the 'day' as their unit. The Comanche tribe of North America counted in 'suns' and Greenlanders counted in 'nights'.

Who first worked out how long a year is?

More than 3,000 years ago, the priests of Babylon were skilled in astronomy and kept accurate records of the passing of the seasons. They calculated how long it took the Earth to complete one year's cycle around the Sun, and worked this out as 365 days 5 hours 42 minutes and 14 seconds. The modern calculation is only 26 minutes and 55 seconds longer.

People born in a leap year on 29 February have to wait four years for their next 'special' birthday. A leap year can always be divided by four with nothing left over. The years 1996, 2000 and 2004 are all leap years.

Why were leap years found necessary?

The Romans based their calendar on the Moon's monthly phases. The Roman calendar started off with 360 days, but was then reduced to only 355. It became clear that the calendar was gradually getting out of step with the seasons. So Julius Caesar ordered a new calendar of 365.25 days. Every fourth year an extra day was added, to use up the quarter-days. This became a leap year. Before the new calendar could begin, an extra-long year was needed to put things straight. The year 46 BC had 445 days and, not surprisingly, was known as 'the year of confusion'.

When did people protest at having 11 days stolen?

Julius Caesar's calendar, named the Julian calendar, was used until the 1500s. By then, it too was out of step. Easter was falling in summer instead of spring. Pope Gregory XIII, head of the Roman Catholic Church, ruled that there should be a new calendar from 1582. Britain kept to the old calendar until 1752. That year, September 2 was followed by September 14. People took to the streets protesting that they had had 11 days stolen from their lives!

Who had two calendars?

People of the Maya civilization in Central America (from about AD 250 to 1500). One calendar had 365 days, divided into 18 months of 20 days, with five 'unlucky' days at the end of the year. Maya fortune-tellers used a sacred calendar with 260 days.

▲ **In an Egyptian water clock, water poured slowly from one pot to another. The Egyptians also had sundials. In Babylon, people marked the face of the sundial into 12 hours. The dial shown here has Roman numerals.**

When were sundials and water clocks used?

Sundials were used as 'shadow clocks' more than 3,000 years ago in Babylon. An upright stick casts a shadow as the Sun's rays alter position during the day. (Remember, this is because the Earth is moving, not the Sun.) Around the stick is a dial marked out with the hours.

The Ancient Egyptians and Greeks used water clocks. There were various types, but they all worked on the same principle. Water dripped slowly out of a container. As the water level fell, so did a float on the surface. To the float was attached a pointer which marked the passing of the hours on a scale.

When were mechanical clocks invented?

Medieval monks needed to know the times for prayers during the day. They wanted a clock that would ring a bell at regular intervals. The machinery that made this possible was invented in the 1300s. Falling weights provided the force needed to ring a bell, and the fall of the weights was regulated by a mechanism known as an 'escapement'. The movement of the escapement gave the clockwork its familiar 'tick-tock' sound.

▲ **John Harrison made the first reliable chronometer, or ship's clock, in the 1700s. It had a slowly unwinding spring inside, so it kept time accurately.**

Were there hands on the first clocks?

Early clocks were intended only to 'strike' the hours, with a bell. They were very inaccurate, losing perhaps 15 minutes a day. But people were not worried about minutes, they needed to know only what hour it was. Clocks struck every quarter-hour, and that was precise enough. After all, there were no trains or buses to catch. Not until the 1600s were clocks with minute hands and faces marked into 12 hours common.

How did the early sailors find their way?

Few seamen in ancient times ventured out of sight of land. The Greeks invented a sundial-like device, the astrolabe, for finding longitude (east-west position) and calculating the time of day. The astrolabe did not reach northern Europe until much later, in the 14th century. Later, sailors made use of instruments called the simple cross-staff and the improved backstaff (1595) to discover their latitude (north-south position) by measuring the precise angle of the Sun above the horizon.

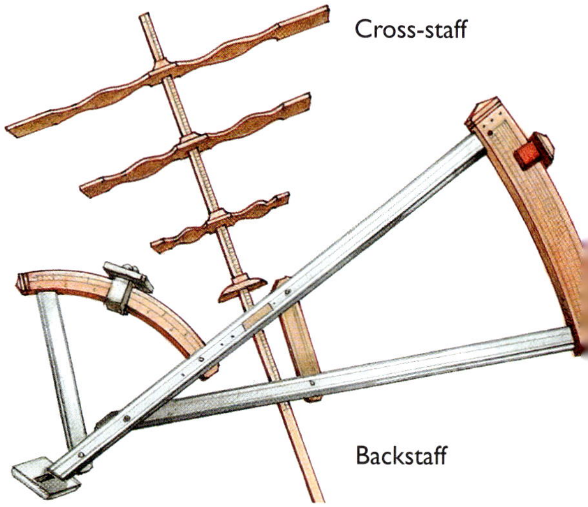

▶ **The cross-staff and backstaff, early navigational instruments.**

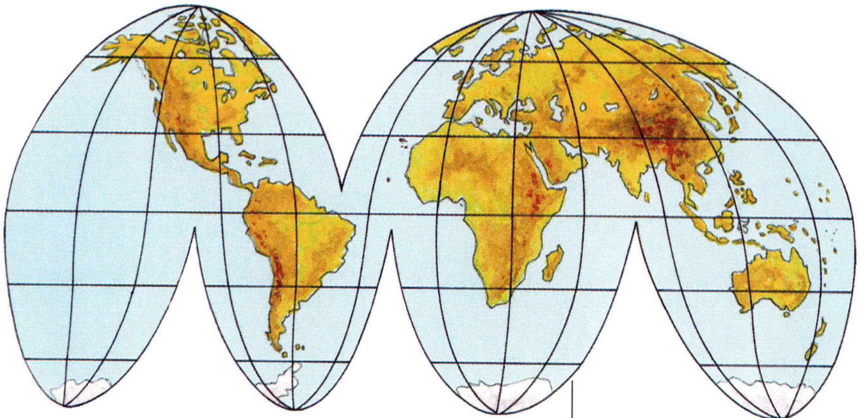

Why is a flat map never really accurate?

A map in a book is flat. But the Earth is round, and its features cannot be drawn accurately on a flat surface. Try peeling an orange, and you will find you cannot lay the skin out flat on a table without it breaking. Every map is drawn in a way that makes some feature (such as area) accurate, but other features (such as shape) less so. This is called a projection.

▲ To make a map on a flat surface, a section of the world's surface has to be shown as if it were flat. It is as if the peel of an orange were cut off and then laid out flat on the table.

Why do air travellers have to alter their watches?

The world is divided into 24 time zones. The time in each zone differs by one hour from the time in the next. East of Greenwich in England (where it is Greenwich Mean Time, or GMT), the time is later. West of Greenwich, the time is earlier. Noon in Greenwich is 7am (5 hours earlier) in New York and 3pm (3 hours later) in Moscow. The United States covers five time zones: Atlantic, Eastern, Central, Mountain and Pacific. Travellers flying west put their watches back on landing. Flying east, they must put their watches forward. So if a flight from London to New York takes five hours, you land at the same time as you set off.

▼ Since 1884, the world has had a standard time: Greenwich Mean Time. In each time zone, time differs by one hour. Travellers crossing the International Date Line gain or lose a day.

When was BC and AD dating introduced?

There are many different systems for dating. Muslims begin their calendar from the Hegira, the flight of Muhammad from Mecca in AD 622. The Christian calendar, now widely used worldwide, begins with the birth of Jesus. Dates before then are followed by the letters 'BC' ('Before Christ'). Dates after then are prefixed by the letters AD (Latin 'Anno Domini'or 'Year of Our Lord'). AD dating was suggested by a monk-mathematician named Dionysius Exiguus in AD 525. It was much later that BC was used, in the 1600s.

How do archaeologists measure time?

Archaeologists uncover the past, layer by layer. Objects can be dated by the radiocarbon method (measuring the amount of radioactive carbon-14 left in charcoal, wood or animal bones). Tree growth-rings also help them, especially using the bristlecone pine of California, which can live as long as 4,600 years. Tree-ring dating has helped to correct errors in radiocarbon dates.

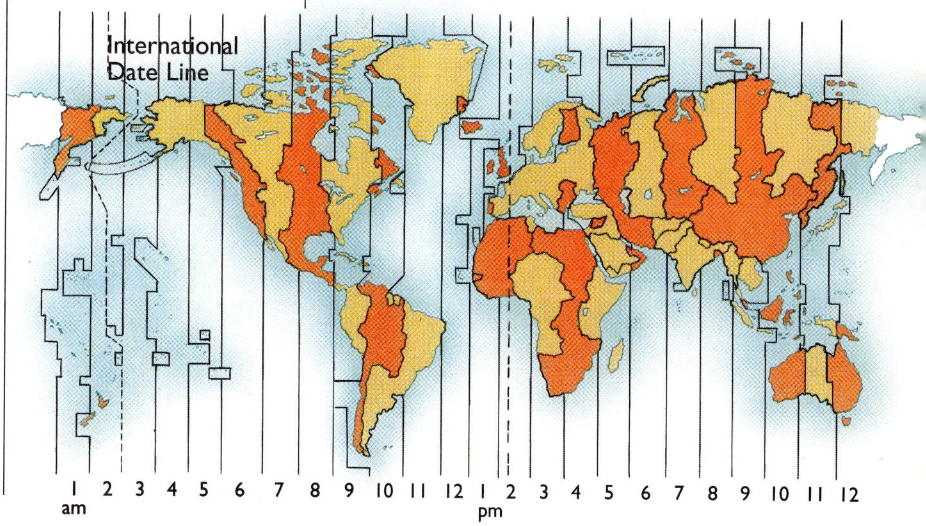

Which clocks are the most accurate?

Atomic clocks keep the most accurate time. These are based on the vibration rate of certain atoms. Most atomic clocks use the vibrations of a caesium atom to regulate quartz crystals. Some scientific clocks, incredibly, are accurate to one second in a million years.

Can time slow down?

Albert Einstein (1879–1955) published his *Special Theory of Relativity* in 1905. He believed that length, mass and time were all affected by motion; and he thought that nothing could travel faster than the speed of light. Near the speed of light, mass would be infinite, length would be zero and time would slow down almost to a stop.

What are light years and parsecs?

Space is so vast that ordinary units of measurement such as the kilometre are of little use. Scientists measure the universe in light years and parsecs. A light year is the distance light travels in a year: about 10 million million kilometres. A light year is roughly 3.25 parsecs (one parsec equals 3 x 10^{13} kilometres).

Could we send spacecraft to the stars?

The stars are so far away that travel to them is out of the question – at least for the foreseeable future. The fastest spacecraft yet built would take more than 150,000 years to arrive at even the closest star.

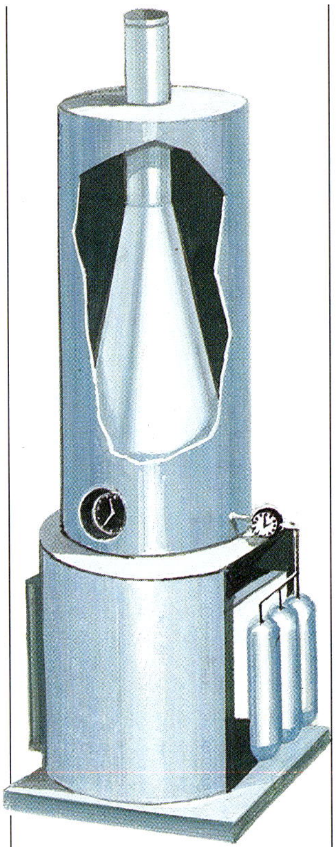

▲ This atomic clock counts the vibrations of light given off by atoms. It should lose less than one second in a million years!

On a 24-hour clock, 9 o'clock in the morning is shown as 0900 and 9 o'clock in the evening is shown as 2100. Train and bus timetables use this system to avoid confusion between morning and evening.

Could we travel through time?

Storytellers and film-makers have made exciting stories about people travelling backwards or forwards through time. Such adventures remain in the world of science fiction. No one has yet built a time machine, and most scientists do not believe time travel is possible.

What is a time capsule?

People sometimes bury containers to preserve various items, as a record of their time. The capsule might contain clothes, photos, tapes, toys, books, even food. The idea is that one day in the future, historians will dig up the capsule and study the contents. There is one extra-large time capsule in the United States which has a car and a motorbike inside!

What is biological time?

Plants and animals follow natural rhythms or cycles (wake-sleep, night-day). Some sea animals even time their activities to the changing tides. An American fish called the grunion, for example, swims ashore to breed at regular 14-day intervals. This rhythm matches the peak tides.

Another kind of time is called geological time. This is measured in millions of years, from the origin of the Solar System through the ageing of the Earth.

How old is the universe?

The universe is about 15 billion years old. Scientists work out the age by measuring the rate at which distant stars have cooled down since the universe began. Some scientists have suggested that stars may cool down more slowly than was thought, so the universe may be even older.

When did people first decide the universe was changing?

Only in the 20th century have scientists shown that the universe is changing all the time. Before then, it was thought that the universe had always been exactly the same. In 1948 a group of scientists put forward the idea of a 'steady-state' universe, which has always existed and will always exist. Now the idea has little support.

SPACE FACTS

Time and distance in space are just mind-boggling.

- The Solar System (the Sun and its planets) is about a million times wider than the diameter of the Earth.
- Our galaxy, the Milky Way, is about 100 million times wider than the Solar System.
- The Andromeda Galaxy is the most distant star cluster that we can see without a telescope.
- Andromeda is two million light years away. This means that the light from this galaxy began its journey to Earth over two million years ago.
- Astronomers use a measure of time called the cosmic year. This is the time it takes the Sun and its planets to rotate once around the centre of the Milky Way – 225 million years.

How did the universe begin?

Most scientists now think that the universe came into being with a huge explosion, known as the 'Big Bang'. The explosion sent matter flying apart, and the universe has continued to expand ever since. Radio astronomers have picked up radiation that does not seem to come from any single source, but is spread throughout space. They believe this radiation may be the result of the Big Bang.

Who thought of Venus as a lion?

Ancient peoples made the universe the setting for fabulous stories. To the people of Babylon, Venus was a bright shining lion roaming the universe. Every dawn, the great god El killed the lion, only for it to return at night.

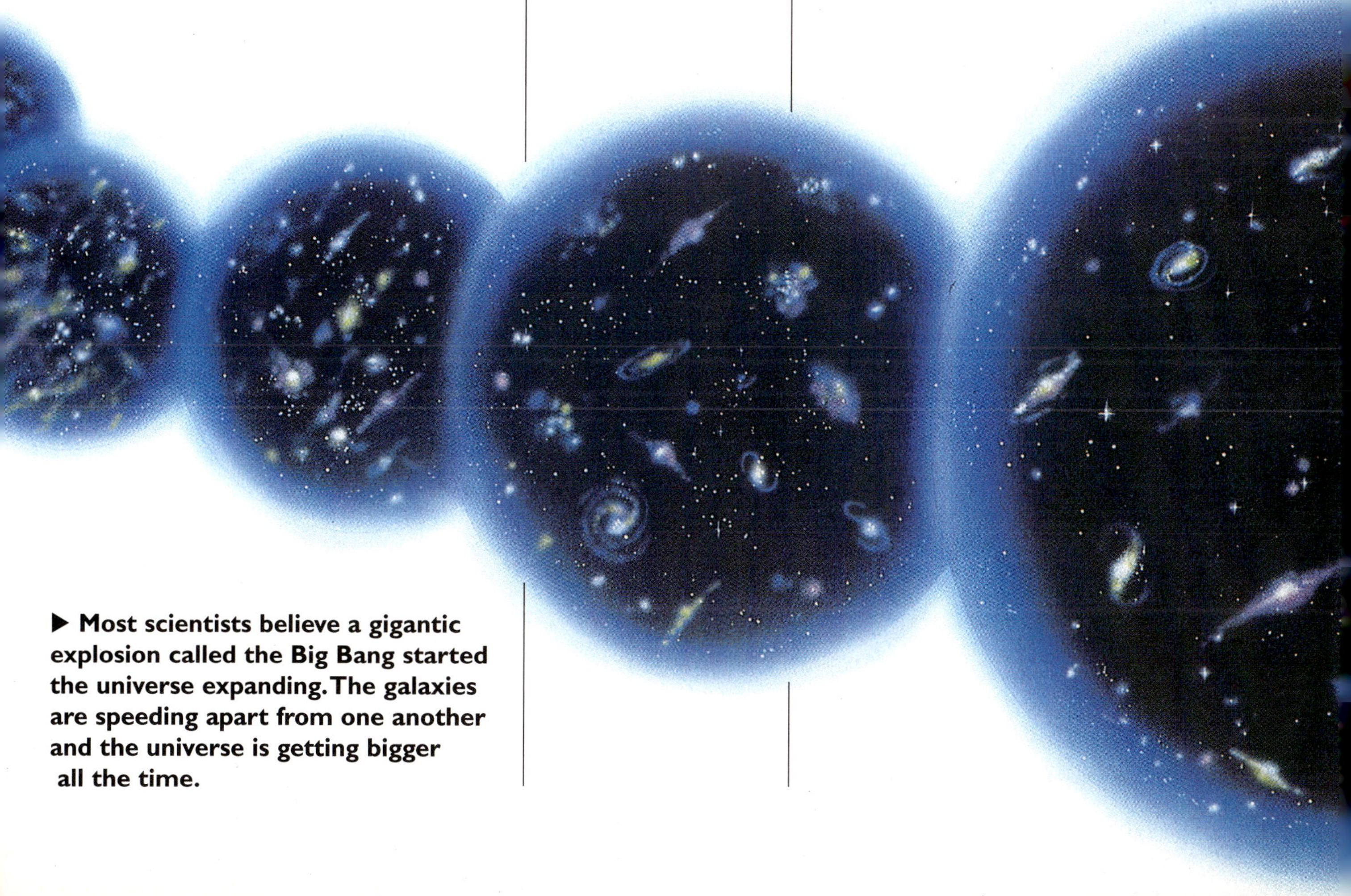

▶ Most scientists believe a gigantic explosion called the Big Bang started the universe expanding. The galaxies are speeding apart from one another and the universe is getting bigger all the time.

Discoveries and Inventions

When were the first tools made?

Long before human beings had evolved, there were ape-like creatures that scientists have named *Australopithecus*, whose remains have been found in southern and eastern Africa. They used sticks and stones as weapons. Scientists have discovered some simple pebble-tools these primitive creatures made more than two million years ago.

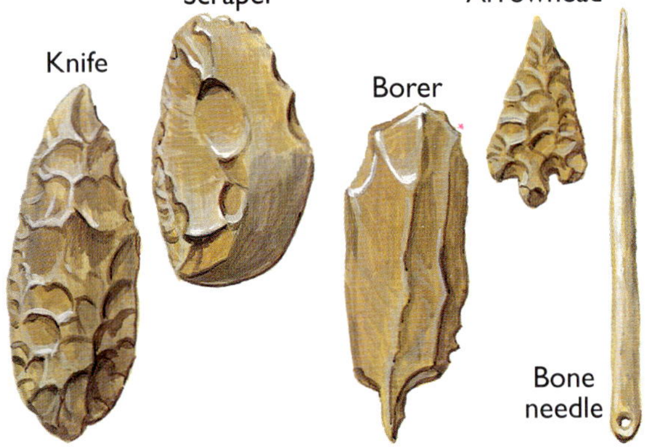

How did people discover fire?

Primitive people feared fire, as animals do. A forest fire, started by lightning, sent them fleeing. Someone, somewhere must have plucked up courage to seize a burning branch. He or she used it to start a small fire for warmth and protection against fierce animals. These first fires were kept burning constantly, for no one yet knew how to make fire using simple tools.

▲ Before the wheel was invented, people used logs as rollers to move heavy stones for building, so perhaps it is not surprising that the first wheels were wooden.

◀ Early people used flint for making tools such as knives, scrapers, borers and arrowheads. They made needles from animal bones.

Who invented the wheel?

No one knows when or where the wheel was first used, but it was one of the most important of all human inventions. The wheel seems to have been invented before 3000 BC, probably in several different places. It may be that wheels were first used by potters to turn clay pots, before they were fixed to carts and revolutionized transport. The first carts had two solid wheels, made from pieces of wood fastened together. Spoked wheels, as used on chariots, were much lighter and a great improvement.

◀ People made fire using a bow drill. As the point of the drill turned rapidly, friction produced enough heat to start wool or dry moss smouldering.

When did the first farmers harvest crops?

Archaeologists in Israel have found flint sickles (tools used for cutting grain) thought to be 13,000 years old. Microscopic examination of the sickle blades shows they were probably used to harvest cultivated, not wild, cereals. If this is so, farming began much earlier than was previously thought. Scientists had previously found evidence of cereal planting in Syria some 11,000 years ago.

How is iron smelted?

Iron was first made by heating iron ore in a furnace with charcoal and limestone. As the charcoal burned, the molten iron ran down and cooled into a solid mass. This 'bloom' was then hammered and reheated to purify the iron. The process of melting down iron ore is called smelting. The 'Iron Age' began about 1500 BC, in the Near East.

One of the most important inventions of all time was the eyeglass. The first recorded statement came from Roger Bacon in 1268 when he wrote about the use of lenses in glasses.

▶ Tipping out a furnace of molten steel. All metals come from ores dug up from the ground. The ore is heated until the metal melts. It is poured into moulds to cool and harden.

When was steel first made?

The Romans knew how to make steel of a kind, and metal smiths in China and elsewhere probably also made steel by accident. During the Middle Ages, Toledo in Spain was famous for its steel swords. Large-scale steel production was not possible until the invention of an industrial steel-making process. This was done by Sir Henry Bessemer, who invented his 'converter' to make steel in 1856.

When were candles first used?

Candles have been in use for at least 3,000 years, and probably longer. They are mentioned in the Old Testament of the Bible and the Romans burned candles made from flax coated with wax and pitch. Beeswax and tallow (animal fat) were also often used.

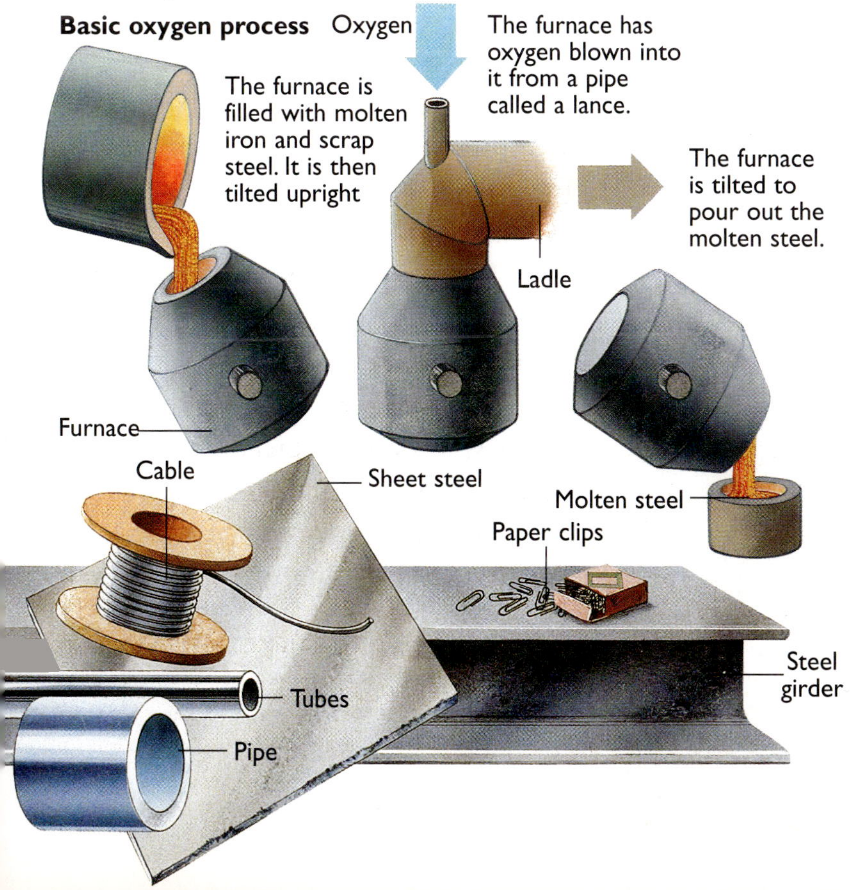

◀ More than half the world's steel is made by the basic oxygen process, illustrated here. The electric arc and open hearth are two other common steel making processes.

Who enjoyed central heating 2,000 years ago?

Wealthy Romans lived in large houses with under floor heating, known as a hypocaust. Slaves fed fuel onto a fire which sent hot air circulating beneath the raised floor of the house. Hot air also made its way through flues in the walls, which allowed smoke to escape. Romans living in parts of their empire far from sunny Italy (such as Britain) must have been grateful for this luxury. The fire also heated water for the bathroom.

How long have people used weighing machines?

Accurate scales or weighing machines are vital for science, and also for trade and business. The Ancient Egyptians had equal arm balances, much the same as are still used today. Such balances have been in use for some 7,000 years!

COMMUNICATING

- Prehistoric people sent messages by using drumbeats, fires and smoke signals.
- The first writing was picture-writing, so people drew pictures to tell a story.
- The people of Sumer in Mesopotamia invented a form of picture-writing about 3500 BC.
- Long scrolls were awkward to carry. So for sending messages, people used wax tablets. They wrote on the soft wax with a pointed stick.
- People in Ancient Rome were able to read the news. A handwritten news sheet of 59 BC was a forerunner of the newspaper.

In Ancient Egypt, few people went to school. Some boys trained as scribes. A scribe's job was writing. He had to learn more than 700 hieroglyphs. Spelling tests were a nightmare!

Who were the first people to use paper?

Paper was first made in China about 2,000 years ago. Before the invention of paper-making machines in the 1800s, each sheet of paper was made separately by hand. The only machines involved were trip hammers, driven by water wheels. These ground rags mixed with water into a pulp. The pulp was then put in a vat, and a wire screen was dipped into it. The screen picked up a thin coating of pulp. It was lifted out, shaken, and laid on felt, and was put in a screwpress to press out the moisture. Each sheet was then peeled off the felt and hung up to dry.

▼ Egyptians making papyrus. Papyrus is made from a kind of reed. The stages of the process turned the reeds into a smooth paper-like writing material.

1 Paper-makers cut and peeled the reeds.

2 They cut the reed stems into thin slices and laid them in rows, one on top of the other.

3 They hammered them until the sticky plant juices glued them together.

4 Next they used a smooth stone or a special tool to rub the surface of the papyrus paper smooth.

5 Finally, all the pieces of papyrus paper were glued into a long strip and rolled into a scroll.

When were cannon first used in battle?

The Chinese invented gunpowder rockets, but cannon were not used for battle in Europe until the 1300s. The early guns were clumsy and fired solid cannon balls. Often their metal barrels exploded under the force of the gunpowder, doing more damage to their own side than to the enemy.

▲ This early cannon of the 1400s fired solid stone balls. It could not shoot far, but it could knock down castle walls.

Why did Leonardo's flying machine never fly?

The Italian Leonardo da Vinci, who invented between 1452 and 1519, dreamed up inventions that were centuries ahead of their time. He drew plans for a submarine, a parachute, an armoured vehicle something like a tank, a helicopter and a flying machine. His flying machine was never built, for no engine existed to power it. The age of light, powerful motors was still several hundred years away.

In 1482 Leonardo da Vinci wrote to the Duke of Milan that he could build portable bridges, cannons, ships, as well as armoured vehicles and catapults!

What was the first steam engine used for?

In 1698 an English engineer named Thomas Savery devised 'an engine for the raising of water and occasioning motion to all sorts of mill works'. His engine was put to work pumping water from the shafts of tin mines in Cornwall. It worked by cooling steam so that it condensed, creating a partial vacuum which 'sucked up' water through a pipe.

Who was called 'Father of the Steam Age'?

The Scottish engineer James Watt (1736–1819) is said to have been inspired to improve the steam engine by watching a kettle boil. In 1764 he was trying to repair a model steam engine of the kind invented by Thomas Newcomen (1663–1729). Realizing how inefficient this kind of steam engine was, Watt added a separate condenser to make it more powerful. He also worked out how to change the up and down motion of the beam engine into rotary motion, suitable for driving machinery. These improvements earned James Watt fame as the 'Father of the Steam Age'.

▶ James Watt improved Newcomen's steam pumping engine, making it more powerful. This is his 1775 version, which was soon at work in factories throughout Britain.

Who built the first reaping machine?

In the 1830s Cyrus Hall McCormick of the USA invented a horse-drawn machine to cut grain. The mechanical reaper was followed in the 1850s by the first combine harvester.

When were fertilizers first used?

Farmers have always used animal manure to restore the goodness in the soil. It was not until the 1800s that they began applying chemical fertilizers. In 1842 John Bennet Lawes of Britain found out how to produce super-phosphate from rock and this was the beginning of the chemical fertilizer industry.

How deep was the first oil well?

The Chinese were able to extract oil from below the ground 2,000 years ago, but the first modern oil well was drilled in Pennsylvania, USA, in 1859. The pioneer driller was Edwin L. Drake, who bored through 21 metres of rock to strike oil. This was 30 years before the first car. The oil was burned in oil lamps.

Who was the most inventive inventor of all time?

This title probably belongs to the American inventor Thomas Alva Edison (1847–1931), with more than a thousand inventions to his credit. Among them were the electric light bulb, the film camera and the phonograph, which was an early form of record player.

The best-attended single-day sports event in the world is a car race – the Indianapolis 500. It is called 500 because the cars must cover 500 miles. The oval track was made from 3.2 million bricks which earned it the name the Brickyard, as it is still called.

▼ Cars rolling off one of the first assembly lines in the United States.

When were cars first built on an assembly line?

Until 1914 cars were built one by one, as wagons had always been. A group of workers finished one car before starting on the next. The American industrialist Henry Ford changed all this by introducing the first assembly line into his factory. Cars moved along an automated conveyor system. Each part (seats, engine, wheels and so on) was put on in turn as the conveyor moved along carrying the car bodies. Instead of taking 13 hours to build a Ford Model T car, it took only one and a half hours using the new assembly line. So the cars cost less.

▶ The Model T Ford first appeared in 1908. It became America's most popular car.

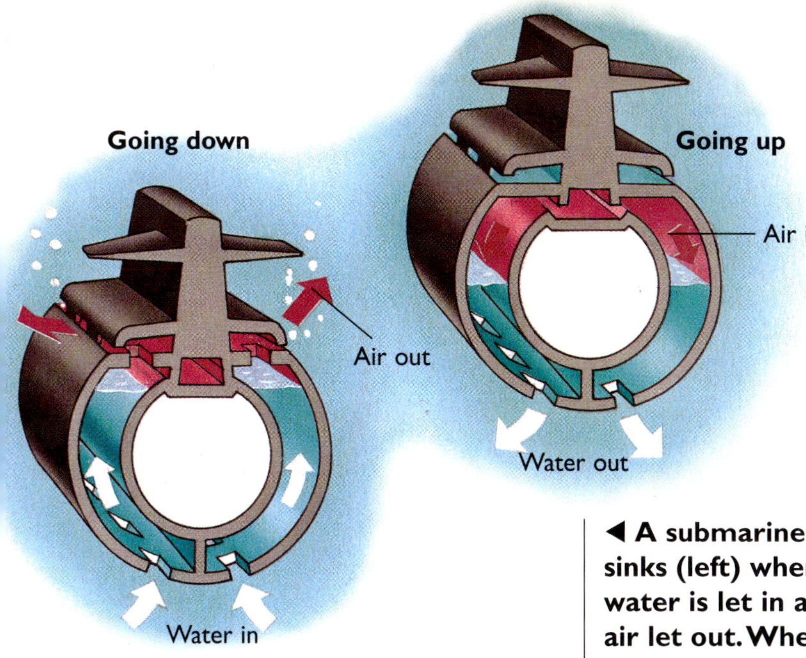

◀ A submarine sinks (left) when water is let in and air let out. When air blows water out, the submarine rises (right).

How does a submarine dive?

A submarine dives by flooding ballast tanks with water. The tanks are hollow spaces between the craft's inner and outer hulls. When the submarine is about to dive, valves are opened to let seawater flood the tanks. The submarine loses buoyancy and dives. To surface, water is expelled from the tanks by blowing in compressed air. This makes the submarine more buoyant, and it rises.

What is an aqualung?

Skindivers have ventured below the sea since ancient times, but they could stay below only for as long as their breath allowed. A diver in heavy diving gear relies on air pumped down through a hose. Not until the 1930s was self-contained diving gear invented. Divers carry air in bottles on their backs, and breathe through valves in their face masks. This aqualung equipment was developed by the Jacques Cousteau of France.

Without the lift (elevator) the modern skyscraper would never have been built. The World Trade Center in New York City needs 244 lifts. Each of these can travel at up to 485 m per minute – about 30 km/h.

Why were there no skyscrapers before the 1880s?

The taller a stone building is, the thicker must be the walls at its base, to support its enormous weight. This fact limited the height of buildings until the 1880s, when steel frameworks were tried for the first time. In 1885 the Home Insurance Building in Chicago was the first building to have walls which were not load-bearing. It was held up by a metal skeleton of girders and, though only ten storeys high, was the forerunner of the skyscrapers for which American cities became famous. By the 1930s, buildings of 100 storeys, such as the Empire State Building in New York, were possible.

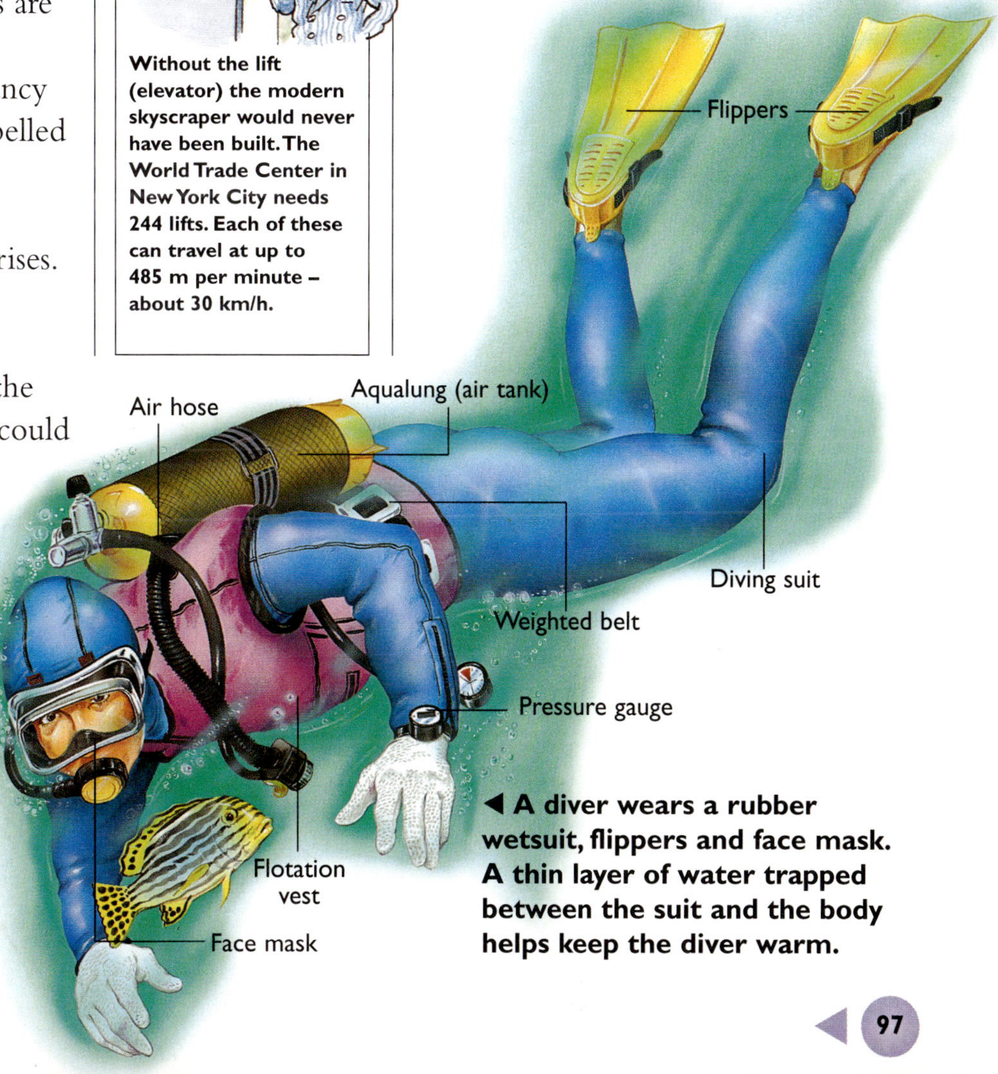

◀ A diver wears a rubber wetsuit, flippers and face mask. A thin layer of water trapped between the suit and the body helps keep the diver warm.

How does a refrigerator stay cold?

When a liquid evaporates (becomes a vapour, or gas) it takes heat from its surroundings. Inside the coils of pipe in a refrigerator is a gas, such as ammonia. This gas is heated and then cooled. Cooling turns the gas into a liquid. As the liquid passes around the refrigerator pipes, it absorbs heat and becomes a gas again. Each time this cycle is repeated, the refrigerator becomes colder inside.

Food goes bad because of the activities of tiny bacteria. Such bacteria multiply rapidly when the temperature is higher than about 10 degrees Celsius. At lower temperatures the bacteria reproduce less rapidly and food keeps fresh longer.

When were frozen foods first sold?

Long ago, people realized that snow and ice kept food fresh. But until the 1800s there was no way of making ice. Before then, winter ice was cut into blocks and stored in ice houses but by the summer it had all melted. In 1834 Joseph Perkins discovered how to make ice artificially.

◀ Modern plastics are light yet strong, ideal for children's toys. Millions of copies can be made from a single mould, in virtually any colour.

Alexander Graham Bell invented the telephone, but he also produced a kite which could carry a person; in 1917 he built a hydrofoil boat which reached 113 km/h.

▼ The iceman delivering ice blocks was a familiar sight before people had refrigerators and freezers at home.

What was the first plastic?

In 1862 a chemist named Alexander Parkes showed a new discovery at an exhibition in London. The new substance he had made was cellulose nitrate, which he called 'Parkesine'. It was the first plastic, a tough material. Parkesine was later renamed celluloid and developed by an American, John Wesley Hyatt.

When were aerosol sprays first used?

The aerosol spray can was invented in 1941 by an American, Lyle D. Goodhue. The container (containing paint or hairspray, for instance) also contains a propellant – a gas under pressure. The gas, mixed with the contents, sprays out when the button on the can is pressed. It is important that aerosols contain only gases that do not damage the atmosphere.

Transport and Communication

What was the earliest vehicle?

The most ancient of all vehicles is perhaps the sledge. This was used in Stone Age times, and not just in snow. Putting a load (such as an animal killed for food) on a sledge made it easier to drag, because the smooth wood produced less friction as it rubbed against the rough ground. Putting runners on the sledge made it even easier to drag. One day someone added wheels and made the first cart.

Who built the first steam-driven vehicle?

A French soldier named Nicolas Cugnot built a carriage driven by a steam engine in 1763. It had three wheels and Cugnot thought it would be useful for hauling heavy cannon. Unfortunately, it was very slow and after a few test runs, it went out of control and somehow overturned. His superiors decided to stick with horse-drawn artillery and Cugnot's ill-fated machine was locked up for safety.

How did the *Rocket* outstrip its rivals?

Steam locomotives that could run under their own power on road or rails were developed in the early 1800s. In 1829, British pioneers gathered to race their steam locomotives at the Rainhill trials. George Stephenson's *Rocket* hauled a train weighing 20 tonnes at a top speed of more than 55 kilometres per hour. The *Rocket's* three rivals were no match for it and it was later used on the Liverpool–Manchester railway. George Stephenson became engineer for several of the railways that rapidly sprang up.

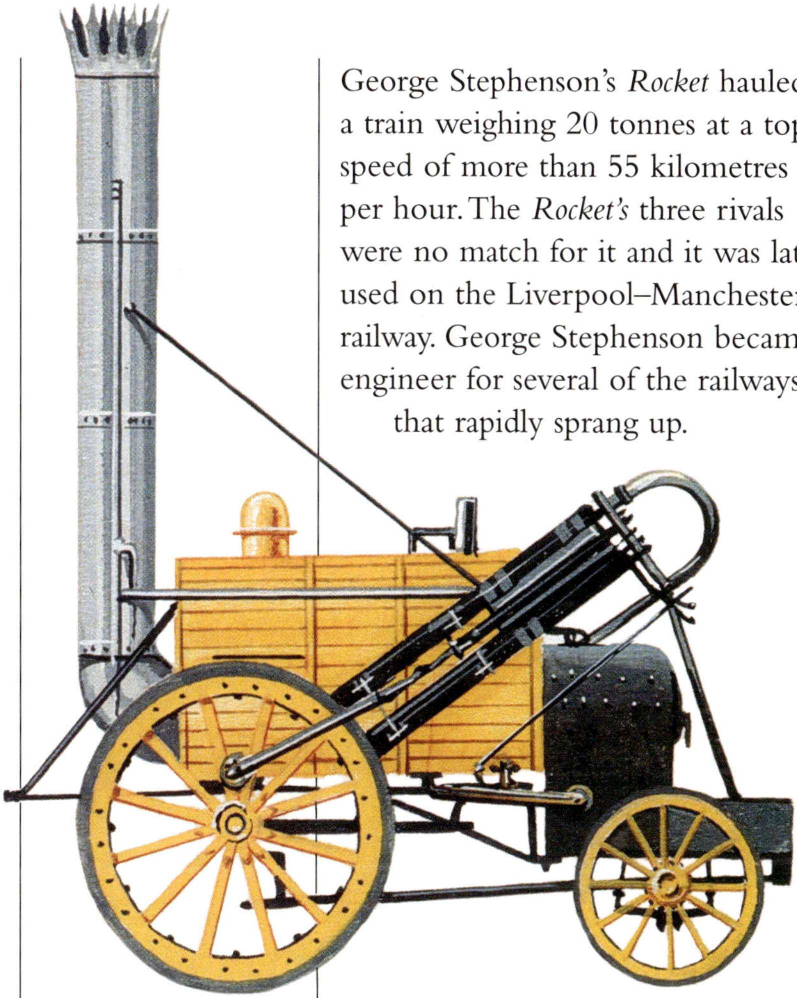

▲ Stephenson's *Rocket* was the fastest steam locomotive of its day. Inside its boiler were five tubes, so more water was heated. This meant more steam drove the *Rocket's* pistons.

When was the world's first electric railway opened?

In 1879 a 274-metre stretch of electric tramway was opened in Berlin, Germany. It was the brainchild of Werner von Siemens. Four years later, his brother Wilhelm opened an electric railway in Northern Ireland. By the 1920s electric lines were operating throughout the world. Electric trains are now so advanced that the French TGV train has exceeded 500 kilometres per hour.

When did the modern bicycle appear?

Several improvements in bicycle design in the 1800s brought about the shape we know today. The pedals were moved from the front wheels to a position between the wheels and a chain drive was added. Wire-spoke wheels, sprung saddles, gears, ball-bearings and a free-wheel device were other important changes made by the 1880s. Last to be added was the pneumatic (air-filled) tyre.

Who built the first internal combustion engine?

In 1863 a Frenchman named Etienne Lenoir designed an engine which burned coal gas. He used it to drive a cart. In 1864 the Austrian Siegfried Marckus built a similar engine that used petrol vapour, and designed an electrical ignition system.

When did the first motor vehicle take to the road?

The first motor vehicle powered by a petrol engine was a three-wheeler built in 1885 by Karl Benz, a young German engineer. His first trial run in his 'horseless carriage' ended in an accident, when he drove it into a wall. The same year as Benz tested his machine, Gottfried Daimler, working less than 100 kilometres away, built a motor cycle. By 1886 Daimler had produced his first car. It had a single cylinder engine and a top speed of 29 kilometres per hour.

▶ Karl Benz built his first car in 1885. It had three cart-style wheels and was steered by moving the front wheel.

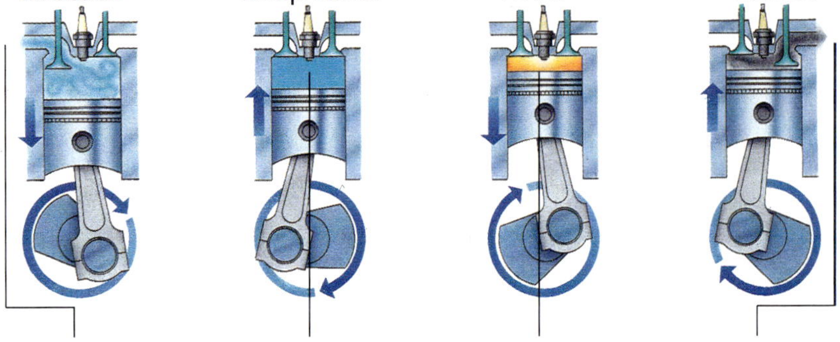

▲ Inside a four-stroke petrol engine. The up-and-down piston movement is changed to a round-and-round movement of the drive shaft linked to the wheels.

In 1865, just after the first steam coaches appeared on the road, the 'Red Flag Act' ruled that any car should have someone walking in front of it carrying a red flag!

What makes a car engine go?

The power of the car engine comes from an explosion. If petrol is mixed with air and then ignited by a spark, it explodes. In the internal combustion engine, the explosions are controlled inside cylinders. Each explosion pushes a piston downwards. The pistons are connected to a series of shafts which in turn are connected to the wheels of the car.

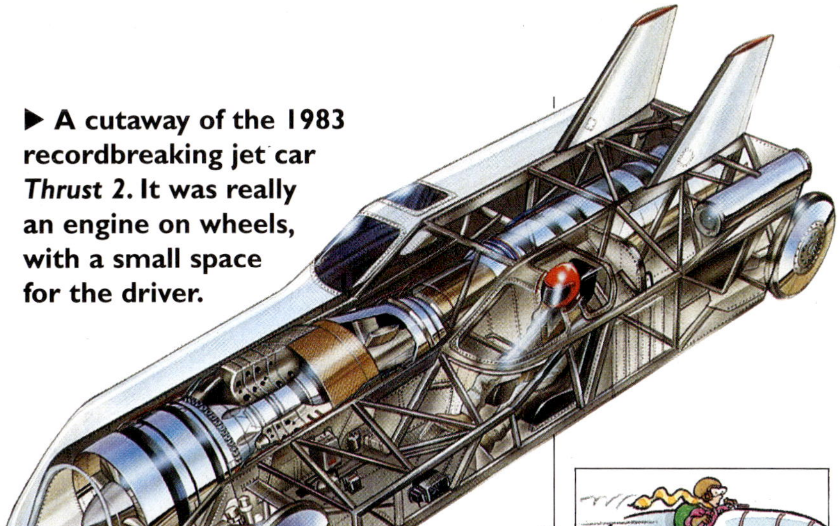

▶ **A cutaway of the 1983 recordbreaking jet car *Thrust 2*. It was really an engine on wheels, with a small space for the driver.**

How fast can a car travel?

Cars fitted with rocket and jet engines can travel much faster than those with ordinary petrol engines. In 1997 Andy Green set a new record in the jet-engined *Thrust SSC* with a top speed of 1,149 kilometres per hour.

What were the first boats like?

The earliest boat was probably a floating log. Then people learned how to build rafts by lashing together logs or bundles of reeds. They hollowed out tree trunks to make canoes. The first boats were driven by paddles. Sails came later.

▲ **The first boats were dug-out canoes made by hollowing out tree trunks, reed boats and rafts made from planks of wood.**

The very first car to go faster than 100 km/h did not run on oil but was battery-powered. It was called *La Jamais Contente*. Amazingly, it did this about 100 years ago in 1899.

Surface-piercing hydrofoil

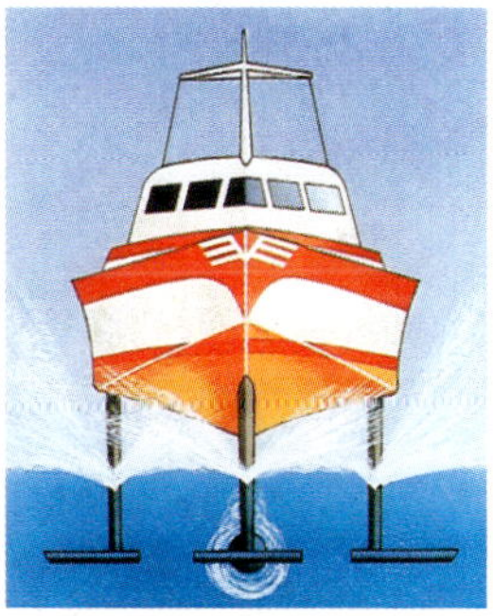

Fully submerged hydrofoil

▲ **Hydrofoils can skim over water at more than 110 km/h. There are two types of hydrofoil, each having a different foil shape.**

When did ships first have rudders?

Early ships were steered by a large oar hung over the stern. Chinese vessels were probably the first to be fitted with a rudder, and by the 1200s ships with rudders had appeared in Europe.

Who built the first steamboat?

By the late 1700s inventors in several countries were experimenting with the new power of steam to drive ships. In 1783 a French nobleman, the Marquis de Jouffroy d'Abbans, built a boat whose paddles were worked by a steam engine. He called it the *Pyroscaphe* (meaning 'fire-craft') and tested it successfully on a river. It was the first steamboat.

Who invented the steam turbine?

The high-speed steam engine was made possible by Sir Charles Parsons, a British engineer who invented the turbine in 1884. Steam was passed through the blades of a series of spinning rotors, which converted the steam's energy into fast circular motion. Parsons built a steam turbine-powered launch *Turbinia* that startled naval experts in 1884.

Why can a hydrofoil travel faster than an ordinary speedboat?

A hydrofoil has special legs, or foils, beneath its hull. When motionless, the hydrofoil floats low in the water like a normal craft. But at speed it lifts up on its foils. This reduces the friction between the hull and the water.

Who were the first people to fly?

Over the centuries, many brave but misguided experimenters have tried to fly. We know of nobody who succeeded before November 21, 1783 when two men, Pilatre de Rozier and the Marquis d'Arlandes, flew in a Montgolfier hot-air balloon above Paris. Their historic flight lasted 25 minutes.

Why did Orville Wright lie on his stomach during the first aeroplane flight?

The Wright brothers, Wilbur and Orville, made the first sustained flight in a powered craft when their *Flyer 1* took to the air on December 17, 1903. It had a home-made petrol engine set on the right-hand wing. To keep the plane stable, the pilot (Orville, on the first historic flight) had to lie on the left-hand wing.

Can aircraft fly without engines?

A glider is an aeroplane without an engine. It stays aloft by diving at a very flat angle, or by soaring on rising currents of warm air.

▲ Two brothers, Joseph and Etienne Montgolfier, built the world's first hot air balloon to carry people into the air.

The parachute may have been used as long ago as the 1400s. Drawings made then show cone-shaped canopies, with people dangling underneath.

When did jets first fly?

Piston engines were found not to work well at high altitude, where the air is thin, nor at very high speeds. A new type of engine was needed. As early as 1930 a British engineer called Frank Whittle had patented a jet engine design, but the first jet plane to fly was German. This was the Heinkel He 178 which was tested in 1939. British and American jets flew soon afterwards, during World War II.

How does a helicopter fly backwards?

A helicopter's rotor blades act both as wings and propellers. To hover, or to fly upwards, the blades are kept flat. To fly forwards, the blades are tilted forwards so that they 'bite' into the air. To move backwards, the rotor blades are tilted towards the tail.

How does a jump-jet hover in mid-air?

The *Harrier* is an example of a vertical take-off or 'jump-jet'. It has four swivelling nozzles which direct exhaust gases from the jet engines.

◀ The *Harrier* takes off and hovers with its jet nozzles pointing downwards. To fly forwards, the pilot simply swivels the nozzles to direct the jet thrust backwards.

Who first sent a radio message across the Atlantic Ocean?

Guglielmo Marconi, an Italian engineer, developed the idea of wireless telegraphy – sending messages in Morse code by radio. The Morse signals were produced by a series of electromagnetic shock waves. The first message sent across the Atlantic Ocean by Marconi consisted of a single letter – S – in Morse code.

Who invented the telephone?

People knew that it was possible to send speech along a wire as early as the 1600s. Two cans linked by a length of string will show you how. But the modern telephone was first demonstrated by Alexander Graham Bell in 1876. His equipment used two electromagnets which picked up vibrations in a thin sheet of iron (the diaphragm). The vibrations were caused by the sound waves from a person speaking. This principle – the changing of sound waves into electrical signals – explains how the telephone works.

Who took the first moving pictures?

The first cameras needed a very long exposure of the photographic plate – as long as 15 minutes for one picture. To make moving pictures, film must be exposed much faster, at around 16 frames (or exposures) a second. In 1877 Eadweard Muybridge set up 12 cameras alongside a racetrack to settle a bet. A horse's owner wanted to know if his horse lifted all four legs at once while galloping. Muybridge's cameras proved that it did. He fixed the still photos on a moving wheel and then projected them with a magic lantern to make it appear that the horse was galloping.

IMPORTANT DATES

Communication Firsts

- 1826 Invention of photography, Joseph Niepce (France).
- 1837 Electric telegraph, Samuel Morse (US).
- 1876 Telephone, Alexander Graham Bell (Scotland/US).
- 1878 Microphone, David Edward Hughes (England/US).
- 1888 Kodak camera, George Eastman (US).
- 1895 Wireless, Guglielmo Marconi (Italy/England).
- 1927 First talking picture, *The Jazz Singer* (US).
- 1929 Electronic television system, Vladimir Zworykin (US).
- 1956 Videotape recording, A. Poniatoff (US).
- 1962 First TV pictures across the Atlantic, Telstar (US).
- 1979 Compact disc, Sony (Japan) and Philips (Netherlands).

▲ An early model of the telephone. The inventor, Alexander Graham Bell, first used the device to call for his assistant's help in another room.

Who took movie cameras out of the studio?

In France, the Lumière brothers pioneered outdoor filming in the 1890s. Their cameras (in which the film reel was turned by a handle) were light enough to carry. They also reduced the speed at which film was exposed to 16 frames a second rather than the 48 frames a second used by earlier pioneers such as Edison. This saved film and reduced flickering. Moving picture shows became popular with the public.

How were television pictures first sent across the Atlantic?

In 1962 the Telstar communications satellite relayed TV pictures between North America and Europe for the first time. A network of communications satellites now orbits the Earth to provide worldwide live television coverage.

When were video recordings first made?

Copies of TV programmes had to be kept on film until the invention of videotape recording in the 1950s. The tape stores the image as a sequence of magnetic signals. Videotape made possible the 'action replay' of sports events. Video cassette recorders became popular from the 1970s.

SCIENCE QUIZ

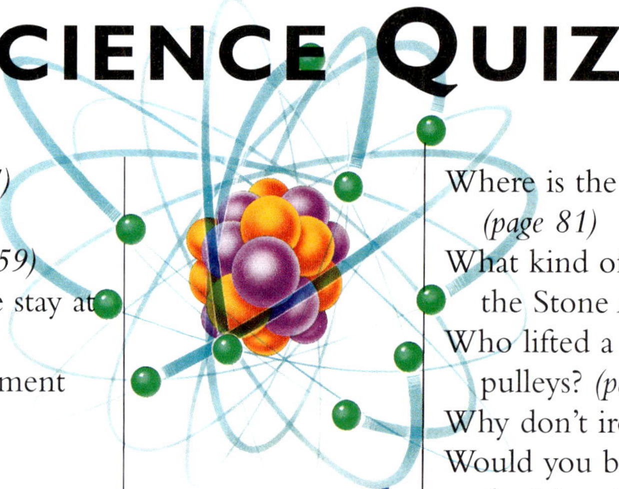

Can you see an atom? *(page 57)*
What are electrons? *(page 57)*
What is nuclear energy? *(page 59)*
How does a nuclear submarine stay at sea for so long? *(page 60)*
What is the most common element on Earth? *(page 61)*
What are crystals? *(page 62)*
What is rust? *(page 63)*
Which famous chemist lost his head on the guillotine? *(page 63)*
How is brass made? *(page 64)*
Why are airships filled with helium? *(page 65)*
Why did Benjamin Franklin fly a kite? *(page 66)*
Why do electrical cables have rubber outsides? *(page 67)*
Is a dry battery really dry? *(page 68)*
What is a lodestone? *(page 69)*
What makes a light bulb glow? *(page 70)*
What was the first electronic computer? *(page 71)*
Why do shops use bar codes? *(page 71)*
What are the primary colours of light? *(page 72)*
Why is a mirror image the wrong way round? *(page 73)*
How were X-rays discovered? *(page 75)*
Which makes most noise: a rocket or thunder? *(page 76)*
Could you sing on the Moon? *(page 77)*
Who invented the phonograph? *(page 78)*
Where do all living things get their energy from? *(page 79)*
Why does a saucepan handle get hot? *(page 80)*

Where is the world's thickest ice? *(page 81)*
What kind of machines were used in the Stone Age? *(page 81)*
Who lifted a ship out of water using pulleys? *(page 82)*
Why don't iron ships sink? *(page 83)*
Would you be heavier or lighter on the Moon? *(page 84)*
Why do we count in tens? *(page 85)*
What are perfect numbers? *(page 86)*
Why do we have leap years? *(page 87)*
Why did early clocks have no hands? *(page 88)*
Why do archaeologists look at old trees? *(page 89)*
How long would it take to travel to the nearest star? *(page 90)*
Is the Milky Way bigger than the Solar System? *(page 91)*
When did the Iron Age begin? *(page 93)*
How did the Ancient Romans heat their homes? *(page 94)*
What did Thomas Savery invent? *(page 95)*
Who invented the electric light bulb? *(page 96)*
Who developed the aqualung? *(page 97)*
Which was the first plastic? *(page 98)*
When did the first car driver take to the road? *(page 100)*
Who built the world's first steamboat? *(page 101)*
How long was the first manned balloon trip? *(page 102)*
Who made the first telephone call? *(page 103)*
When were people first able to tape TV programmes? *(page103)*

INDEX

Page numbers in *italic* refer to the illustrations. Numbers in **bold** refer to volumes.

C

D

E

Q

R

S